"Reading through Parul's cancer experience evoked from sadness to laughter, fearfulness to hope. Ultimately, it's a very and very honest story of survival from breast cancer. Started as a diary, Parul covers her journey chronologically and then shares her experience of the support she sought and experienced throughout her recovery. Her family and friends had a crucial role to play, demonstrating the unpredictability of responses to a life threatening condition. Cancer still provokes a myriad of reactions and uncertainty, not only for the person going through a cancer diagnosis and treatment but everyone around them. The dynamics of relationships invariably change. Some become stronger while others struggle to survive. Understanding how family and friends could make a difference to Parul, will offer insight and awareness to the reader, giving them confidence to either ask for or offer support and practical help.

Parul shows enormous strength and courage in her quest to regain control over her body and her life, and to find a new 'normal'. Over the years I have met many people affected by cancer yet I found Parul's story was still incredibly moving and humbling. She has invested so much of herself and emerges as a strong, determined woman with everything to live for. This book offers hope and useful advice for anyone affected by breast cancer."

- Beverley van der Molen,
Macmillan Information and Education Officer,
Paul's Cancer Support Centre and St George's University Hospitals
NHS Foundation Trust and author of *Taking Control of Cancer*

My Cancer Journey

A rendezvous with myself

PARUL BANKA

BALBOA
PRESS

A DIVISION OF HAY HOUSE

Balboa Press books may be ordered through booksellers or by contacting:

Balboa Press
A Division of Hay House
1663 Liberty Drive
Bloomington, IN 47403
www.balboapress.com
1 (877) 407-4847

Because of the dynamic nature of the Internet, any web addresses or links contained in this book may have changed since publication and may no longer be valid. The views expressed in this work are solely those of the author and do not necessarily reflect the views of the publisher, and the publisher hereby disclaims any responsibility for them.

The author of this book does not dispense medical advice or prescribe the use of any technique as a form of treatment for physical, emotional, or medical problems without the advice of a physician, either directly or indirectly. The intent of the author is only to offer information of a general nature to help you in your quest for emotional and spiritual well-being. In the event you use any of the information in this book for yourself, which is your constitutional right, the author and the publisher assume no responsibility for your actions.

Any people depicted in stock imagery provided by Thinkstock are models, and such images are being used for illustrative purposes only. Certain stock imagery © Thinkstock.

Print information available on the last page.

ISBN: 978-1-5043-2740-4 (sc)
ISBN: 978-1-5043-2742-8 (hc)
ISBN: 978-1-5043-2741-1 (e)

Library of Congress Control Number: 2015901519

Balboa Press rev. date: 6/8/2015

To Abhi...
And his love, that makes this life worthwhile.

Contents

Foreword

I first met Parul while working at Cambridge University Press, in the bike shed, of all places. She smiled at me as we struggled to get our bikes out of the over-crowded bike shed and her face lit up. It is this warmth and generosity of spirit that struck me and this is something that has carried her through the rough times. First coping with the prospect of such a life-changing event as hearing for the first time that you have cancer, and then with the various stages of the treatment.

But she has found the strength to realise how the whole experience has changed her into what she calls a 'better' person. Someone who came to terms with things that irked her in the past, and learnt to let go of the pain they caused. I am sure this will strike a chord with many of us, of how a difficult period of our lives has helped us to get in touch with our feelings and make sense of the past.

Born, raised and educated in India, Parul came to the UK two years before she discovered she had breast cancer. When she relayed her news to family and friends back home, people were not only shocked but fearful of what the future would hold. She underwent the cancer treatment in the UK.

One of Parul's aims in writing this book is to change people's view of what cancer means and to use the experience as a force for good. The first half of the book provides an insight into how treatment hits and punctures the body, how it demands every ounce of strength to retain any form of normality, and the different ways in which she and others coped.

The second half is more spiritual, as it's more about how the experience has changed her as a person – some of this comes down to a change of pace, as she moved into the slow lane, with time to reflect on past relationships and to understand how important it is to treasure loved ones. She used the opportunity to work on herself and adopt several changes. For Parul, the most dramatic change happened during the Cancer Support Group meetings, where she found the experience of connecting with people who have been through cancer very empowering – I'll leave you to find out about that yourselves.

PS: She makes a mean cup of Ginger Tea (chai), say yes if she offers you one. You won't regret it.

- Sarah Keefe
Friend and confidante

With gratitude...

I stood in an alley,
All alone and a little scared
The wind blew hard and
The autumn leaves flew here and there.

I felt cold and uncertain
Vaguely, I knew what I had to do
But the road ahead was intimidating,
It seemed to demand lots of daring.

And so I stood there,
Clinging to my thoughts,
'I'll be strong like always,' I said
Only this time I didn't feel too sure.

I gingerly raised my left foot,
To take the first step
'What if I tumbled?
And fell over?'

I felt off-balance,
While I stood with my foot in the air,
When an angel hugged me and said,
'Let me take care of you here.'

Encouraged I took the first step
Ah, putting my best foot forward,
Shame that I still felt unsure,
As I raised my other foot forward.

'I must take the next step,'
I heard that in my head
When another angel flew to my right
And tightly grabbed my hand.

And so I beamed
Flanked by them on each side
And holding their hands
I took the first stride.

We talked, while we walked,
We laughed crazily loud.
Frequently, we joked
And at each other, a lot of fun we poked.

Do not be fooled,
The journey was difficult by every measure,
But we joked and fooled around,
While we aimed to find the treasure.

My life was at stake,
I knew I must keep my chin up,
No way that this opponent could win
I knew I must not give up!

And so the battle started.
'We shall fight to the finish,' I screamed.
'I am going to be a tough adversary,
Don't you giggle at me like this!'

The beast was enraged,
It guffawed and made its move,
I lost balance and bawled,
And it daggered me in the cold.

I fell down, I bled and groaned,
'I have to get up,' I coughed
'It is MY battle and not my angels'.'
But my breath had slowed.

In flew a huge mother angel
She grabbed us and far away she flew,
She held us tight in her arms,
Determined not to let us fall through.

After a while, she placed us down
While she caught her breath,
She looked tired, and frail
She looked old and hurt.

But she looked fiercely determined
To beat the monster called cancer
These three angels were:
My husband, my brother and my mother.

Acknowledgments

This book has been possible only because I am fortunate to have some amazing people in my life. Such was their love and care for me during the darkest time of my life that I had to share their story. I had to tell the world what amazing things love and kindness can do.

I am grateful to Alastair Cunningham, the author of the Healing Journey programme, and Paul's Cancer Support Centre, London for granting me permission to reproduce some of their work in this book.

Thank you to the various therapists at Maggie's Wallace Centre at Cambridge. You were the first support centre I had ever visited. Thank you for welcoming me and giving me the confidence to visit a support centre again.

Thank you to Ella Titman, Pauline Withers-Born and Petra Griffiths, my mentors at the 'Coping with Cancer Stress' course at Paul's Cancer Support Centre for your guidance. Thank you to the rest of the team at Paul's, especially Beverley van der Molen, Bridget Cambridge, Catherine Chadwick, Daniel Pereira, Emma Craig, Honor Brogan, Patrick Browning and all the therapists. Thank you for wrapping this dire cancer experience in a bundle of warmth and care. Thank you to Petra and Beverley in helping me to improve this manuscript.

Thank you to Christopher Woodward, Deborah Slaughter, Eve Warren, Gosia Gorna, Nadia Brydon and all the therapists and pals at The Haven, London for looking after me.

I am immensely grateful to my proof-readers and editors at PaperTrue, Anna and Meg, for their expertise and commitment to editing this book. Thank you for your insightful questions that prompted me to think more deeply about my cancer experience. Thank you for making me laugh with your comments and helping me add humour to this book.

To Virginia Morrel and David Yoder at Balboa Press, my publisher, who worked with me relentlessly to ensure that this book sees the light of the day. I am thankful to the rest of the Balboa team who worked behind the scenes and contributed to this book.

To the most amazing healthcare team, especially my consultants, Dr Parto and Dr Charles, who looked after me during cancer. I know that you are the best although, I wouldn't mind if someone else who has been through cancer wants to call their healthcare team so! Thank you...it is owing to your skill that I am alive and well to share my story.

To my homeopath Lorraine Smillie, who lovingly read my manuscript and helped me to improve it, in addition to creating magic with her homeopathic potions.

Thank you to my lovely friends Caroline Clark, Christopher Salter, Jenny Dennehy, Liz Aram, Roya Aram, Sarah Thompson and Sonia Markham for inspiring me with your strength. Thank you for the opportunity to learn from each one of you. Thank you for your understanding and your friendship. Let's continue beating the hell out of cancer! Also, thank you to Liz Aram and Caroline Clark for suggesting improvements to the script as well as for your encouragement and the several book chats we have had.

To all my work colleagues and friends who wished me well and kept me in their prayers. You are the proof that good wishes and prayers work. I consider myself extremely fortunate that I would need several pages, if I try to write every name here. So, my friends who shall be nameless here, you have a very special place in my life and you are very much treasured.

To all those wonderful people who touched my life during this journey – you have amazed me, you have grounded me, you have humbled me and you have time and again, given food for thought to the writer within me.

Thank you to Sarah Keefe for playing a pivotal role in this book. Sarah, thanks for being there for me – as a friend, as a confidante, as a guide and very importantly, for providing invaluable inputs to the book. Thank you for writing the Foreword to this book.

To my friends Madhura Nene, Rashid Merchant, Rukmini Iyer and Shrivallabh Kulkarni, who encouraged me to write my experience and share it. Thank you for your confidence in me.

To my mum-in-law, Nirmala Banka, who ardently prayed for my recovery from cancer.

To my parents Rajendra Kumar Goel and Prabha Goel, my brothers Sachin Goel and Dinesh Goel for taking this journey along with me. Thanks for your love and for telling me that we could do it together, just when I needed to be told so. Thank you for making this cancer journey less painful than it would have been without you.

To my darling niece, Ananya, for your enthusiastic ideas and sheer faith in me. I am so grateful for your love and so proud of the person you are. I hope that I make you a little proud with this book.

No amount of thanks will be sufficient for my husband, Abhishek, or Abhi as I call him, who was there for me unconditionally. Thank you for being with me every single moment and supporting me: be it during the difficult times of cancer treatment, be it rejoicing in surviving cancer, or be it in supporting me in writing this book, right from the inception of the idea until the final execution. Thank you for helping me to find beauty in myself – despite all the scars. Thank you...for everything!

To the rest of my family, near or far, especially Subhadra and Rekha and my Banka family who kept me in their thoughts and prayers.

To my reader: As you invest your precious time and effort in reading my story, I sincerely hope you feel that you are not alone in this journey. While every cancer case is different, there are certainly a few things they have in common when it comes to treatment. Cancer is much bigger than a word or a medical condition. It is something that has not only affected me physically and psychologically, but has also changed me as a person...and this change happened for the better. If your life has been touched by cancer, I wish you good luck and strength galore. May the Higher Powers be with you. I feel privileged in being able to share my story with you....Thank you!

When I first heard on the phone that Parul had been diagnosed with cancer, my mind froze. All I could think was that my daughter would die, probably, in the next 40-45 days. I was scared and I cried.

The only thing that was stronger than my fear of losing her was the desire to make the remaining days of her life as comfortable as possible.

Prabha, Parul's mum

Introduction

I am 34 (I know my birthday is just a few weeks away, but let's call me 34 and not 35). I am 1.56 m tall, an average height for women in India. I am the youngest child born to my parents, and their only daughter amongst three children. We grew up in a middle-class family in India, where our parents worked hard to make ends meet, to send us to expensive private schools, and later to pay for our university education.

In India nothing is provided as a benefit from the State (and if it is, it is of such quality that you usually don't want it). You need to be well-educated and earn well, if you fancy having things that make life comfortable: a house, a car, a gym membership, fashionable clothes, etc. Most of the healthcare is private, and therefore you need to be able to afford it, to get the treatment. You crucially need to study and earn well, in the country that I am from. And so, like many young children from middle-class Indian families, I have been a sincere student who studied well, and a high-performing professional who worked hard.

I worked hard because it felt like the right thing to do. I worked hard because I was a firm believer in the theory of *Karma* – keep doing what you must, and you shall eventually achieve what you are meant to...until the 10th of September 2012. Until this day, the whole concept of *Karma* had fitted well with the rational side of my brain: good grades in exams can be achieved by studying; it is possible to be a top performer by doing your job well. But when this day came, what I failed to figure out was: what *Karma* gets you included in the frightening statistic of 1.08%?

Out of the new cases of breast cancer reported every year in the UK, 0.44% come under the age group of 10 to 29 years, 1.08% are in the 30 to 34 year age group, 2.7% fall in the 35 to 39 age group, 15.62% in the 41 to 49 group, 47.39% in the 50 to 69 group, 24.32% in the 70 to 84 and 8.4% in the 85+ age group. I never knew these specific numbers until I became one of those numbers.

It strikes me now how little I knew about breast cancer, the most common cancer affecting women in the UK, the country to which I moved about three years ago from India. I knew breast cancer existed, but I didn't know much about it. Was I so arrogant as to think that I was immune to it, that it could not happen to me? No, I never thought that could be the case. I believe that anything can happen to anyone at any time. There are no guarantees, and life does not come with insurance, no matter how big a premium you pay for it every year. Yes, anything is possible in this wide world – but cancer? Unfortunately, the answer to this question is yes too.

More about Cancer:

Breast cancer statistics in the UK[1]:

Age Range	Breast cancer %
0 to 04	0
05 to 09	0
10 to 14	0
15 to 19	0
20 to 24	0.06
25 to 29	0.37
30 to 34	1.08
35 to 39	2.75
40 to 44	5.98
45 to 49	9.43
50 to 54	11.13
55 to 59	10.45
60 to 64	13.95
65 to 69	12.05
70 to 74	8.42
75 to 79	8.60
80 to 84	7.31
85+	8.42
All Ages	100.00

Probability based on the average number of new
cases per year, Females, UK, 2009-2011

---

[1] Cancer Research UK. "Breast cancer incidence statistics." Last modified May 2014. http://www.cancerresearchuk.org/cancer-info/cancerstats/types/breast/incidence/#age. Last accessed December 05, 2014.
And
Cancer Research UK. "Cancer stats explained." Last modified October 2013. http://www.cancerresearchuk.org/cancer-info/cancerstats/cancerstats-explained/#How. Last accessed December 05, 2014.

As per the above data, the chance of someone my age being diagnosed as a new breast cancer case was 1.08% – a tiny probability. And yet, there I was – one of the people who formed these statistics in 2012.

Now if someone talks about low probabilities in my presence, I laugh out. The remotest 0.0001% is also some person!

SECTION I

(Dedicated to that phase of cancer treatment when 'things were done to me' and made me feel that I had little or no control over my life!)

The heads-up

My cancer journey began when I discovered a lump in my left breast. I asked my husband Abhi to check if he could feel the lump too. He could, and I decided to go and see my GP in Cambridge the following week. My reasoning was: if the lump was harmless, then it would be good to get the confirmation; and if it was not, then I needed to know as soon as possible.

At this point, Abhi thought I was being a hypochondriac. He didn't suspect anything untoward. He chose to remain blissfully unaware of the bad things diseases could do, and therefore for him, the possibility that the lump could mean bad news just didn't exist. While it was OK to be aware of the medical conditions that exist in the world, he thought, it made no sense to imagine that they could happen to us. Well, I wasn't about to adopt the same attitude, because I understood medical conditions slightly more than many others. With a four-year full-time degree in pharmacy, I had come to appreciate the phenomenal range of medical conditions that exist, and I understood that they could happen to anyone. Therefore, for me, the probability was 50% – it was either good news, or it was not. Even though Abhi was certain the lump wasn't anything serious, he didn't stop me from seeing the GP.

When I met my GP, I voiced my concern: I had a history of fibroadenoma (benign breast lumps) and was concerned about this one, because it felt different. I am not sure if my GP completely shared my anxiety, but he did nonetheless refer me to a specialist immediately, someone I wanted to go to at Addenbrooke's Hospital in Cambridge. This quick referral was partially because the UK has a tremendous focus on the diagnosis and cure of cancer. The GPs try to make sure any suspected case of cancer is referred to a specialist as soon as possible. The specialist I requested was Dr Parto, who had removed one of my fibroadenoma lumps eighteen months ago. Through this previous experience, I was familiar with the surgeon's skill and expertise.

I went to consult the specialist. While I waited for my turn at 9:00 am on the 10th of September 2012 at Addenbrooke's Hospital in the scenic city of Cambridge, I looked at the various people in the waiting hall. I wondered how many of these people had found symptoms that were perturbing to say the least. After a while, I saw Dr Parto briskly walk into the clinic. Since I was first on the appointment list, I prepared to hear my name being called out.

The nurse came and called my name shortly afterwards. When I got to the examination room, I expressed my desire to specifically see Dr Parto. I told the nurse about the earlier operation and they understood my request to continue treatment with the same surgeon. They assured me that they would check if Dr Parto was available and sure enough, after a few minutes, there he was.

My appointment lasted just fifteen minutes, but he asked me to stay back for some tests and scans. The first ultrasound scan seemed to go on forever. The radiologist stared at the screen, which to me looked like an indistinct blur of black and white waves. She asked me to wait while she called in the senior doctor, and then they both stared at the screen for a long time. I felt uncomfortable and asked if everything was OK. They replied that they wanted me to go for some more tests immediately.

So I was sent for a mammogram[2]. The machine's squeezing was hurtful and I was disgruntled at the thought of my precious boobs being hurt so badly. I had never heard anyone describe the experience of getting a mammogram, and so I was taken aback by the pain. I had somehow assumed that it would be like any other scan – a CT scan or an X-ray. But then I stopped thinking about the pain, because there was a more intense turmoil going on inside my head. After the mammogram, I was led back to the ultrasound room for biopsy samples and more scans. The radiographer told me that they usually took samples for biopsies from lymph nodes larger than four centimetres in size. However, in my case, even though the lymph nodes were only three centimetres wide, they wanted to collect the samples for investigation. They asked for my consent, but I wanted to know why they wanted to take samples even though I fell below the minimum threshold. They said that they wanted to be sure.

This heightened my sense of suspicion. The process of taking the biopsy sample was painful, although the local anaesthetic was a life-saver! I think that more than the process, it was the size of the needle that alarmed me. During the process, I fixed my gaze on the computer screen and tried to follow every single movement made by the needle.

A suspicious lump in the breast, several scans for which I did not have appointments (especially in an NHS hospital which is always busy with patients), radiographers staring at their computer screens forever, and finally my consent being requested for a biopsy even though the size of the lymph nodes was below the usual threshold – everything put together signalled bad news to me. I held onto every word they said.

---

[2]   Mammogram: A mammogram is a low-dose x-ray of the breast tissue. It is a test to look for early breast cancers.
Macmillan Cancer Support. "Your mammogram appointment and what to expect." Last modified August 2014. http://www.macmillan.org.uk/information-and-support/diagnosing/how-cancers-are-diagnosed/breast-screening/your-mammogram-appointment-and-what-to-expect.html. Last accessed April 09, 2015.

They talked about some calcification that they saw on the screen and I asked, 'Is that a bad thing?' They said 'no', and a hippopotamus-like silence filled the room again. Anaesthesia, cuts, pain, shoving, and lot of staring at the screen followed. When the doctor had finished the biopsy scans, she said, 'You get dressed, and we'll have a little chat over a cup of tea.' Now I was in an NHS hospital, and I wondered – since when did NHS doctors have time to have a chat with a patient over a cup of tea on a Monday morning? The NHS healthcare team had always treated me with warmth, but the idea of having a cup of tea with them felt a bit out of place.

I was given a choice of tea, coffee or hot chocolate, and the nurse strongly suggested that hot chocolate was the best. I went with her suggestion and she quickly came back with a mug of hot chocolate and handed it to me with a huge smile. I sipped it gratefully, and tried to relax after two and a half hours of physical pain, anxiety, and tests. The radiologist came in and gave me further information about the investigation that I had just undergone. But all I wanted to know was: was there any bad news? Was the lump in my breast something that I needed to worry about? I knew that the doctors would not say anything unless they knew for sure; and I understood that. But I just needed to know... I needed to know what I was up against.

The doctor understood my impatience and said, 'Next week when you come for the reports, please expect to find some cancerous cells'. There it was – almost as clear as black and white. She had confirmed the last thing anyone wants to hear – that they have cancer. My worst nightmare had just been confirmed. I briefly thanked the doctor for her time and honesty, picked up my belongings, and left. I was quiet and in no mood to engage in any further conversation.

Once I was out of the consultation room, I called Abhi immediately and stammered into the phone that the doctor thought I had cancer. It was time for Abhi to be shocked; he was livid, 'How can the doctor say something like "You have cancer"?'

'Errr... they saw the texture of the lump on the ultrasound.'

'But how can they say something like "You could have cancer"?' he screamed.

I told him about the scans and that I was calling from the hospital. The ironic thing was: when the doctors were silent, I wanted them to say something. When they did say something, I wished that they had kept quiet.

Thanks to my ability to hold myself together during difficult times, I managed to compose myself, at least on the exterior, during the twenty-minute bicycle ride to the office. I was three hours late and there was work to do. I did not have luxury of sitting and crying over what I had just learnt about my condition!

My team were waiting for me. I told them that I had been at the hospital for the investigation of a breast lump, and that immediately triggered responses about how some of them had had to undergo extra tests when they had discovered lumps in their bodies. The only difference was that they had been given clearance, and I had been given a heads-up for cancer: the Big C. The discussion caught heat, and somehow I did not feel like participating. For me this was not a general discussion about a medical condition, where people shared experiences while they took a break from work. This was something that was about to change my life, and I doubted that the change would be for the better.

The 10th of September was also the day my evening Spanish classes started. When I entered the classroom at 8:00 pm, I had a lot on my mind. On any other regular day, I would have had lots of fun in class while connecting with different people and learning the language. But this day was different. I tried to keep the day's events tucked at the back of my mind, and concentrate on the lesson. It was a difficult thing to do.

I was required to go and collect the biopsy reports on the following Monday. I had a week before I got the results. Abhi and I decided to spend the week preparing for the meeting of our lives. If only I had studied so well in school! ☺ But then, what lies at stake decides how far we go for a particular thing, doesn't it?

We browsed the internet and spoke to several people about breast cancer. After four days, we knew so much about the condition, and were so frightened by most of it, that we started getting bogged down. There were tales of what cancer can do, the misery it causes, and the bleakness of the cure. I came across several blog discussions where people had written about their cancer experiences. Some said things like, 'I had breast cancer ten years ago, and I am still here.' The emphasis on still being here seemed enormous. The life expectancy for breast cancer survivors seemed short – ten years or so! There were stories about success too, but they were few and far between. We soon became so perturbed that we decided to stop reading about cancer. Anyhow, we had read everything we needed for the discussion on the following Monday.

I confided in my brother, Sachin, about what had happened at the hospital. I sent him links to some online information about breast cancer. The more he read about it, the more his restlessness grew. He also discussed cancer with a few of his colleagues in the US, where he lives. One of his colleagues, who had had an experience with cancer as a primary carer, said, 'Sachin, you guys are about to embark on a very difficult journey. It will be so difficult that it could drive you crazy.' Thank you for the information – but it was rather demotivating! Sachin became hysterical after this conversation. Before the week was over, he stopped reading about cancer, as most of the tales were sad.

Waiting for the results was harrowing! It felt like the longest week of our lives.

A few days later, it was the 15th of September and my birthday. We spent the day in Cambridge, shopping at our favourite store, John Lewis, and spent the evening with our friends from India. I bought three tops: purple, lime green, and my favourite red. It was a good day. We put aside what we were going through and had fun. It appeared that we would have enjoyed ourselves more if we had not had this nagging fear in our heads. But on that day, the need to be happy and be grateful for being alive seemed paramount to me. I was prepared in my heart for the bad news simply because of the *vibes* I had received from the doctors during the tests. I did not know what lay ahead, and that was why living that day was so important. We finished my birthday with cake. Our friends had placed a magic candle on the cake, and each time I put it out, it would come back with a poof! It seemed a silly game but we had so much fun. It helped us take our minds off the imminent Monday.

Only one day remained between me and the potential confirmation of cancer.

More about Cancer:

<u>The symptoms of breast cancer</u>[3]**:** Cancer can be tricky to diagnose, as in many instances it stealthily sneaks up on people. I consider myself lucky that my cancer showed up distinctly.

The following are the key symptoms of breast cancer:

- a lump in the breast
- a change in the size or shape of the breast
- dimpling of the skin or thickening in the breast tissue
- a nipple that's turned in (inverted)
- a rash (like eczema) on the nipple
- discharge from the nipple
- swelling or a lump in the armpit.

In fact, we need to know what is normal for our bodies. As soon as we notice a change, a visit to the GP is well worth our time. I would rather be considered paranoid than delay the diagnosis of an illness that could kill me.

---

[3] Macmillan Cancer Support. "Signs and symptoms of breast cancer." Last modified October 2013. http://www.macmillan.org.uk/information-and-support/breast-cancer/diagnosing/how-cancers-are-diagnosed/signs-and-symptoms/index.html. Last accessed April 09, 2015.

The confirmation

Finally, Monday came and we went to the hospital. As we waited for our turn, I watched the other women sitting in the Breast Unit reception. Most of them were accompanied by family or friends, and I noticed that Abhi and I appeared to be the youngest people there. This was not a compliment in the current situation; it only meant that we were about to face the bad news earlier in our lives. It also told me that cancer shows no mercy, it does not discriminate – people old and young, rich and poor, of every religion and skin colour – any one of us can get it.

My thoughts were interrupted by the nurse, who escorted us to the consultation room. Dr Parto came in and gently started the conversation. I knew instantly that something was different. On every previous occasion, this doctor had come to the point straight away. He is indeed a man of few words. But that particular day, he came in and said, 'Mrs Banka, as you know, you came to see us last week, and we called you in today for the results.' He was starting to build a preface. I braced myself for the bad news.

I remember that moment in clear detail. I remember that I was wearing a red top. I remember exactly how I was sitting – I was leaning a little to the front with my hands slightly clasped in my lap. Abhi was sitting to my right. Dr Parto carried on, 'I am very sorry to say that you have been diagnosed with aggressive grade 3[4] breast cancer'. I had been expecting to hear the C word – but the accompanying adjectives were not expected and made little sense. As I tried to comprehend these words, the doctor went on to add that based on the location and nature of this particular cancer, a mastectomy[5] looked inevitable.

A mastectomy! Now, that was an even bigger shock. I'd been expecting that the cancer had been caught at an early stage, and was unnerved at the strong possibility (rather the heads-up) of a mastectomy. I loved my boobs, and suddenly here was a doctor telling me that one of them would need to be cut off and separated from me forever. It felt like a violation or an assault, to which I was being subjected. But I had no time to mourn over it. There was something more important that I needed to know.

'What are the chances that I will survive?' I asked.

The doctor responded, 'We are going to undertake treatment with an intention to cure.'

'Yes, but that does not answer my question. What do the statistics say about the survival rates? I just want to know what the chances are that I will survive!'

---

[4] Macmillan Cancer Support. "Staging and grading." Last modified August 2013. http://www.macmillan.org.uk/information-and-support/treating/treatment-decisions/understanding-your-diagnosis/staging-and-grading.html. Last accessed April 09, 2015.
And
Macmillan Cancer Support. "Understanding breast cancer in women." Last modified October 2013. http://be.macmillan.org.uk/Downloads/CancerInformation/CancerTypes/MAC11616BreastwomenE10lowrespdf20131101.pdf. Last accessed April 09, 2015.

[5] Macmillan Cancer Support. "Types of surgery for breast cancer." Last modified October 2013. http://www.macmillan.org.uk/information-and-support/breast-cancer/treating/surgery/surgery-explained/types-surgery-breast-cancer.html. Last accessed April 09, 2015.

God damn it! Why can't the doctors use plain English? I said in my head.

Dr Parto answered, 'Out of five people, four survive'.

'Cool! So, we are looking at an 80% chance that I will survive. That's a high percentage,' I said, so relieved that I found myself thinking out loud. I believe I saw a slightly startled look in Dr Parto's eye. Maybe he thought I was crazy, or that I was in denial, or that I did not understand what he was telling me. I suddenly sounded relieved, just after being diagnosed with aggressive grade 3 breast cancer! Well, people who know me well would not have been surprised by this. My friend Nikhil called me the undying optimist. I think that in the larger scheme of things, I was just happy to be told that I wasn't dying.

Dr Parto also told us that the lymph nodes did not show any sign of cancer; the results were negative for malignancy. This was brilliant news, as it meant that the cancer had not spread beyond the primary site, which was the lump in my left breast.

He had already organised a meeting for us with the oncologist. He gave us five minutes to assimilate the information. Saying he would go and check if the oncologist was ready to meet us, Dr Parto walked out of the room. The nurse followed him.

Abhi and I were left alone in the room. I hugged Abhi and I wept. This was mad, it was impossible. A mastectomy! Aggressive grade 3 cancer! Abhi held me tight and cried silently too.

Abhi and I have known each other for more than a decade. He is tall and thin, and I am short and, shall we say, not quite so thin. He devours chocolate every day and gains no weight. I seem to put on weight just by buying all that chocolate for him. I enjoy cooking and hate cleaning up, and he's fine with cleaning up and hates cooking (works well for us). He loves reading business magazines; I read often, but rarely business magazines. He accepts many ideas and values because they are handed down to us in the name of tradition and culture, whereas I must challenge everything that I am asked to do. He chose to study the quantifiable, finance, whereas I studied the unquantifiable, human behaviour. He specialises in negotiating contracts, while what works for me is connecting with people by talking. We may be as different as the East and West, but we are in sync on critical things: being able to make each other laugh, and standing by each other when it really matters.

And so, that day in the little consultation room at the hospital after being told that I had cancer, Abhi and I held each other and shed precious tears. This was the only time Abhi cried during my entire cancer experience, and it was the first time I cried. I don't know why we both cried at that moment: was it the diagnosis of a serious illness or the fear of mortality associated with it? Was the 80% chance of survival not good enough? Was it because something had just kicked us in the guts without warning? Was it because our safe world had so swiftly fallen apart like a house of cards? Was I crying for the difficult time ahead of me, and the potential loss of a breast – or was I crying for the pain to which Abhi would be subjected? Was he crying for me, or was he crying because there was a (20%) chance that he might be left alone? Was I crying because I might not grow old with him and be there to laugh at the silly things we had done together? Was I worried if anybody else would understand Abhi like I did – would anybody else know how he felt about things even before he knew it himself? Did we cry because his presumption that bad diseases happen to other people had just been ridiculed? Whatever the reason, we held each other silently and the pain gripped us.

I wouldn't cry for a very long time after this, as I would be too busy getting on with the treatment.

We got hold of ourselves in a couple of minutes, as we knew that Dr Parto could come back into the room any moment. When he walked in, he saw my red eyes. I am sure he understood that I had been crying. He said that the oncologist, Dr Charles, was ready to meet us.

I was given a thick information pack to which I could refer later. It had information on the diagnosis, about breast cancer, and the primary points of contact and support services available at the hospital for cancer patients. It also had the contact details for Dr Parto, who would be my breast care specialist during the treatment.

We were led by the nurse to Dr Charles's office. Dr Charles is probably about 50, English, and an extremely patient man. He began by explaining the diagnosis to us. 'Breast cancer', 'potential mastectomy', 'aggressive grade 3 tumour', and 'immediate need to start the treatment' were the key phrases that I gathered from him.

'What next?' I asked.

He replied that he would recommend immediate chemotherapy, followed by surgery and radiation therapy.

'Do you think that my condition is curable?' I asked.

'To cure would be the intention, although we need to perform a few more scans to establish the extent of spread of cancer in your body.'

'Right... and... what are my chances of survival?' I wanted to know, although Dr Parto had already given us the statistics.

'About 80%.' The same answer. Then Dr Charles asked, 'Do you have children?'

'No.'

'Do you want to have children in future?'

I paused. 'Why? Is my answer to this question related to the treatment?'

13

'Yes, it may affect a few decisions.'

Dr Charles added gently, 'I'd like you to know that about two-thirds of women retain their fertility, and about a third of women lose it during the treatment.'

This conversation was getting more difficult every moment. Being asked whether I wanted to have children, right after being told that I had cancer. This was definitely not the best time to make such an enormous life decision.

When it came to fertility, I had faced a difficult situation over the last year. A massive fibroid had developed in my uterus. It is not a very common thing for fibroids to grow to this massive size. I happened to be one of the exceptions! Due to the size and complexity of the fibroid, a hysterectomy had looked inevitable, as removing only the fibroid could lead to severe complications. The very idea of a hysterectomy filled me with searing loss, dread, and anger. I felt as if the choice of being a parent was being snatched away from me. What I did with this choice was my prerogative – but I couldn't bear to think of losing that possibility.

But then, thankfully, I was referred to two doctors, who together performed a long operation on me and successfully removed the fibroid, while leaving the uterus intact. I had just been on the verge of losing my fertility and had managed to retain it. This experience had really prompted Abhi and me to think seriously about parenthood. In fact, we were booked in to see my surgeon, who had sorted out the uterine fibroid, in three weeks' time to discuss this further. But before *that* could happen, here I was – being told once again that I might lose my fertility, this time because I had cancer!

I had a flurry of emotions and thoughts – I felt overwhelmed and empty deep inside me at the same time. I avoided looking at Abhi, because I was scared that I would shatter into a million pieces, and yet I was so thankful that he was there with me. I could feel him right next to me and that gave me enormous strength to carry on.

I gathered my thoughts and drew in a deep breath. I tried to focus on what Dr Charles was saying. I heard myself say, 'Well, I am not sure if I want children in the future. We have not had children so far by choice, although we come from a society where there is an enormous social pressure to have children – because we felt that we were not ready to be parents. But – if you are asking me to make a decision now – yes, I'd like to have this option in the future.'

'What about egg-harvesting? Is that an option we have?' All the reading that we had done in the previous week was helping me to ask the right questions.

'That is an option, although I would not recommend it,' Dr Charles replied. 'Your cancer is an aggressive grade 3 type, which means that it has the potential to grow very fast. Harvesting eggs or embryos typically takes three to four weeks. I am not comfortable with such a delay in starting your treatment. This type of cancer can do a lot of damage, if not stopped immediately.'

'Do I need to speak to another oncologist for a second opinion?'

Looking back, I think this was a rude thing to ask Dr Charles. But he has such great empathy that he did not mind this question even a tiny bit. He could understand what we were going through, that we were afraid and naturally wanted to avail of the best course of action. He said that a second opinion would not be necessary, as he had discussed my case with four other oncologists at the hospital.

He suggested that we meet Dr Raj, a senior gynaecologist at the hospital. Dr Raj also specialised in the In-Vitro Fertilisation (IVF) treatment. Dr Charles had already booked the earliest possible appointment with Dr Raj for us, at 4 pm on the same day. He suggested that I take a couple of days to assimilate all this information, make a decision about the embryo harvesting, and then come back to him.

Irrespective of whether I decided to go for embryo harvesting, they needed to establish the extent of the spread of the cancer and baseline the case. So I booked an appointment to see Dr Charles that Friday, the 21st of September. I told him that I would like to undergo the treatment privately, but would need to speak to my insurance company to ascertain if cancer was covered in my policy.

Dr Charles very kindly wrote out the exact diagnosis (in medical jargon) that I should communicate to the insurance company, BUPA. He also advised me on important details that I should clarify with them.

We said goodbye to Dr Charles and said that we would be in touch with him. We knew this was the beginning of a long association. During that one morning, we had met the two doctors who would go on to become my life-savers. I may not be alive or well today to tell my story, if it weren't for the efforts and skill of Dr Parto and Dr Charles.

It was 12 noon, and we still had four hours before we could see Dr Raj. Abhi and I hadn't expected to be at the hospital for so long. Clearly, we knew nothing about how cancer treatment is approached and what it comprises. We went to the cafeteria and bought some food – a huge blueberry muffin and two cups of tea. We carried our tea to an unoccupied table and sat down. There was so much going on inside my head. Abhi was quiet. I sipped my tea quietly and ate the muffin. Strangely, the muffin tasted weird – I usually enjoy them but it was different that day. Abhi chose not to eat at all. I ate whatever I could and binned the rest. After finishing the tea, we went out. It was time to break the news to the family.

It was autumn and a gusty wind was blowing. Using mobile phones was not allowed in most parts of the hospital, and so we stepped out of the hospital to call up the family. It was difficult to talk on the phone, with my voice broken up by the wind and by the difficult diagnosis.

Sachin was the first person we called. Since he knew about the heads-up for cancer that had been given to me last week, he had been eagerly awaiting a call from me, to find out what the reports said. I had missed two calls from him, and I knew that he was going crazy with all the waiting.

The call went through. He picked up and shouted, 'Where have you been? What did the doctors say?'

'Cancer is confirmed.'

There was a pause.

'And it is not just cancer but aggressive grade 3 cancer.'

'How many grades are there?' he asked.

'Three.'

Another pause – longer than the one before.

'We have been speaking with the doctors since morning. They say that based on the size and position of the tumour, a mastectomy is inevitable. I know this is real and I am trying to be strong. But I'm scared. I don't know what "aggressive cancer" really means. It definitely sounds intimidating. I thought that I found the lump early, but they are already talking about a mastectomy. This is crazy.' My voice choked.

Sachin freaked out. We had been expecting cancer, while of course hoping that the initial heads-up would prove to be wrong. But we were not prepared for the 'aggressive' version.

I immediately told him that the doctors thought that they would be able to save me; there was a good 80% chance. I repeated that, more than once. I knew he would be worried about whether I would make it, and I wanted him to know about the high survival rate right at the start.

But he asked, 'Did the doctors say that there is just an 80% chance'

He was concerned that they had said just 80, and not 100. He was scared that I could fall into that 20%.

My eyes welled up as I spoke to him on the phone. I was choking, while I tried to be calm so that I could talk to him. He said that together we would battle it, and things would be fine. *I hope so!* I thought.

I asked him if he could share the news with our parents and our eldest brother, Dinesh. He agreed. That took a burden off me, as far as repeating the same thing was concerned, on that devastating day. I wished that there was an opportunity for me to break the news to my family in person, but with us dispersed in different countries, it wasn't possible. I really didn't want to use video chat to share this news with them. Maybe I was aware of my vulnerability, scared that I would crumble as if I were made of sand when I saw them. I decided that it was best to leave the communication to Sachin.

> *The day had just begun in the US when the phone rang. I had been waiting for this and sprang to answer the phone. On the other end, there was my sister and she said, 'The doctors have confirmed cancer.'*
>
> *No training in this world prepares you to receive such news. My mind and body became numb and time seemed to freeze. Everything looked blurred, hazy, and uncertain. There was an upheaval of thoughts in my mind. Soon the initial shock was overtaken by anger: Why my family, and why my sister? Once the news had sunk in, the worst of all emotions surfaced: F-E-A-R. Fear of the uncertainties that lay ahead, fear of what came next, and the fear of losing my sister. I felt helpless because I didn't have the power to change anything or to somehow make her cancer go away.*
>
> *I struggled with my emotions. Eventually, my mind and body were exhausted; I couldn't hold back anymore, and I cried. I searched for answers. I wanted to know why it had to happen to us, but all I got was a cold vacuum.*
>
> Sachin, Parul's brother

At 4 pm, we went back in to meet Dr Raj. We were to discuss the option of egg harvesting with him. He told us that because we were married, it would be embryos that would be harvested, and not eggs. We were OK with that. We needed to know more about the process and he very kindly explained it to us. The key things that we understood were: my body would need to be stimulated, using drugs, to release eggs. The eggs would be fertilised with Abhi's sperm, and the resultant embryo would be harvested and stored in the embryo bank.

'Great," I said. "What is the timeframe required for this procedure?'

'Three to four weeks, definitely not less than three weeks.'

'But Dr Charles says that he is not comfortable with that kind of delay in starting my treatment. He says that the damage that this cancer can cause in three or four weeks' time can be humongous.'

'Yes, I have spoken to Dr Charles and am aware that he is not comfortable with the waiting. But the decision is yours; it depends on what your priorities are.'

I knew that I laughed when Dr Raj said this. I said, 'I am aware that it is my decision, but I need to be alive to have a baby later on. What is the use of going through embryo harvesting, if I do not survive cancer?'

'So, what are your priorities?'

I turned to Abhi, 'Do you want to answer this?' I felt exhausted, and thought that Abhi could take over the conversation.

'We would like to retain the fertility. That will be our priority,' he said.

I was stunned at this response. In fact, this was the most shocking moment of that day. I could not believe that in our present situation, Abhi put fertility above everything else – above me! It felt like the biggest betrayal, more severe than the one that my body had subjected me to. His few words had broken my heart into a million pieces.

I was shattered – but this was my treatment, and my life! I decided to take charge.

'Sorry, my priorities are different, and they are: first, survival. Second, saving the breast – I don't want to have a mastectomy. And third, after my life and hopefully my breast are saved, I want to have the option of other nice things in life, like the option of having a baby.'

Now, it was Abhi's turn to be surprised. He looked at me and said, 'Obviously, the first two points that you said are the topmost priority. There are no second thoughts about them. That's why I didn't even mention them.'

I was so relieved. *I* was Abhi's number one priority. *I can battle this situation with him on my side*, I thought.

I turned to the doctor and continued the discussion, 'Even though you say that the decision is mine, I will do what my oncologist thinks is best, because he is the one who understands cancer, not me.' While it was my decision to make, I felt that I did not in reality have much choice, since starting treatment as quickly as possible was the necessary thing to do in my case.

We also spoke a little about future support through IVF for conceiving, if I happened to be amongst the 66% of women who retained their fertility.

In case I happened to fall among the remaining one-third, I could consider adoption or surrogacy. It was quite useful to speak to Dr Raj, as he is from India. He really understood the social and the cultural aspects that affected us. He suggested that in the future, we could look at the option of egg donation: someone in the family could do it, and it would be a very special and a very, very personal gift. He also told us that there are egg banks, and we could take an egg from one of the banks and use Abhi's sperm to fertilise it.

Taking in all this information, I said, 'I completely understand that I need to decide the next course of action, but can you help me arrive at the right decision, please? I want to choose the option that is most rational.'

Dr Raj replied, 'If your priorities are so clear, it should not be difficult to make the most rational decision.'

'OK – in that case, we will go ahead with Dr Charles's recommendation.'

I felt guilty when I made this decision. I felt that I was choosing myself over my baby. I had conflicting emotions in my mind, and it was strange that I felt so. Abhi and I had always thought that we were just not ready to be parents. But when I made the decision about starting the treatment without harvesting the embryos, I felt stressed. There was a chance that I could lose my ability to have a baby, and it just felt wrong that I should put myself before my baby.

However, in my heart I knew that it was the right decision to make, because as I said before, to have a baby, I needed to be alive!

My experience with the NHS hospital had been brilliant. They had processed all my tests at a supersonic speed, delivered the results with such great empathy, and had given me as much information as I needed to make decisions about the treatment.

We reached home by 7 pm, feeling absolutely drained. Sachin had already shared the news about cancer with our parents and Dinesh. Dinesh was waiting for Abhi and me to get back home, so that he could speak to me. He was in shock, as the diagnosis had caught him unawares. Although Sachin had given him all the details, I had to reiterate them. He was finding it difficult to believe that this was happening to me. He needed to hear everything again to process the information.

Soon after speaking to Dinesh, I went to attend my second Spanish class. I felt confused and numb as I left for the class. The earlier events of the day had exhausted me mentally and physically. I reached the class early, and while waiting there, I realised that I had completed the wrong exercise for homework. Hurriedly, I started working on the exercise that I should have done. I think all the anxiety about cancer had caused that goof-up. From 8:00 pm to 9:30 pm, I had a strange concoction of thoughts about cancer and the Spanish lesson in my head. While the class was interesting, I was distracted. I just hoped that I would be able to continue attending the classes along with taking the treatment, as I really wanted to learn the language. I had been able to secure a place in the class after waiting ten months. After such a long wait, I was happy to take the course of my choice, but it was just difficult for me to concentrate.

My life had changed, officially. I was a cancer patient.

More about Cancer:

Staging of cancer[6]: The different stages of cancer describe its size and the extent of its spread. The part of the body where the cancer begins is called the primary site.

Breast cancer is divided into the following four stages:

- Stage 1 – The size of the cancer lump is smaller than, or equal to, 2cm across, and has not spread to the lymph nodes in the armpit.
- Stage 2 is divided into two stages:

  o Stage 2A – The lump is smaller than 2cm across but has spread to the lymph nodes in the armpit; or, it's bigger than 2cm (but under 5cm) and hasn't spread to the lymph nodes; or, the cancer can't be found in the breast but is in the lymph nodes in the armpit.
  o Stage 2B – The lump is smaller than 5cm and has spread to the lymph nodes in the armpit; or, it's bigger than 5cm but hasn't spread to the lymph nodes in the armpit.

- Stage 3 is divided into three stages:

---

[6]   Macmillan Cancer Support. "Staging and grading." Last modified August 2013.   http://www.macmillan.org.uk/information-and-support/treating/treatment-decisions/understanding-your-diagnosis/staging-and-grading.html. Last accessed April 09, 2015.
And
Macmillan Cancer Support. "Understanding breast cancer in women." Last modified October 2013. http://be.macmillan.org.uk/Downloads/CancerInformation/CancerTypes/MAC11616BreastwomenE10lowrespdf20131101.pdf.   Last accessed April 09, 2015.

- o Stage 3A – The cancer can't be found in the breast, the lump is under 5cm in size and the cancer is in the lymph nodes in the armpit, which are stuck together; or, the lump is bigger than 5cm and has spread to the lymph nodes.
- o Stage 3B – The cancer has spread to tissue near the breast, and may be attached to the surrounding skin or muscle. There are usually cancer cells in the lymph nodes in the armpit as well.
- o Stage 3C – The cancer has spread to the lymph nodes in the armpit, below the breastbone, near the neck, or under the collarbone.

- Stage 4 – The cancer has spread to other parts of the body, such as the bones, liver or lungs. This is called secondary or metastatic breast cancer.

Grading of cancer[7]: Grading refers to how the cancer cells look under the microscope, compared with normal breast cells.

Grade 1 (low-grade) – The cancer cells look similar to normal cells and grow very slowly.

Grade 2 (moderate-grade or intermediate-grade) – The cancer cells look more abnormal, and grow slightly faster than normal cells.

---

[7] Macmillan Cancer Support. "Staging and grading." Last modified August 2013. http://www.macmillan.org.uk/information-and-support/treating/treatment-decisions/understanding-your-diagnosis/staging-and-grading.html. Last accessed April 09, 2015.
And
Macmillan Cancer Support. "Understanding breast cancer in women." Last modified October 2013. http://be.macmillan.org.uk/Downloads/CancerInformation/CancerTypes/MAC11616BreastwomenE10lowrespdf20131101.pdf. Last accessed April 09, 2015.

Grade 3 (high-grade) – The cancer cells look very different from normal cells, and tend to grow quickly.

I was aware of the signs of breast cancer. Therefore, as soon as I noticed a lump, I went to see my GP. I strongly believe that my awareness saved me. Mine was an aggressive grade 3 cancer, and it could have done irreparable damage if I had ignored the lump, even for a few weeks. I understand that it's tempting to postpone a visit to the doctor because you are scared of the bad news. But don't be – because if it is bad news, the sooner you know it, the easier it will be to manage.

Stay aware, stay safe, and stay alive.

Embarking on the journey to get beyond the Big C

Reality struck as I received a letter from the hospital that explained my condition in medical terms:

Diagnosis: Self detected, triple-receptor positive breast cancer.

Background: September 2012, 33 mm LUOQ mass (previous fibroadenoma site).

Biopsy confirmed T2Nx Grade 3 carcinoma, ER 8/8, HER2 3+ invasive breast cancer and a negative lymph node.

The medical terminology made the cancer look more grotesque and complicated.

I wrote to the insurance company, BUPA, the very next day to enquire if cancer was covered under the policy. It was. I decided to take treatment at Nuffield Health Hospital, Cambridge, which was very close to my place of work. I had never seen anyone go through cancer treatment before and I did not know how feasible it would be for me to work. But I intended to continue working, and hoped that the treatment would not be much of a hindrance. At the same time, I decided that I would let my life go on as 'normally' as possible. I would try to work, exercise, cook, have fun, and not be bogged down with cancer. I resolved that I didn't want pity or sympathy from others. I wanted them to treat me like they had always done: treat me as myself. I didn't want any leeway because of cancer. Secretly, I also hoped that I wouldn't need any concessions because of the new beast in my life. I was happy to receive wishes for a speedy recovery, and accepted people expressing how sorry they were to hear about my news; but pity? No, thank you.

We had recently moved to Hitchin, and I had yet to finish the paperwork for registering at a local surgery when I was diagnosed with cancer. Therefore, I happened to still be registered at Cambridge for the cancer treatment. I also worked in Cambridge, so I planned to coordinate hospital appointments as per my work schedule. Hitchin is a little town, tranquil and scenic. From Hitchin to Cambridge is a thirty-eight minute train ride, but overall I took about an hour and a quarter to reach the office or hospital at Cambridge once I stepped out of home.

The next day was precious. It was the only day over the next fifteen months or so when I would be well (I knew that cancer was gnawing at me from the inside, but on the surface I was well), not affected by any medicines, and with no hospital appointments. The actual treatment would run for about fifteen months, but the first eight months would be intensive; and then afterwards, I would be on oral tablets for five years.

I saw Dr Parto on Thursday, the 20th of September 2012, and he asked me to undergo a full-body MRI scan. We needed to find out if the cancer had spread to other parts of my body. The result would have a great impact on the future course of action, and the prognosis (the likely outcome of the treatment). This was also the day my regular and immensely frequent visits to the hospital began. Dr Parto organised an appointment for the MRI scan for me, which was very helpful. I think that my doctors were trying to give me all the support that they could, to get the treatment started as soon as possible. The result of this scan later came out as negative – the cancer had not spread to other parts of my body and was limited to the primary site. Awesome news!

Since Monday, when the cancer had been confirmed, each visit to the hospital had been followed by a phone call from Sachin and a video chat on Skype with Dinesh. They were elated at the results of the MRI scan. As a family, we were holding on to each instance of positive news to keep our morale up. My parents had still not spoken to me. They, and I, needed time before we could discuss my medical condition. Sachin continued to act as the messenger, sharing information with them.

21 September was the day on which I communicated to Dr Charles my decision about starting the treatment immediately. We spent time discussing the next steps.

Thursday: (a) A small operation would be done to insert something called an implantable port[8] into my body. An implantable port is a thin, soft plastic tube that is put into a vein in the chest or arm, and has an opening (a 'port') just under the skin. It allows medicines to be injected into the vein, or blood to be taken from the vein. The tube is not visible to the naked eye, but the port looks like a round coin placed just beneath the skin. This port would be used to inject all the drugs intravenously. It would do away with the need to put an IV drip into my arm each time I had to undergo treatment. (b) We would start with four weekly Zoladex[9], to switch off my ovaries. We hoped that this would prevent my ovaries from getting damaged, and would be an essential step in preserving my fertility. It would also prevent the ovaries from producing oestrogen[10] (a primary female sex hormone), because they

---

8   Macmillan Cancer Support. "Implantable ports." Last modified October 2012. http://www.macmillan.org.uk/information-and-support/treating/chemotherapy/being-treated-with-chemotherapy/implantable-ports.html. Last accessed April 09, 2015.

9   Macmillan Cancer Support. "Goserelin for breast cancer (Zoladex®)." Last modified January 2013. http://www.macmillan.org.uk/Cancerinformation/Cancertreatment/Treatmenttypes/Hormonaltherapies/Individualhormonaltherapies/GoserelinBreast.aspx. Last accessed December 05, 2014.

10   Wikipedia. "Estrogen." Last modified October 2014. http://en.wikipedia.org/wiki/Estrogen. Last accessed December 05, 2014.

would get switched off. My cancer was oestrogen positive, and therefore blocking oestrogen made sense. (c) I would have a blood test, to baseline my blood count.

Friday: I would have the first session of chemotherapy. My drug regimen for chemotherapy would be FEC-T[11]. Each of these letters stands for the name of a drug. The first three cycles of chemotherapy would comprise 'FEC', all the three drugs. The last three cycles would have only 'T'. We were looking at six chemotherapy cycles, of three weeks each. This meant that I would be on chemotherapy for the following eighteen weeks. Six cycles of chemotherapy are fairly common for breast cancer. Different types of cancers may have varying numbers of chemotherapy cycles. I shared with Dr Charles that I had tickets booked to travel to India in December. He told me that I would not be allowed to travel.

'Does this mean that I can't travel to India to meet my family?' I asked.

'Yes,' was his succinct response. 'Not this year.'

I must have looked disappointed, because he went on to explain the reason. He said that during chemotherapy, I might urgently need access to healthcare. If I was unable to get it, this could be very risky for my health. There was no way he would allow me to board a ten-hour flight. I was told to get the tickets cancelled. We weren't happy about it, but it had to be done.

---

[11] Information about FEC-T: FEC-T comprises initials of the chemotherapy drugs used: F – Fluorouracil, E – Epirubicin, C – Cyclophosphamide, T – Taxotere® or Docetaxel
Macmillan Cancer Support. "FEC-T chemotherapy." Last modified January 2014. http://www.macmillan.org.uk/Cancerinformation/Cancertreatment/Treatmenttypes/Chemotherapy/Combinationregimen/FEC-T.aspx. Last accessed December 05, 2014.

Dr Charles further explained the side effects of chemotherapy. The main side effects that I was to expect were:

- Severe fatigue and weakness
- Severe sickness (vomiting, nausea)
- Severe constipation
- Severe mouth ulcers
- Complete hair loss

These side effects, except the hair loss, would start setting in immediately after the start of chemotherapy.

We booked a time for the operation on Thursday, and so chemotherapy was scheduled to start the following week, on Friday.

Over the weekend, I wrote to my good friends Madhura and Rukmini (Ruks), who live in India, about cancelling our plan of travelling to India in December and why this was. My email dropped a bombshell on them. Madhura, in particular, jumped out of her skin. She has always treated me like her little sister, and the pain she felt on receiving the news was unfathomable.

Abhi broke the news to his sisters. They, in person, passed it on to their parents. The cancer diagnosis was a bolt from the blue for everyone in the family.

I also spoke to my parents – eventually! I had spent the last week gathering substantial information about my condition, and they had spent it coming to terms (as far as they could) with the diagnosis. They asked me to be strong, and I requested their help. I asked if Mum could come over and look after me during the chemotherapy. 'Of course I will,' she said. It was such a relief to hear this. While I didn't know how poorly I would be during the treatment, I knew that there would be difficult times ahead. I had been feeling worried about Abhi, and a little guilty about putting him in a difficult situation with my illness. He had a demanding job, with a long daily commute to London, and I felt guilty about adding to his burden. I was happy that with my parents' support, part of his burden would be relieved. At least he wouldn't have to worry about the daily chores like cooking or washing. There would always be food on the table when he came back from work.

It would be some weeks before Mum could travel to the UK. Indians need a visa to visit the UK, and it takes approximately two to three weeks to get the tourist visa processed. I told her that Abhi and I would do the paperwork for the visa over the next couple of days and initiate the process.

On Monday, the doctors found a slot available for me, a day before the scheduled date. They wanted me to start the treatment as quickly as possible. They were worried about what a grade 3 tumour might be doing, or about to do, to my body. So now the port would be inserted a day earlier, on Wednesday, and the first round of chemotherapy would be on Thursday. I called up Sachin and told him about the new schedule. He said that he would fly in for my first treatment. I tried to dissuade him, but he would not budge. He lives in Washington, DC, and wanted to fly to London at one day's notice. He was the only person in my family who had a visa to travel to the UK, and therefore he was the only one who could visit me straight away. He boarded the first flight out of Washington for London on Tuesday, and reached our home at Hitchin around midnight.

All of us were nervous about the next day, Wednesday. We chatted until late in the night, and eventually went off to sleep. We had to leave home at 6:00 am - the real journey for the Big C was about to start.

On Wednesday, an implantable port was inserted under my skin, just below the collarbone on my right arm. This would be used for the next fifteen months, for intravenous treatment. The needle that would be used the next day had been left inside, and would be removed after the first chemotherapy. It was a simple operation that was performed under sedation. However, the cut took a month to heal and I took several months to get used to the new insertion in my body. For the next eight months, I would not sleep leaning on my right hand side, as I found the port obstructive after turning onto my side. I would need to change my sleeping position. Once the port had been inserted, Zoladex was given to me, and the blood sample was taken.

It would be some time before Sachin, Abhi, and I found the time to process everything emotionally.

Wait...did I forget to feel?

Considering everything that had just happened, I was surprisingly calm. I understood the facts clearly, and I was neither in shock nor in denial about the cancer. I didn't feel like a victim, either. I understood that cancer is an illness, albeit a difficult one. Considering myself a victim wouldn't help, that is not a good frame of mind to be in. I was not devastated either. I definitely was confused about the *Karma* bit, but I didn't feel angry about the diagnosis. Lots of people think, 'Why me?' But interestingly, when the cancer happened, I never asked this question. I never blamed God for giving me cancer, nor did I whine about how 'life is not fair'. I think what was happening to me *was* life, working in its own peculiar way. As I turned to find answers within myself, I knew that I must use cancer as an opportunity to do something – I was not very clear what exactly this would be, but it would definitely be something. I felt ready to embark on the roller coaster ride that lay ahead of me.

But I also felt overwhelmed. There was too much information to process, and too many tasks to sort out. There were tasks at home, tasks at work (because I would have to take leave when chemotherapy started), and tasks sorting out the insurance, and amidst these was a hospital visit every day.

I soon became busy doing what had to be done. I understood that I had a key role to play in my recovery, and the sooner I took ownership for my well-being, the better it would be. All my emotional readiness and rational ownership grew in parallel with coping, at an emotional level, with my newfound status of being a cancer patient.

34

Different people may find different mechanisms for coping. For some people, knowing very little about cancer and what it can do works for them. Me, I wanted to seek as much information as possible. Even about difficult or obscure aspects of the treatment, I chose to be well-informed. This made me feel more in control of the situation, as it meant that I could make rational decisions. While I had become part of the cancer statistics without any choice in the matter, I resolved to become part of the survivors' statistics. *I will survive*, I decided, *and be part of that 80%*. I decided to do everything that would be required to kick cancer's butt out of my life.

We have two options, medically and emotionally: give up or fight like hell.
- Lance Armstrong

Bring on the chemotherapy!

The ugly duckling

Thursday, the 27th of September 2012: This was the day I experienced chemotherapy for the first time. The Oncology department at Nuffield Health Hospital, Cambridge has several nurses who specialise in chemotherapy treatment. The chemotherapy nurses need to have a particular number of years of experience as a nurse, followed by a course in chemotherapy, and experience working as a chemotherapy nurse. These nurses would play a very important part in my treatment over the next five months.

My appointment was at 3 pm. We planned to board the 1:47 pm train from Hitchin to Cambridge. Just as we were about to leave for the hospital, the doorbell rang. There was a delivery for me. My brother Dinesh, his wife Subhadra, and their children Ananya and Dev had sent us a huge bouquet of flowers, to wish me good luck as I started the chemotherapy. The bouquet had arrived just in time, and I felt all pampered to receive flowers from my family all the way from the US.

When we got to the hospital, Lorraine, the Head Nurse, came to us and explained the entire treatment and the process in explicit detail. She also got me 'consented', which means that I agreed to the treatment.

Jane C was my first chemotherapy nurse. Jane is a warm and bubbly English woman. She entered the room where I was waiting for my first chemotherapy treatment, pushing a heavy trolley of medicines. She was carrying loads of medical paraphernalia on it. Amidst syringes, medicines and dressings were kept four injections. Each injection was *huge* and the size was rather unsettling. They contained the chemotherapy drugs,

FEC, which would be administered for the first three cycles of my therapy. The injections would be given manually through the port inserted under my collarbone. Jane told me that because it was the first chemotherapy session, she would go slowly with the speed of injection.

Jane asked me not to look at the huge syringes, as it was clear that they were intimidating. 'Ready?' she asked.

'Yes, let's do it,' I said.

Jane and I chatted (like girls do), and Abhi dutifully clicked pictures. I wanted to capture the entire journey of cancer in photographs. Jane asked me if the organisation where I worked was supportive, because of my health condition. I replied in the affirmative, and went on to explain what a fabulous organisation Cambridge University Press was, how great my employer was and how they cared for staff. I later realised that Abhi was recording a video on his iPhone while I was telling Jane about the Press. What a wonderful unsolicited testimony for the organisation from an employee – impromptu and no marketing gimmick!

In the meantime, Jane had skilfully pumped in the first drug, 'E'. She kept checking with me, asking if I was all right. I felt OK while 'E' was being injected. Then 'F' was pumped in. 'F' caused a severe reaction. I felt as if my head was on fire. My nose turned watery and I squirmed in bed like crazy. Jane called in Lorraine and they mutually agreed that the reaction was as expected. I behaved like a monkey (so I think, although Abhi did not produce any video evidence corroborating this) for about twenty minutes. I held my head tightly; I almost felt like it would explode with the burning sensation! Gradually, the reaction settled down. Jane proceeded to pump in the third drug, 'C'. We were done by 6 pm.

When the chemotherapy session was finished, I was handed a medicine bag. It looked like a take-away packet from a restaurant that could feed a family of three! It held the medicines that I was supposed to take during the chemotherapy cycle. This is how my medicine chart looked:

Medicine	Breakfast	Lunch	Evening	Bedtime	Purpose	Other information
Ondansetron 8mg tablets	X		X		To prevent sickness	Take regularly for 2 days after chemotherapy
Dexamethasone 2mg tablets	X X		X X		Steroid	Take regularly for 2 days after chemotherapy
Domperidone 10 mg tablets	X X	X X	X X	X X	To prevent sickness	Take regularly for 5 days after chemotherapy, then take as needed
Start on day 8 of chemotherapy						
Ciprofloxacin 250 mg tablets	X		X		Antibiotic	For 7 days
Fluconazole 50 mg capsules	X				Antifungal	For 7 days
Movicol sachets					Laxative	Twice a day

My medicine chart during chemotherapy cycle I

I had to take medicines for the first two weeks: Fourteen tablets per day on the first two days, eight tablets per day for the next three days, and three tablets per day for the next seven days; plus a huge load of Movicol sachets. The third week would be free of medicines. Hurray!

The chemotherapy cycles were three-weekly. The first week after the chemotherapy was the one in which the side effects were most severe. The second week was when my body was at maximum risk of infection, as my immunity would be very low. Unfortunately, chemotherapy drugs kill not only cancerous cells but also healthy cells. Red blood cells and white blood cells get targeted too, and their count starts dropping as the chemotherapy sessions progress.

The third week was the one for recovery. At the end of the third week, I would have the next session of chemotherapy, and the three-weekly cycle would start again.

Chemotherapy can seriously weaken the body's ability to fight infections. This is because chemotherapy temporarily reduces the number of white blood cells in the blood. We were asked to watch out for the signs of infection, and were required to contact the doctor immediately if we spotted any of them.

A key sign to look out for was a raised temperature, above 38°C or 100.4°F at any time, or else above 37.5°C or 99.5°F at two readings taken an hour or more apart. We constantly monitored my temperature throughout the eighteen weeks of chemotherapy. On occasions when the thermometer recorded a number higher than the normal 98.6°F, the stress levels at home shot up like the mercury in the thermometer. If the number increased in two successive readings, all of us would get edgy. A drop in the temperature was a welcome relief. To avoid infection, everybody at home, including me, took special care to maintain hygiene. Some of the simple things that we religiously followed, and that really helped us, were:

We all took flu jabs, so that we wouldn't catch an infection in the winter. Nothing was touched in the kitchen without first washing our hands with soap. Any use of the bathroom was followed by thoroughly washing our hands. (With all this washing, our consumption of hand wash increased exponentially, but it was well worth it.) The kitchen was cleaned with an anti-bacterial agent every day, to get rid of unwanted intruders on the countertops. We kept a physical distance from anyone who had obvious infections – my colleagues and friends used to be extremely careful about this when I was in their vicinity. If one of them had a runny nose, they would not shake hands with me or hug me. Such simple care from others was really helpful.

Lorraine and Jane had repeatedly asked me to look after my mouth and oral health. I must take care that I clean it properly and not allow any phlegm to accumulate. They repeated this instruction so many times that I got really curious about the deposition of phlegm due to chemotherapy. As it turned out, I would understand the significance of this instruction three days later. I would soon find out how stressful phlegm can be. I guess nothing is easy when the word 'cancer' is involved, which rightly contributes to the dreadful image of the disease.

After my first chemotherapy session that Thursday, we started our journey back to Hitchin in the car. I remember speaking to Abhi's mum over the phone on our way back. Sickness had started setting in by then, as we were driving. By the time we reached home, I was very sick and breathless. The evening was difficult. I threw up three times, and found it difficult to breathe. There was a lot of drama at home that evening. Nausea alternated with breathlessness, tiredness, weakness, and a general feeling of being unwell. The side effects of chemotherapy had started, and the cure was soon to become tougher than the Big C itself!

The next two weeks were probably the worst weeks of my life. I slept poorly at night, and woke up with a terrible weakness and sickness. I took the medicines to combat the sickness and they made me feel worse. In went more medicines, and I felt awful. I continued throwing up, again and again. Rushing to the bathroom to puke became a regular feature of my day. Unfortunately, I didn't have the strength to attend my Spanish classes anymore, and had to pull out of the course.

Because of the Zoladex, menopausal symptoms had also started affecting me. It was time for the hot flushes, night sweats and low moods to start setting in. Hot flushes were like my body's personal moments of confusion. Like when at a retail store, I was indecisive about buying a top with a cowl-shaped neck or a V-shaped neck, or when I was confused about whether I should order Indian or Chinese take-away. Similarly, hot flushes were the moments when my body couldn't decide how it should respond to the sudden increase of heat in my body. It couldn't decide whether it would make more sense to throw off my warm clothes or keep them on – when the temperature was freezing outside, at less than 0°C! These symptoms would stay with me for a good twenty months. I would have to strive really hard to ensure that my moods did not bother others, including Abhi. I knew that I ran the risk of bottling up my emotions for the worse, but I could not be an encumbrance on anyone.

The hot flushes, night sweats and overall hormonal imbalance left me with severe insomnia. Before I had cancer, I could fall asleep in the blink of an eye, no matter whether it was day or night. However, with all the treatment I was taking, sleep became a luxury for me. I would toss and turn in bed for hours and not be able to sleep. The hot flushes were so bad that I found myself drenched in sweat several times during the day as well as night. They also interrupted whatever little sleep I could get.

Surprisingly, something good came out of these long insomniac nights. In order to fill all the extra time I found when I was awake, I started pouring out my experience of cancer in words. This was a small catharsis during an unimaginably difficult time. My writing began with the objective of creating a personal memoir, something I could refer to later. Of course, I assumed that there *would be* a 'later' for me.

Hope is a good thing, maybe the best of things, and no good thing ever dies.
- Andy Dufresne, the character played by
Tim Robbins, *The Shawshank Redemption*

Three days went by, and then in the middle of the third night, I suddenly felt severe chest pain. I was still sleepy, and felt confused. Then it occurred to me... what if it's not a chest pain, what if my heart is giving up? I flapped my arms frantically to wake Abhi. I did not know if I had enough time before the pain took over me and before Abhi woke up. The pain intensified and I felt that my heart was sinking. Abhi awoke, and held me tight. The pain lasted for about fifteen minutes, during which I am not sure how I managed to last! Although the pain subsided, Abhi spent the next forty-five minutes reading about the drug regimen that I was on. It was our first heart scare. But unfortunately, he did not find any further details. Eventually, we decided to call the hospital the next day, and went back to sleep.

I made a call to the hospital next morning, and they asked me to come over for an ECG. Sachin and I reached the hospital in the afternoon. Since I had simply walked in without an appointment, the hospital took me in only after they had finished seeing their day patients – at 6 pm. The ECG report was normal, and my heart was given a clean bill of health. Thank goodness!

On the fourth day, my mouth started developing phlegm and ulcers. By the end of the first week, I had a tongue that felt swollen because of phlegm deposits. While this had begun with minimal discomfort, the feeling of a swollen tongue kept on increasing. By the end of that week, I felt that there was very little space in my mouth; most of it felt occupied by the tongue and by phlegm. This congested space in my mouth had a new companion in the form of ulcers. By the middle of the second week, my mouth was full of severe ulcers. The inner lining of my cheeks turned white, ulcerated, painful and swollen. It had become difficult to eat regular food, because it hurt the mouth. Things like apples and cornflakes went out of reach, as they felt too hard. My favourite fruits, oranges and clementines, burnt the ulcers, and so did the berries. I started soaking bread in tea before consuming it. Untoasted bread took the place of toast, as the latter scratched my sore mouth. For someone who loved to cook and eat food, it was a miserable time!

It was day twelve, and after dinner, the soggy inner lining of the mouth came out – all of it. For some time, it felt good; I was happy to see the ulcerated skin go. What I forgot was that this bared my cheeks and that they would be even more exposed to the food. The following morning was different, to say the least. I tried to brush my teeth, and could hardly move the brush in my mouth. My mouth would not open as my cheeks were so sore.

I somehow managed to brush and came to the dining table. It was breakfast time, and Abhi served bread with butter and tea. Anyhow, it was not possible for me to drink hot tea anymore, it hurt my mouth. I picked up some bread to take a bite and groaned in pain. The mouth would just not open; it was jammed. I tried to move my jaw with my left hand while I held bread in the right, but it would not budge. I needed to eat breakfast, as I was on a huge dose of oral medicines in addition to the chemotherapy drugs that were already causing chaos in my body. With stronger determination, I picked up bread, forced open my mouth with my hand and took a small bite of bread. Eating those two slices of bread was probably one of the most painful experiences during my chemotherapy treatment. It took over half an hour to eat them. I felt sad while I ate. My mouth hurt and I felt as if I would not get through this ordeal. I cried while I chewed and that made me feel worse. Finally, the breakfast was over and I decided to eat only when I felt really hungry.

I had to change my toothbrush and toothpaste. When the ulcers developed, I could no longer use a regular brush, as it hurt my teeth and gums. Sachin suggested that I try a baby toothbrush. Abhi went to Boots pharmacy the next day and bought a soft toothbrush for little children, and also some bubblegum flavoured baby toothpaste. I missed the strong mint flavour, but nonetheless, carried on using the baby tooth paste. Thankfully, the ulcers reduced during the third week.

All through the three weeks, the sickness and nausea persisted. There was always heaviness in my chest. There was a familiar feeling of rebellion inside the pit of my stomach. Only in this case, the origin of the rebellion was not in my mind but in the rest of the body. It was the chemotherapy drugs that were spinning my system into a state of nausea and sickness. Throwing up in the basin became a routine thing, and I began to grow accustomed to it.

The weakness and fatigue had engulfed me immediately after the treatment began. I tried to manage cooking whenever I could, but it was not always possible. Sachin and Abhi did a good job of cooking, and of looking after me. Sachin also continued to be the main channel of communication with our parents and Dinesh. They obviously had many questions, and were very concerned about how I was faring with the treatment. He constantly kept them apprised of my situation.

Simultaneously, it was time for a metamorphosis to begin – time for me to change into an ugly duckling. The much dreaded hair loss had begun!

I had been used to receiving loads of compliments about my hair: it was thick, dark and voluminous. In the second week after chemotherapy began, I started losing it. The oncologist said that all of it would go, and that later it would come back. The first couple of days were tough. I felt bad that I was losing my pretty hair. I was not ready to let go of it. Dr Charles had said that people moved on pretty fast as far as losing hair was concerned, and I must admit that I had found this slightly difficult to believe. When the hair loss had not started by the end of the first week, I had begun to silently hope that it would not happen. I mentioned this to Dr Charles, and he plainly said that I was wrong: the hair loss *would* start and I *would* lose all the hair. (At that moment, why on earth was I briefly reminded of Liam Neeson in the movie *Taken*: 'I *will* find you and I *will* kill you'? But then, do you really need a reason to think of Liam Neeson?) I was disappointed to hear that the hair would go. My face dropped.

Now that it was confirmed that I would lose my hair, I could choose to either wear hats, or a wig. For some reason, I didn't want to have a wig. I think the decision was partly motivated by the fact that I thought that I would be comfortable moving around with a bald head. I chose two pretty and fancy hats online, with help from Abhi and Sachin, from Suburban Turban, a company that specialises in making hats for cancer patients. I wanted to ensure that I received the hats before the hair loss started. There are several other companies that sell hats for cancer patients. Suburban Turban were brilliant, just like most of the people who were part of my Cancer Journey.

I called up the store and placed the order. One of the hats had a peak, and the other was in the turban style. The lady who took my order suggested that I should also order a bedtime hat. This hat was rather simple, and I had not even considered ordering it. But simply based on her suggestion, I took one of those hats too. The hats arrived in a couple of days. I tried them on, and while they looked pretty, they hurt my sensitive scalp. There was some elastic that had been used to keep their shape, but that was too much for my skin to bear. Eventually, it turned out that for the following eight months, I wore the bedtime hat that I had bought on the lady's recommendation. I didn't wear the hats of my choice for even a day. When I needed a replacement because the hat had worn out, I ordered a similar one again. I am so grateful for the suggestion to buy that simple hat. I wore it even at night, because I was cold without it. It would be my constant companion until summer arrived.

The physical process of losing hair started soon after, and it looked as if I was moulting. I had always hated hair being strewn over the floor. I would pick up the strands of hair and bin them. Thankfully, both the men at home were fully supportive while I continued to leave strands of hair everywhere. If I lay down, the pillow and the bedsheet were coated with hair. If I was sitting, the sofa would grow some hair too. When I changed into different clothes, I found several strands all over my clothes.

That was just the beginning. As the hair thinned, first just a few strands fell out, and then it fell out in clumps. One day I was in the shower. I applied soap, worked up the lather, scrubbed, and turned on the shower to wash it off. Swoooosh, came out the water jet, and I was suddenly shrouded in hair. Every bit of my body had hundreds of strands stuck to it. I almost screamed in horror. Somehow, it was a scary sight. I called out to Abhi and he rushed to the bathroom. My eyes welled up with tears as I said, 'Look.' He saw and we both knew it was time to say goodbye to my pretty hair. I looked scared, with hair all over me, and Abhi offered to help wash it off and clean up the bathroom. But I chose to do it myself. I had figured out that the journey ahead would be difficult, and I could not afford to be weak. With a deep breath, I turned on the shower at the highest speed and let hair gradually slide down my body. Half an hour later, there was a thick layer of hair on the floor of the shower cubicle. I reached out for the fountain shower, washed my feet one at a time, and stepped out gingerly. I picked up a tissue roll, collected all the hair in sheets of tissue paper, and threw them in the bin. *It was time to let go!*

When I came out of the shower, I found Sachin and Abhi were quieter than usual. They empathised with my pain and were sad to see me in this situation. I was grateful for their understanding.

It was also time for Sachin to return home. While he was with us, his wife Rekha had been managing their home and looking after their children all by herself. Sachin would not have been able to come to the UK without her support. His being away from home must have put so much pressure on her. I fully appreciate that it must be stressful to manage a home and children – their school, extra-curricular activities, parent-teacher meetings, and also their emotional needs – all of this, along with a demanding full-time job! I am thankful to Rekha for her support. While Sachin was happy to get back home and be with his family, I could clearly see how uncomfortable he was about leaving me during the treatment. He was in a dilemma – to leave or not to leave? I assured him that I would be able to look after myself, with Abhi's help, as we were getting used to our changed schedules and the treatment. After spending many days in this quandary and staying with us for three weeks, Sachin flew back to the US. I felt blessed to have such strong support from my family. His presence at our place had also enabled Abhi to attend office regularly. Thank you, Sachin, for making this journey easier than it would have been without you.

Back to the hair loss story – The process of hair loss was so physically painful that I wanted it over as soon as possible. The pain had become particularly bad one Saturday evening. We researched it online, and found a simple solution to this problem – cutting the hair short! But in the tiny town of Hitchin, where we lived, no shops are open on Saturday evenings. I called up my regular hair dresser, but only managed to reach her voice mail. 'Maybe she is with a client and will return the call,' I thought, but she did not. She had closed shop rather early that evening. We managed to somehow get through the night, and on Sunday morning, after breakfast, Abhi took the matter – and a pair of scissors – into his own hands. With the scissors from the stationery kit (we didn't have the ones for cutting hair), he started working on my hair. We talked about the many movies in which we had seen people cut their own hair, to change their identity. You've probably guessed by now that Abhi and I are movie-lovers. We placed the laptop in front of us, and clicked some pictures.

I still had an awful lot of hair, despite the incident in the shower that I had been through a few days ago. Abhi had never cut anyone's hair before, and didn't know where to start. He was a little overwhelmed, and as he was wondering how to tackle my hair, I snatched the scissors from his hands and began chopping my hair off recklessly. The objective was to cut off as much hair as possible. When I had done my bit to make my head lighter, I handed the scissors back to him. Abhi tried to recollect all the hair-cutting experiences he had had (as a customer) and began to work. After an hour and a quarter, he was done. I looked different, in short snazzy hair. People could not even guess that the haircut had not been done professionally, and I said to Abhi, 'The things that people do for love; they even become barbers.' ☺

There were huge patches of baldness on my head now. People could look at the scalp and guess that I either had a medical condition or was undergoing some treatment. My scalp was very tender, as the hair follicles were hurting. The follicles were strong enough not to fall out themselves, but not strong enough to resist external pressure. So some hair fell out at night, from the friction of the pillow. To help speed up the hair loss, Abhi pulled out clumps of my hair. (It didn't hurt when he did that.)

Looking back, I do think that a wig would probably have been nice too. I just missed my perfect opportunity to turn into a blonde or a brunette, or to try something more whacky, like purple or orange hair! Of course, bald is sexy too (think Natalie Portman in *V for Vendetta* or Demi Moore in *G.I. Jane*) and don't let anyone tell you otherwise.

When I went through the hair loss experience, I realised what Dr Charles had meant by 'Once you lose your hair, you soon forget about it, as so much else is going on.' Losing hair is a petty thing, and so is looking pretty. In the context of cancer, survival and being able to be cured is what matters the most; being with the people you love is the key, and everything else is secondary. On a practical note, the pain while losing hair was so terrible that I wanted it to go. I was allowed to take paracetamol, but only in case of an emergency, as paracetamol can mask a temperature. In chemotherapy there is always a risk of infection, which, as you can imagine, is dangerous. The first sign of an infection is fever, and paracetamol would mask it. Therefore, I couldn't take the painkiller and had to suffer the severe pain of neuropathy during the hair loss for four weeks... absolute madness!

Some people may think that losing hair is not such a big deal, if it is part of the treatment that could prolong your life (I was told this just yesterday). But in reality, it can be a big deal for the person who is going through it – if they don't like what they see when they look at themselves in the mirror, it can be not just unnerving but depressing. Unfortunately, the time frame of losing and re-growing hair can stretch up to several months, which does not help an already low level of confidence. There can be other reasons why some people may find hair loss difficult to cope with. There are people who do not cut their hair for religious or cultural reasons. So, while you may wonder why the person in front of you is being difficult about losing hair which will grow back, the actual reasons can go deeper.

Therefore, if you are interacting with a cancer patient, can you please try and be sensitive about the hair loss?

My nails had turned blue by the end of the first cycle. They had become vertically ridged, and horizontal lines had also developed on them. A blue colour, with several ridges and lines, did not make a pretty sight at all. This couldn't qualify as the poorest work of nail art. My nails looked terrible. Period.

I could have tried to hide some of the dirty-looking colouration with nail varnish, but I was advised by my healthcare team to apply the transparent colour, so that *I would know what was going on underneath!* Therefore on a Saturday morning, Abhi went out on a hunt for transparent nail polish, and apparently he had to go to four shops before he could find some. Soon the nails turned brittle, and with the slightest provocation, they broke. The changes in my nails progressed and they started looking weirder as the chemotherapy continued.

The metamorphosis into the ugly duckling phase had definitely started.

When the cancer diagnosis was confirmed, I had shared the news with only a few people: some of my close friends, and the management team of the project on which I was working. I had less than ten days between the confirmation and the first chemotherapy treatment. After the first chemotherapy session, I took leave for a week, and worked from home during the second week. When I went to the office in the third week, my hair had thinned and was short (the haircut that Abhi had given me). People were surprised to see such short hair so suddenly. In less than a week, I had developed several patches of baldness. It was obvious that something was going on with me. I talked candidly and honestly about the diagnosis, if anyone asked me.

The news about my cancer spread fast. Many people came up to me, expressed how sorry they were to hear about the diagnosis, and wished me good luck with the treatment. They shared stories about cancer that had happened amongst their family and friends – Suddenly, I knew of dozens of people who had cancer! There were all kinds of stories: the ones with hope, the ones with long periods of remission, the ones where the prognosis was not positive, and also the ones where people had lost their loved ones to cancer. Cancer seemed to be omnipresent. Every day, I came back home and shared the new cancer stories with Abhi. These stories made us feel that we were not alone, and that we would get through this mess. The support I received from my colleagues at work was fabulous and I am immensely grateful for it.

When we had begun the treatment, a mastectomy had looked inevitable. My consultants constantly monitored my health, in between the chemotherapy cycles. After the first cycle had finished and before the second session of chemotherapy, I went to the hospital to see Dr Charles so that he could gauge how I was coping with the treatment, and if he needed to make any changes. Dr Parto also performed an ultrasound on me. He was surprised by what he found. The tumour had shrunk by over 85% in volume! He said that such a drastic reduction happened only in about 10 to 15% of cases.

'Mastectomy?' I asked.

'Yes. The tumour is still big, and a lumpectomy is not feasible. Not yet,' he said.

'Maybe by the time we finish chemotherapy and I go into the surgery, the tumour will have reduced enough. *Insha'Allah[12],*' I said.

I was holding onto the brilliant result from the first chemotherapy cycle, and being hopeful. At times, I wondered if I was giving myself false hope – but nonetheless, it was important to carry on being hopeful. People may have different levels of comfort as far as a mastectomy is concerned. I knew that I would feel devastated at the loss of a breast. Dr Parto had mentioned that if a mastectomy happened, we would discuss reconstruction surgery. I tried to see the silver lining in the free tummy-tuck that the process would bring, but I couldn't cheer myself up. Of course, I knew I might be forced to come to terms with it eventually, looking at the big picture, but it would be a difficult position for me to attain. The lines below reflect my thoughts in those 'Oh God! Pleeeeease save me from a mastectomy!' moments:

Ah, Cancer!

It does not know how to discriminate.
It does not care about the colour of your skin –
Black, or white, or a shade in between –
It cares nothing for which Gods you worship,

---

[12]   Insha'Allah: Insha'Allah is Arabic for 'Allah willing' or God willing. It is used when speaking about plans and events expected to occur in the future and indicates submission to God.

51

Or whether you have a God at all.
It cares nothing for how you will battle alone,
Or how, with you, your loved ones will moan.

It takes away what it sets eyes upon.
It takes away the breast it desires –
It cares not whether a baby suckles at it,
Or if a lover's lips will miss it
It cares not whether you will cry
Each time you look at yourself in the mirror.
Or how frantically you will search for your booby
While it decays in some hospital's lobby!
It cares not whether you will love yourself less
Or if your relationship will be in a mess.

At times cancer shows itself in your body,
At times it attacks with stealth, unknown.
At times it wins hands-down,
At times it allows you to be.
But your life continues on its terms –
Marked with changes and apprehension.

Cancer does not discriminate,
It cares nothing for who you are.
It simply takes what it desires.
Ah! The mighty cancer!

I continued to worry about the mastectomy as the days progressed.
Cycle II was about to start, and I was already dreading it.

The bald and the beautiful

I had survived the first three weeks of chemotherapy, and the thought of having a severely ulcerated mouth one more time made me wince. Jane, who was from Zimbabwe, was my chemotherapy nurse for the second treatment. She worked at Addenbrooke's Hospital and was called to Nuffield whenever they needed more chemotherapy nurses. She was fabulous. She gave me lot of information about cancer, particularly prostate cancer. She was a very skilful nurse, really good with needles. She told me that her native language was Shona. I laughed and told her that in my language, Hindi, *Shona* is a word of endearment, used for someone you love enormously, like a partner or lover or even a child. She was fascinated with this information. She laughed out loud when, after a few minutes, I addressed Abhi as 'Shona'. I picked up her infectious laughter and laughed too. Who said that I couldn't have moments of happiness, even if I had cancer?

My blood was checked. I was lucky that none of the counts fell below the acceptable levels during my treatment. A normal blood count meant that I could go through the chemotherapy sessions uninterrupted, which was nice. Any interruptions would have caused delays and unnecessary stress.

Cycle II was similar to Cycle I, but with less intensity. Abhi decided to work from home for the next two weeks, so that he could be around if I needed help.

The fatigue had accumulated within me since the chemotherapy had commenced. I had taken the first week off, after the first cycle of treatment. Sitting idle or resting throughout the day was a new experience for me. My project work was also piling up, and because I was taking leave intermittently, my manager had not been able to arrange for a replacement. During the days that I was on leave, I felt bad that I could not work. I tried to work, but the tiredness consumed me. The feeling of being useless and not in control of my own life surfaced time and again. I shared these feelings with Abhi, and he assured me that I wasn't useless or a burden on him or anyone else. Often, he tried to pep me up. I saw how hard he was trying to support me, and promised myself that I would not give up this fight.

When Abhi was due to go for a regular haircut, I told him that I would like to go with him and get my remaining hair shaved off. A bald head would look better than a few vagabond strands on the head, I reckoned. Abhi called up his usual barber shop, and asked the barber, 'Would you shave off my wife's head? She's undergoing cancer treatment and has lost quite a lot of hair already.' The barber was quiet for a moment and asked, 'By the way, do you mean to say that you want to get the *hair* shaved off?' 'Yes, of course, the hair on the head – not the head!' The barber let out a sigh of relief, and said that he could do it. Abhi told him that my scalp was very tender, but the barber reassured him that he would shave my hair off without hurting me.

We finished breakfast the next day and went to the barber shop. We waited for our turn, and I could not help but notice the different types of hair there: the blonde, the black, the thick hair and the thin hair. I was about to lose all my hair and it was as if, for the first time, I became really conscious of what it was to have hair. I chatted with the barber's daughter as we waited. Soon after, it was my turn. I mentioned to the barber that we had called the previous day about shaving my hair. I reminded him of a sensitive scalp and he told me not to worry. He sat me down and, with a feather-light touch, started shaving off whatever hair remained on my head. When he was done, he took out a moisturiser and gently applied it on the scalp. My new look was complete. I was the new bald and beautiful!

We walked back towards home and before we went in, Abhi clicked some pictures of me. He put his arms around me, and I drew towards him in anticipation of a hug. He pulled me towards himself, but before I could ensconce myself in the safest place I know, he exclaimed, 'You have a mole on your scalp!' He was excited at his new discovery about me. He held my finger and directed it to the mole that had been hiding under the hair all these years. We giggled about the new mole like it was the funniest thing on earth.

Soon my expenditure on shampoos and conditioners would be zero. I would spend less time in the shower, and no time at all on brushing my hair. There would be no bad hair days for about a year. I would not go for haircuts or worry about how I wanted to get my hair done. I would not spend money on waxing or threading either. In our tiny town of Hitchin, I didn't know even a single place where eyebrow threading was done. Most of the salons waxed eyebrows. I used to go to a salon in Cambridge for threading, and typically took after-work appointments. No more of these troubles! The hair loss was not just on my head, but over my entire body. I felt great about my super-waxed body! I thought about later, when my hair would re-grow – I guessed I would take some time to get adjusted to it. I would be a strong candidate for the laser treatment for hair removal, if only I could afford it! If I used make-up, I would have saved the money on mascara too; but I was not really a make-up person (at least not until I attended the 'Look Good, Feel better' programme, but more on that later).

I had mentioned to Ruks earlier that I was sad about losing my hair. She commented that I had a fabulously shaped head, and that I should show it off. 'How do you know?' I asked. She could not possibly have discovered the perfect shape of my head while it was hidden under a crown of hair. I *knew* that she was trying to cheer me up and didn't read too much into what she said.

I went to see Dr Parto for a regular consultation after the hair loss was complete. He asked me how I was, and I told him about the hair loss. He responded, 'You have a perfectly shaped head, just show it off.' I was rendered speechless at this compliment. I am sure he has worked with innumerable cancer patients. He must have seen many bald heads. I was happy to receive the compliment, and it definitely boosted my morale. I said to myself, 'All right Ruks, so you knew what you were talking about.' ☺

It is a shame that I lost hair in not only such a painful but also such a useless way. My oncologist, Dr Charles, had mentioned that I could consider cutting it short, but I had thought that if I was going to lose it in a couple of weeks, why bother at all. With so much going on in my life, surely a haircut was the last thing on my mind. If this is how you have been thinking, please beware – It would be wise to learn from my experience.

After the hair loss happened, I found out that many cancer patients proactively shave off their hair. This saves them the physical agony of losing hair. If I had done so, maybe I would not have had to suffer the migraines that I did. Shaving does not necessarily prevent the follicles from hurting afterwards, but it might have helped to reduce the pain, in my case. As we learnt later, chemotherapy had probably damaged the nerve endings of my hair follicles. This caused severe nerve pain, leading to terrible migraines. We guessed this because many people suffer from migraines, but very few feel pain in the hair follicles.

I also found out that many cancer patients donate their hair, aware that they will soon lose it. The donated hair is used to make wigs for other patients undergoing treatment, which is not necessarily for cancer. My hair was beautiful, and it would have made a lovely wig. It was a shame that I had binned my hair instead of transforming it into a wig, due to my ignorance.

I have now decided that when my hair grows back, I will consider donating it. A length of about ten inches can be used to make a wig. It will be my little contribution to those fellow beings who are fighting difficult illnesses.

My intention is simple: I want to do my bit to cheer them up. During the treatment, they will have many bad days, and the wig may cheer them up on a few of those. When a medical condition takes away somebody's pretty hair and their looks change for the worse, they may feel more confident wearing my hair on their head. While my preference is to donate my hair for cancer patients, I understand that cancer patients usually wear synthetic wigs. A natural wig is expensive, and also takes about twelve weeks to be prepared. A cancer patient rarely knows three months in advance that they will need a wig. But patients with other long-term hair loss conditions will be able to use my hair.

I remember meeting a young girl who was undergoing treatment next to me, at the hospital. She had come there with her mum. We started chatting and after a while I asked her, 'So, what drug regimen are you on for chemotherapy? Did you not lose your hair? It looks gorgeous.' She giggled, 'Now that's my favourite question. I absolutely love it when people think this is my real hair.' With a twinkle in her eye, she went on to explain to me that her husband had shaved off her hair. Fortunately, she did not have to suffer from a painful scalp, like I had when the hair loss had set in.

The hospital's chemotherapy day unit had so many patients hooked to machines for intravenous treatment. Each individual machine bleeped, and it was chaotic. We were all very ill there, but a few patients looked awfully ill. The man sitting to the girl's left barely looked in his early twenties, but he was absolutely emaciated. The lady on my right was very old and I wondered how her frail body coped with the strong chemotherapy drugs. In such a stressful hospital environment, I was so happy to see that little twinkle in the girl's eye; her happiness was such a positive thing to witness and share. That very moment, I decided that I would start donating my hair to making wigs that may be used for other patients.

If you are someone whose life has been touched by cancer – whether it is yourself or someone amongst your family or friends who have it – can you make this little donation, for the benefit of patients suffering from hair loss? It will not cost you anything extra. Who knows, it may help them get through another difficult moment or day?

If you live in the UK and are interested in donating hair[13], you could visit Banbury Postiche (http://www.wigsuk.com/) and the Little Princess Trust (www.littleprincesses.org.uk). The Little Princess Trust specifically works for children affected by cancer and other conditions.

It was the third week of the chemotherapy cycle and I was in the office. I opened my lunch box and started eating – cabbage and parathas[14] packed for lunch. The cabbage had not turned out great, but I could eat only home-made food, so I continued eating. But the food tasted weird and it smelled weird too. Then it dawned upon me...I could definitely taste cabbage, but I tasted something else too – it smelled like the tablets used in the dishwasher. I was eating cabbage intermingled with the aroma and taste of dishwasher tablets! Please don't think that I had had any experience of tasting dishwasher tablets before this day, but I think that was how my food tasted!

---

[13] Cancer Research UK. "Hair donation and wigs." Last modified July 2014. http://www.cancerresearchuk.org/cancer-help/about-cancer/cancer-questions/hair-donation-and-wigs. Last accessed December 05, 2014.

[14] Parathas: A type of Indian bread typically cooked fresh at home before consumption.

As per the routine, I went to see Dr Charles after work so that he could check how I was doing. I knew there would be several such appointments, and so I asked Abhi not to accompany me to the hospital unless there was something critical to be discussed. I wanted to look after myself and take as much of the load off Abhi as possible.

I shared the dishwasher-tablet-eating experience with Dr Charles. I am sure he must be used to listening to many such weird experiences from his patients. Of course he had a scientific explanation for this, but I remember how much I laughed while I narrated this experience and distorted my face multiple times. The nurse laughed with me and we had a good time. Abhi asked me later if the doctor had laughed, and I said no. Maybe he wanted to, but thought that it was rude to laugh at the plight of a patient who had just narrated how she tasted dishwasher tablets in her food!

Soon after the dishwasher-tablet-eating experience, my olfactory sense developed beyond what I would have desired. I am not sure if this sense was compensating for the loss in my taste buds. But we came to a point where I could smell just about anything that was placed in my vicinity. If someone opened the fridge in the kitchen, I could smell the cheese in it while I was in another room. If food had been stored in plastic containers, I could not eat it, because I would get the smell of the plastic and the soap. We did have quite a lot of problems with this particular development. I found that I could eat food off porcelain dishes, if the food had not been preserved for too long. Food packed in aluminium foil was OK too. But this severely curtailed what I could carry to work, as no plastic containers could be used. This is how things remained for a good seven months.

I love watching movies and TV shows on vampires. Vampires are believed to have heightened senses. Their senses of touch, hearing, scent, and sight are depicted as being extremely strong in most of my favourite shows. In our home, I was the newbie with the vampire senses.

With all these crazy changes in my life, I couldn't help wondering yet again: if the cure made me so ill, how bad could the disease be? I wondered how difficult it must be for people who suffer with cancer, when it affects the normal functioning of the body. Thankfully, in my case, the cancer had not manifested as any major symptoms that made me feel ill. Well, it could also have been very risky – since there were no symptoms, the diagnosis could have been delayed. I am so glad that the hypochondriac in me went to see the doctor in time, and was diagnosed with the Big C before it was too late.

The second chemotherapy cycle was coming to an end. My mum was on her way to London on the 5th of November, just before the third chemotherapy cycle, and Abhi was supposed to go and pick her up at the airport. She played an immensely important role in my treatment and recovery, as she was my primary carer for the five and a half months that followed.

My mum is well-educated and a homemaker. She was the main impetus that drove her children to study and achieve their goals in life. She is someone who is constantly working towards some goal. When we were little, her goal was to ensure that we studied well. Her goals evolved as we grew up. In fact, I imbibed the habit of goal-setting from her so ardently that Ruks had to bring to my attention that I was overdoing it. When I was a member of Toastmasters[15] (a not-for-profit organization dedicated to improving people's communication and leadership skills), I had a clear timeline by which I wanted to complete a particular certification level. In fact, many times I planned my speeches with dates, and worked with the executive committee of the club to get speech slots on those dates.

---

[15] Toastmasters International. "Who we are." Last modified 2014. http://www.toastmasters.org/About/Who-We-Are. Last accessed April 09, 2015.

At the moment, my mum's goal was to ensure that she gave me the best possible care during my cancer treatment. While she had travelled both within and outside India before, this was the first time she had travelled alone outside the country. She does not speak English, but that did not deter her from boarding the flight and coming to London on her own. She was also very unwell when she came to London – her knees needed replacement surgery. They got jammed every now and then, and did not support her weight well. In her current condition, taking every step was a nightmare for her. There were so many occasions when she would try to move, but her knees would not budge. She would literally stand frozen wherever she was. Despite her critical condition, she had decided that the knee replacement surgery could wait for another six months. My parents lived separately for three months while she was here. I am certain that must have caused significant disruption in their personal lives. I remember one of my colleagues saying that it was amazing that my family could afford to drop their lives and be with me during the treatment. I responded, 'It is not that they could afford to drop their lives and come here, but that they chose to drop their lives to be with me.' Life is all about the choices we make for ourselves, or for our loved ones, isn't it?

Abhi and I will be eternally grateful to my mum for looking after me and genuinely being there for us when we needed help.

Thank you, Mum.

Late one evening, Mum saw me working at the laptop. She wanted to know if I was doing office work. I told her that I was writing about my cancer experience, because I wanted to keep it as a personal memoir. She asked, 'Will you get it published too?' I was not prepared for the question. Until now I had not thought about getting my experience published. I said no. After a while, I asked her rhetorically, 'Do you think I should explore the possibility of getting my notes published?'

The idea of getting my cancer experience published had just been planted in my head by Mum.

There is something else that this little exchange shows. There are some Asian cultures that attach stigma to an illness like cancer. I had also felt that stigma in the reactions of some people I knew when they learnt about my disease. But the fact that my mum suggested that I could get my experience published indicates that she thinks differently. She has always had a mind of her own, and doesn't necessarily follow what others think is right. This is a very big deal, in a collectivist culture like India. What society thinks is an important consideration for most people in India, and it takes substantial courage to go against the tide. My mum is definitely one of those brave people, and this is something invaluable that she has passed on to us: the courage to stand up for what we believe is the right thing to do, even if others disapprove of it.

As my diary gradually progressed, two out of three 'FEC' cycles were coming to an end. It was time for the final treatment of 'FEC'.

More about Cancer:

The blood counts: Along with destroying cancer cells, chemotherapy can also affect healthy cells being made in the bone marrow. Therefore, the blood needs to be checked before each chemotherapy session. The counts for the following blood components must be right, before the treatment can be given.

Haemoglobin: If the haemoglobin count is low, a person can feel lethargic, breathless, dizzy, have headaches and fainting, or have a paler complexion. Such a condition may require a blood transfusion, or a course of iron tablets.

White blood cells (WBCs): A low white blood cell count means that the body's immune system is depressed. An overly high count suggests that the body is fighting an infection. In the first three chemotherapy cycles, my WBC count was lowest 7-10 days after the treatment. In the last three cycles, it was the lowest 10-14 days after the treatment.

Platelets: Platelets control clotting, and stop bleeding. Therefore, a low platelet count can cause abnormal bruising.

While undergoing treatment, I had seen people struggling with severely reduced WBC counts, which meant they contracted infections and needed antibiotics. I am glad that I didn't have to go through this.

Am I dying?

There is a saying in India that roughly translates to, 'God likes to call good people back to himself sooner.' In other words, good people live shorter lives, and bad ones live longer. No, this has no correlation to science or research. I am not sure how the saying originated, but when a young person dies, you can often hear their loved ones say this.

I believe (I know it is true) that I am a good person, but I don't want God to call me back early on in my life. He will have to manage for several more years without me.

The third session of chemotherapy was to take place on the 8th of November 2012. I was hoping that the third cycle would be less eventful than the second. The side effects had been less in the second cycle as compared to the first, and I was expecting a further decrease. So, with that expectation, Abhi and I went to the hospital on the 8th of November 2012. Perpetuara was my nurse. She is from Zimbabwe. We wanted to start the treatment as we always did – by taking a sample for the blood test. But the port did not bleed, which meant that no blood could be taken from my body through the port. It is important for the port to bleed back, because it shows that the port is in the right place and has not been dislocated. Perpetuara flushed the port line several times. She increased the flow rate by injecting the saline at a faster rate, so that any blockage in the port line would get unclogged. No result. The enzyme, Fibrillin, was pumped in to unblock the line. Same result – nothing. More enzyme was pumped in. More waiting. But the port still did not bleed back. The wait went on until 6 pm. We were asked to come back the following day, for a lineogram. A lineogram is a scan that checks whether the port is in the right place. I was very disappointed that the third chemotherapy had not happened on the designated day. Having chemotherapy at all was frustrating enough; not being able to have it as per the schedule was even more frustrating. On Friday, the 9th of November, I went for the lineogram. The results came back fine, and I was given an all-clear for the chemotherapy treatment. The port did not bleed, but because the lineogram was all right, they decided to go ahead with chemotherapy. Sree, an oncology nurse from India, looked after me. Since it was the third chemotherapy session, the drugs were administered at a faster rate, and I was able to return home after a few hours.

My mum had been at our place for a week now and she made a remarkable observation. She noticed that I felt better when I ate at frequent intervals, but if I didn't eat for more than two hours, I started getting unwell. In the beginning, we all laughed about it. We joked that even during cancer treatment, when my mouth was full of ulcers, all I wanted to do was eat. It felt funny that while so many people lost their appetite during cancer treatment, I was different. But gradually, we realised that Mum's observation was correct. There were so many instances when I started feeling weak, but eating some food helped me recover quickly. Mum also suggested that I should try to get out of bed on time in the morning, no matter how rubbish I felt. I should eat something, and go back to rest later. While it was hard getting out of bed on most mornings, her suggestion worked really well. What my body needed was a constant inflow of energy.

It was the 14th of November 2012, the day following Diwali[16], and six days after my third chemotherapy session. I had been feeling unwell since the day before. We had celebrated Diwali, but getting through the festive preparation and ceremonies had been such a humongous effort. The tiredness and the feeling of general illness continued into

---

[16]   Diwali: The festival of lights, an important Indian festival.

the following day. At about 8 pm, I started feeling an intense chest pain. Something stabbed at my heart furiously and I writhed in pain. After a while it felt as if someone was squeezing my heart. Abhi had just come back from the office. He came to the bedroom, where I was lying, and saw that I was in pain. My mum came and sat by my bedside too. I asked Abhi to hold me tight where the pain was, but it just kept getting worse. I kicked my heels in pain, but the hurting would not subside. I began choking for breath. Mum and Abhi were scared to their bones. They saw me battling horrendous pain and all they could think was that I was dying! It definitely felt that way. By 8:30 pm, the pain had worsened so much that I could not bear Abhi's touch anymore. I tried to hold myself where the pain was, but it was just too painful. The heart region palpitated hard; I thought I was having a heart attack.

Abhi called up the hospital (as we had been instructed) and spoke to the Chemotherapy Unit. Abhi tried to explain, but he was clearly babbling. I remember him saying, 'My wife is very unwell. She has a severe pain in the breasts.' 'In the breasts?' they asked with surprise. Abhi replied in the affirmative. They sounded confused. Amidst all the pain, I reached for the phone and said that the pain was not in the breasts but in the heart region, beneath the breasts. I also said that I was worried I was having a heart attack. They said that they would be in touch as soon as possible.

The hospital staff contacted Dr Charles, and he called me back immediately. Abhi answered the phone but Dr Charles insisted that he wanted to speak to me. He asked me to talk him through what was happening to me. I remember saying, 'Doc. This is going to sound really funny but I feel as if someone is drilling through my chest, deep into the heart. The pain is moving downwards into my gastrointestinal tract too. I am squirming with pain and unable to lie in one position. I feel that my heart is giving up.' I resisted telling him that what I really felt was that I was dying! He listened intently and said that I was down with a severe gastrointestinal tract spasm, oesophagitis.

Even amidst such severe pain, I was amazed at how quickly Dr Charles separated my vivid imagination of being 'drilled' from the medical facts. *Hmmm... must have heard that one before!* I thought. By the time I finished speaking to him, I felt less wound up. I was confident that I had access to sound medical advice and that Dr Charles would take care of me. He also advised me to drink some cold milk straight from the refrigerator. Milk neutralises the acid in the stomach, and helps relieve the symptoms. I drank it twice but felt nauseated, rushed to the bathroom and threw up. What came out was not milk, but a perfectly bowl-shaped cheese slice that I looked at in bewilderment. The milk had curdled and it had taken the shape of my food pipe, in less than ten minutes! This suggested that there was abnormally high acidity inside my intestines. Once the bowl-shaped curdled milk was out of my system, I felt better.

Dr Charles also suggested that we buy an antacid. Our town did not have a pharmacy that remained open beyond 10 pm. Abhi had to rush to Stevenage, the nearby town, to get the medicine. He called for a taxi and jumped into it even before the driver had chance to pull over. He gave the address of the pharmacy and told the driver to drive fast. Just as they were about to reach the pharmacy, Abhi asked the driver to wait for a couple of minutes so that he could use the same taxi to get back home. The driver was not too sure; he said that he should not be parking in that area, and could not afford to wait beyond a few minutes. Abhi promised that he would be back within a couple of minutes. The driver had figured out that something was wrong: this man was rushing, at 10:30 pm, to the pharmacy store located in the nearby town, in extremely cold weather.

Abhi had been in touch with the store manager, and by the time he reached the store, he knew in which aisle the medicine was kept. He stormed into the store, rushed to aisle number four, and picked up two bottles of Gaviscon. He paid at the counter and was out of the store in less than two minutes. The taxi was waiting and he jumped back in and started the journey back home. After a couple of minutes, the taxi driver asked him what was wrong. Abhi told him that I was extremely unwell and that he needed to get my medicine for an emergency. The driver asked what the medical condition was, and Abhi said, 'Cancer.' The taxi driver was stunned. He exclaimed, 'Your wife has got cancer? At such a young age? Oh my God!' He was really sorry to hear that. He banged on the accelerator, and as his car careened through a dark street he said, 'Don't worry, I'll get you home as fast as possible.' When they reached home, the taxi driver did not want to take money from someone who was out in the middle of a cold winter night for his wife who was suffering from cancer. He finally agreed to take less money, and Abhi was able to get home.

So much for wishing and hoping that the third cycle would be easier than the previous two cycles. *What on earth happened to the law of attraction*[17]*?*

It is amazing how quickly I developed the 'life must go on' attitude with cancer. The oesophagitis incident had happened soon after my mum arrived in the UK. This particular experience caught her off-guard. Since the trouble had started brewing around 8 pm, we had not had the opportunity to finish dinner. After seeing me suffer so badly, my mum froze and was not really in a position to cook dinner. She said that she could not cook, and that we should all probably sleep. But that wouldn't have helped either. Abhi had come back from work and had not yet eaten anything. I needed to eat something regularly, otherwise the acid built up in my system, further deteriorating my health. Mum had not eaten anything either.

---

[17] Law of attraction: The Law of Attraction may be defined as: *I attract to my life whatever I give my attention, energy and focus to, whether positive or negative.* Losier, M. 2007. *Law of Attraction: The Science of Attracting More of What You Want and Less of What You Don't.* Great Britain: Hodder Paperbacks.

When I saw that she was too shaken, I asked her to help me out with cooking. I went to the kitchen and fixed a meal, with her help. I rolled the chapattis[18] while she cooked them. She had prepared the curries in the evening, so they were ready to be eaten. When Abhi came back, I was just finishing up the cooking. He was momentarily surprised to see me cooking, but he figured out what must have happened. We quietly finished the meal and went to bed, for yet another very difficult night ahead of us.

After the oesophagitis episode, the rest of the third cycle comprised an incredible amount of antacids and indigestion remedies. Instead of buying Gaviscon[19] from a pharmacy, we started buying it from Sainsbury's with our regular groceries, and the Sainsbury's website showed it under our 'usual items'. I finished one bottle of Gaviscon after another. One bottle lived on our dining table and another on my bedside table, while one more was kept in my office drawer.

I had stopped eating spicy food and yet even plain food would trigger indigestion, time and again. A constant heaviness sat on my chest, just where the heart is, and also at the same spot at the back. It always made me wonder if it was my heart that was reeling under stress from the chemotherapy drugs. Would it be my heart that would give away in the end (for the wrong reasons), or was it the gastrointestinal tract that had been abominably traumatized, I did wonder.

And I wondered, yet again – If the cure made me so ill, how bad would the Big C be? Hopefully, during the rest of my life, no matter how short or long it is, I will never have to find out. Amen!

---

18   Chapatti: A type of Indian bread, cooked fresh before consumption.
19   Gaviscon: An over the counter antacid, which is sold at pharmacies as well as supermarkets in the UK.

Dr Parto continued monitoring the tumour after each chemotherapy session. I responded very well to chemotherapy, and the tumour continued shrinking. Our meeting with him after the third chemotherapy session was critical. This was the day he would decide whether it would be a mastectomy or lumpectomy, and therefore Abhi had accompanied me for the appointment.

Abhi and I were nervous. I tried to relax, but I just couldn't. I looked into the eyes of Dr Parto and said, 'Come on, tell me that you are going to save my boob.' He smiled, slightly embarrassed. My language sounded (almost) inappropriate before such a gentleman.

'I understand that you can't commit, but please tell me what is going on with me. I am not going to hold you to your words if things change later. Let me know what looks feasible based on your experience.'

Dr Parto understood my restlessness. He told us that based on my progress, the mastectomy had been ruled out.

We were delighted. His words were music to our ears. Blissful!

He did mention that we might have to explore the options of size reduction. The plan would be:

Step one: He would extract the tumour, and the tissues in its vicinity.

Step two: The surgically removed tissues would be sent to the histo-pathology lab, for analysis.

Step three: If no cancer was found in the biopsy (if they 'got it all'), no further surgery would be needed. However, if even a single cell was found in the lab, I would go in for another surgery. But this would not have to be a mastectomy. It would just be a size reduction. Steps one and two would be repeated, and if any cancerous cells were found again, a third round of surgery might be required.

They could not risk leaving even one cancerous cell inside, otherwise they would multiply and cause a recurrence. It is strange – the kind of things that are discussed during cancer treatment. Here we were – discussing the step-by-step procedure of cutting out parts of my body!

We understood the plan, and hoped that I would not need a second or third round of surgery. *Fingers and toes crossed! My boob will be saved! Hurray!* I felt on top of the world. I was happier than all the happy people in the whole of England put together!

My diary about cancer was progressing well too. The insomnia had been severe during the third chemotherapy cycle, and I had spent most of my hours during the night burping, trying to get some sleep, or writing.

A few days after the oesophagitis experience, I started recovering, and Mum slowly became more used to seeing the difficulties of cancer treatment. On a particular evening, she shared with me how scared she and Papa had been when they got to know the diagnosis. They had thought they would soon lose me.

I remember clearly that I had made it a point to tell Sachin that I hoped to be cured, and that the prognosis was very positive. I had asked him to communicate this message to our parents, and reinforce it time and again. However, Mum said that Sachin had never shared this with them. When I checked with Sachin about this confusion, he told me that he had repeatedly clarified that the treatment should be able to cure me. But *the very word 'cancer'* had scared my parents so much that they were unable to assimilate the information that was being given to them. All that they could think of was that cancer would kill me, and that I may not outlive them. Unfortunately, such is the impact of the C word.

I have no family history of cancer, neither on my father's nor my mother's side. I seem to be 'the chosen one' for cancer. Because we have never had cancer in our family before, my parents thankfully did not have to battle the guilt which many parents feel when a child gets diagnosed with cancer. Being diagnosed with cancer is no one's fault, but many people tend to feel guilty about it. It's a shame that I can't say anymore that there is no cancer in my family!

I have a friend going through breast cancer treatment, who has teenage daughters. Her biggest worry after her breast cancer diagnosis has been, 'Have I passed on the wrong gene to my girls?' This has been an incredibly difficult fear for her to cope with.

Having seen the agony my parents went through, I think that for me, it was probably easier to go through cancer because I did not have children. If I did have children, I would have been so worried about having passed on the cancer gene to them, or of dying and not being there for them. But then, maybe having children would have given me additional strength to beat the hell out of cancer, so that I could be well for them!

The fear of losing me must have been excruciating for my parents, but the whole cancer experience turned out to be for the better in the long run. It reminded them of how precious their children were for them. It is not that they had forgotten this – But it is nice to be reminded of the things and people that are important to us. Cancer was not just my journey; it was a journey that my loved ones took along with me. Together we went through a difficult time, and together we emerged stronger as individuals and as a family.

I had battled half of the chemotherapy. 'FEC' was out; it was time for 'T' to get its teeth into me.

Funny hands and funny feet

The fourth cycle was different, because the new drug Herceptin[20] was being introduced. Herceptin is a targeted treatment for HER2[21] positive breast cancer cells. HER2 is a protein that can affect the growth of some cancer cells. HER2 positive breast cancers tend to grow more quickly than HER2 negative breast cancers. In the fourth cycle, when we moved to the drug 'T' in the 'FEC-T' regime of chemotherapy, there was far more havoc with the skin. T is Taxotere®, the common name for docetaxel.

The Herceptin was administered intravenously on Thursday, and I was kept under observation for a total of six hours, including the duration of the treatment. Abhi waited patiently through all this time. He wanted to be with me at the hospital for the first session with the new drug. Herceptin usually causes flu-like symptoms, and in rarer cases, it can also damage the heart. It reduces the ability of the heart to pump blood effectively. Therefore, it is imperative that a heart scan be performed regularly, every couple of months. Herceptin didn't create severe side effects in the first session. I only felt a choking in my throat, which was resolved through instant medication. The three scoops of strawberry

---

[20] Macmillan Cancer Support. "Herceptin ® (trastuzumab) for breast cancer in women." Last modified October 2013. http://www.macmillan.org.uk/Cancerinformation/Cancertypes/Breast/Treatingbreastcancer/Herceptin.aspx. Last accessed December 05, 2014.

[21] Macmillan Cancer Support. "HER2 positive breast cancer." Last modified January 2013. http://www.macmillan.org.uk/Cancerinformation/Cancertypes/Breast/Aboutbreastcancer/Typesandrelatedconditions/HER2%20positive.aspx. Last accessed December 05, 2014.

ice-cream that I ate after lunch must have helped too. So far, so good. The bigger beast, Taxotere, needed to be tackled on the following day.

It is strange how calmly I write, 'So far, so good.' Such a statement does not mean that all was well and hunky-dory. It just means that in the larger scheme of things, there was no emergency situation and therefore, I was OK. The baseline for being OK had changed for me. I had actually started appreciating what was meant by the age-old cliché, 'What doesn't kill you makes you stronger.'

This reminds me of how several people whom I met during cancer kept saying that I was facing my cancer bravely. Yes, I know I didn't sulk about it all the time and did my best to keep calm – but what other choice did I have? In fact, when I received this compliment from people who didn't really know any specific details about my treatment, at times I wondered if they really understood what I was going through. If they did, they would have been familiar with the stakes involved, and would probably have understood that every cancer patient needs to be brave, to be able to go through what they have to go through. It is a simple equation: either the cancer should be killed, or there is a high chance that it will kill you. Maybe they expected to see cancer patients feeling fragile and devastated. But not being brave would not help a cancer patient get through the treatment or the illness. But enough of this old debate; let's come back to the fourth chemotherapy cycle.

The next day was the first time the new chemotherapy drug 'T' was administered. When I was voicing my concerns about what Herceptin could do (cardiac toxicity), Dr Charles had said that he would be more worried about the new drug, docetaxel, than Herceptin. Dr Charles had never used a worrisome word before, and coming from him, this was slightly perturbing.

Kate, the fabulous chemo nurse, whom I grew very fond of during my chemo sessions, administered the treatment to me. I loved it when Kate looked after me. Somehow I felt less pain with the needles at her skilful hands. I am not sure if it was the extra skill or her pleasant personality that lessened the pain, but it worked its magic on me.

And then came the effects of the drug. Soon after the fourth session, my complexion turned darker. And I don't mean the sultry, beautiful dark complexion, the kind that a person would be happy about. This was the kind of dark complexion that sheaths your skin when it is screaming, '*Hey! I am ill!*'

But it was my hands that underwent the most drastic change. Dr Charles had given me a heads-up that I might feel as if my hands were burnt; the skin might develop rashes and burn-like marks. This sounded intimidating, and yet the intensity remained to be seen, like in the case of every other side-effect. The fourth day after the chemotherapy, my typing went awry. I just could not type properly! I made mistakes, and it felt *funny and different* when I typed. The following day, simple tasks like holding a fork or wiping the table or lifting a mug felt difficult. My hands began to look very red, became painful to the touch, and eventually, by bedtime, I let out a scream at the slightest touch to my hands. The nail beds were the worst. They ensured that I could not do anything that required the touch of my fingertips.

I was amazed, as I realised how much we utilise our nail beds. Typing, lifting a mug of warm tea on a winter morning, being able to peel the wrappers off medicines, breaking the *chapatti* during a meal – everything seemed undoable, almost impossible. Suddenly, countless little pleasures in life were difficult to enjoy. It was not possible to carelessly lift some tea while watching TV. This act now required the utmost precision, wherein I would cup the mug carefully, with both my hands stretched out, as I could not manoeuvre my fingers to hold the mug in what could be called *the normal way*. *Normalcy* looked far away – at least for another ten weeks, until the chemotherapy was finished on the 31ˢᵗ of January. It became torturous to touch anything warm – the feeling of warmth on burnt hands, say with hot food or warm water in the shower, was unbearable to say the least.

Then the skin on my hands started coming off. Very quickly, they looked as if I was in need of a manicure, and subsequently, in a dire need of a manicure. Soon my hands looked as if they had some serious skin disease. My hands looked exactly like a pair of burnt hands losing skin. And I understood what Dr Charles had meant by 'you could feel as if your hands were burnt'. The same thing happened with my feet. The soles got burnt. The skin on my feet turned black, and it hurt just like it was supposed to – like burnt skin. The skin on the soles turned dry and hard. It became so hard that it felt almost like nails. It pricked me hard every time I placed my foot on the ground. Walking every single step became a challenge.

Docetaxel also caused severe muscular pain. The big muscles in the upper back and shoulders became very painful, and the legs and arms hurt too. Being massaged and caressed helped me feel better, but the impact was temporary. At the same time, I developed a weird pain in the head. A shooting pain would start from my forehead, and run through the head down to the nape of the neck. It was rather infrequent when it started, but it soon became more and more frequent. Dr Charles attributed it to some viral infection that I must have picked up in the past.

The changes in the colour of my nails continued. The blue completely changed to brown. The horizontal lines turned into distinct bands. Well, brown nails looked better than blue, but they were still seriously ugly. Dr Charles mentioned that some people lose all the nails from their fingers as well as their toes. *Ouch!* I fervently hoped that I would not be among them. I really dreaded the thought of losing all twenty nails. For the next ten weeks, I would keep a close watch on my nails, and get paranoid if I felt that they were not as firmly rooted upon my body as they should be. Several times, I felt as if the nails were coming off, and I asked Abhi and Mum to check them time and again. I even suspected that some of my nails were loose. But they both seemed to disagree. Eventually, the nails chose to stay on. *Phew!*

Constipation had been my constant companion since Cycle I. Movicol had been helping, but was not enough. So on my request, the doctor prescribed Sena, an Ayurvedic drug, to me. Sena works differently from Movicol, and the two drugs together grudgingly did the needful – opened up the bowels. The accompanying fissure did not help the act, and interfered as much as possible, but it was bliss compared to what another cancer patient told me about her constipation in Cycle IV. She'd had to go to her GP, and he had had to put in a pair of tongs to pull out the faecal matter! Seriously? Apparently, yes!

After hearing about her experience, I was thankful for being able to open the bowels on my own, without any intervention. The little pleasures of life! ☺

The loss of eyebrows began in the fourth cycle. By the third week, they looked poorly plucked. I was losing eyelashes too. There were days when I had to remove eyelashes that had dropped into my eyes as many as ten or fifteen times. Whenever I felt something poking my eye, I knew it was another eyelash.

The first and fourth cycles of chemotherapy were the most difficult ones. The first one had been difficult because the strong chemotherapy drugs had been injected into my system for the first time, and there was a sudden rush of toxicity in the body. The fourth was so abominably tough not only because of the severe side effects of the drug 'T', but also because the previous three cycles had weakened my body. The 'T' and the tiredness that had built up inside me over the months made the three weeks of this chemotherapy cycle so difficult that, innumerable times, I felt that the pain would never stop. The cancer and its treatment were gnawing at me, and there seemed to be no end to the agony and the despair. I had to build a sheath to protect myself from all this internal pain. But there was always one fact, the single most helpful fact in this entire experience: Time does not stop. No matter how long the days and nights appeared, because of all the misery, *they still passed.* No matter how difficult it felt, the next day was another day, and it meant that I had survived one more day of chemotherapy. When coping became unbearable, I simply held on to this optimism and carried on.

This was also the time when I looked my worst. My skin, nails, hands and feet, ill complexion, swollen face due to the high dose of steroids, the total absence of hair which served as a constant reminder of cancer, and my increasing weight – everything contributed to my deteriorating looks.

I looked like a boiled egg. Abhi fondly addressed me as Andu (pronounced 'undo') – a cuter-sounding version of *anda*, which means egg in Hindi. Each time he called me Andu, I felt better about how I looked and we laughed. *Love can do amazing things.*

I knew so many cancer patients who were on the same treatment as I was. Even though several variables were the same in terms of the type of cancer, the grade, the stage, the hormone sensitivity, and the drug regimen, the way we responded to the treatment was absolutely different. There were some side effects that I developed which others didn't, and vice versa. The vast range of how we were all responding to the same drugs was mind-boggling. We drew comfort from each other's stories, and compared notes to learn from each other.

Christmas was approaching. It was the 15th of December, a special day, as Sarah Keefe, my friend and colleague at work, was coming home for the first time. Sarah and I worked well together, and we got along famously. She taught me how to prepare some delicious soups, while I helped her with curries. Our wavelengths matched and we found each other funny and great company. But it was only after my cancer diagnosis that we grew really close. It is remarkable how some people choose to stand by others in their moments of adversity. Sarah was that one friend who was there with me when I was going through my darkest hours. Thank you, Sarah.

We decided to cook bread-potato rolls, some savoury snacks and coconut cakes for her. Bread-potato rolls are Mum's speciality, and she created the magic again with her cooking. However, when I tasted them, they were too salty. I ate some more and realised that it was not just the rolls that were salty, but my mouth too. Apparently, the taste of my mouth had changed, and now it tasted like salt! My lips tasted salty too. By dinner-time, I had applied my common sense to understand that I should be eating food with minimal salt. *Khichdi*[22] with very little salt tasted fine, while my mouth supplied the missing salt. It was an interesting experience for a week; all food tasted as if I was eating plain salt. For a week, I ate food with minimal salt, while I supplied the remaining salt myself. ☺

The heavy dose of steroids which was introduced with the new drug, not only caused me to gain weight but also increased my appetite – and because I ate more, I put on more weight. It was a vicious cycle, but one that I couldn't do much about. Thankfully, I was eating more than usual – I was not one of those cancer patients who lose their appetite, and become weak because of poor nutrition. Gaining weight was better than being malnourished, I consoled myself. Unfortunately, while I gained that weight rather quickly, even after I was taken off steroids, the extra weight just stayed with me.

In the fourth chemotherapy cycle, I stopped writing about my cancer experience. The quasi-burnt hands ensured that I couldn't do any typing. I could only write or type with huge effort, and I ploughed

---

[22]   Khichdi: A savoury dish made with rice and pulses cooked together.

that effort into my office work. It would be a long time before I was able to resume writing my diary.

I was getting ready for the fifth cycle of chemotherapy. Four out of six done – through with two-thirds, just one-third remained.

Skin or cuticle?

I had the fifth chemotherapy cycle on the 21st of December, a Friday. Catherine, a senior chemo nurse, looked after me. I had become very weak now, but Catherine did her best to ensure that I was as comfortable as possible. I tolerated this cycle much better, as compared to the fourth cycle.

From the next day onwards, my office was closed for ten days – for Christmas and the New Year. This helped enormously. I did not have to think about work at all. There was no guilt feeling for not working when the project needed me. The New Year began, and I resumed work. I hoped that I would be able to commute to Cambridge easily, and work full-time.

But within two days, the tiredness got the better of me. Thankfully, the weekend was coming up, and the third week of the chemotherapy cycle, the one that facilitated recovery, was beginning too. I thought again, *From Monday onwards, things should be fine.* During week three, I would return to relative normalcy. However, Monday made me feel tired and by Tuesday evening, I was absolutely knackered. I could not possibly travel to work; the commute of about ninety minutes tired me out, even before the work hours had started. The fatigue built upon itself incessantly and so did the muscular pain. The third week of the chemotherapy cycle was far more tiring than it had been in the previous four cycles.

I worked from home for two days. Unfortunately, there was so much work that whatever time I saved on travel, I had to plough into work. Nonetheless, working without the travel was definitely more convenient.

My skin kept changing for the worse. As the fifth cycle progressed, the skin on my hands and feet became so hard that it felt almost like the cuticles of my nails. The hardened skin continued to peel off. Each morning, I spent about fifteen minutes clipping a few inches of skin off my hands and feet.

By the end of the fifth cycle, I had two thick and distinct brown coloured bands on each nail. The nurse told me on the day of the sixth treatment session that each of those bands stood for each cycle of docetaxel. *This is interesting! This means that I should have one more band after three weeks*, I thought. I was tempted to name the bands Liam and Neeson, after my favourite actor, who makes my heart skip a beat every single time he appears on screen. But when the third band developed, well, what would I name it? It just felt wrong to put anyone else in the same league as Liam Neeson, and so I eventually decided to let the bands just be, without any names!

After the gastrointestinal tract spasm in the third cycle, and the change of the drug in the fourth cycle, the stress levels at home were phenomenally high. Despite my less serious side effects in the current cycle, I was extremely unwell. Mum, Abhi and I were doing our best to hold up, but there were outbursts here and there.

The misguided opinions of other people made one of the difficult days even worse for us. These people had seen someone go through cancer, and that person had been given three sessions of chemotherapy. I was being given six. They failed to understand that every case is different. They didn't know any specific details about either of the cases, but jumped to conclusions. They went ahead and told Mum that my prognosis must be really bad. Instead of the usual three sessions, I was being given six sessions! With extreme concern, they summed up the conversation by speculating whether I would survive the ordeal.

We knew, rationally, that this speculation was stupid. It showed nothing but their ignorance and misconceptions about cancer. It also showed a lack of empathy and a lack of kindness, of the worst kind. They knew that I was going through cancer treatment, and there was no reason for them to go and tell my mum that I might not survive. It was cruel. Even though Mum knew what to think in rational terms, she was deeply hurt. She cried for several hours. I tried to comfort her, but she was aghast at how cruel people could be. How could someone suggest that she would lose her child? The mere thought of me being on 'death row' shook her. Words are powerful, and someone had just used them to cause an upheaval in a shaky boat crossing turbulent waters.

I remained unable to type out my cancer experience during the fifth cycle. And since I had been advised to avoid crowded places during chemotherapy, I could not go to watch the latest James Bond movie, *Skyfall*. Missing a James Bond movie is not cool, but the dashing Daniel Craig would have to wait!

However, all was not sad at the Banka residence in Hitchin: something exciting did happen. I noticed that my hair had started re-growing! It looked more like soft fur than hair, but it was the beginning. I wasn't super excited about the fact that this meant the hair would come back on the rest of my body too. Being clean of hair for four months had been wonderful. But the hair re-growth suggested that my body had begun coming back to normal. *Happy!* ☺

It was time for the sixth and the final cycle of treatment on the 11th of January. What joy!

Frail but free

Our level of motivation to visit the hospital on the 11th of January for the sixth chemotherapy session was very high. We were excited about the final lap of chemotherapy. I spent a long time thinking about this, and revisited the pictures that we had taken on the day of my first treatment. I wore the same clothes: blue jeans, black sweater, and shirt with vertical violet strips. I added a blue and violet scarf, as a much-needed accessory to the winter clothing. For some weird reason, I wanted to wear the same clothes for the first and the last session of chemotherapy.

We took our usual train at 8:22 am, and reached Cambridge by 9 am. As always, we walked down to the hospital. Kate came and said that she would look after me; I was happy. The treatment began at 9:45 am: Saline flush for the line, sample for the blood test, saline flush again, Herceptin injection, and another flush to ensure all the Herceptin went into my blood stream, a strong dose of steroids, another flush, chemotherapy at 12:30 pm, and the last flush from 1:45 to 2:00 pm.

This was a special cycle, as everything worked perfectly. The port line had worked on both sides (flushing in and flushing out) only during the first two cycles. In the third cycle, the nurse had not been able to make the port bleed back, but we had proceeded with the chemotherapy based on the lineogram. The port had not bled in the fourth or the fifth cycle either. But in the sixth cycle, no-one knows how, the port fixed itself and it bled back. I remember telling Kate that it was probably her expertise with needles, and not a stroke of luck, that made everything work perfectly.

Amidst all this, at 12 noon, I had my preferred comfort food at the hospital: jacket potato and a generous helping of beans and cheese, with extra salt and pepper – this followed by three scoops of strawberry ice-cream and a small glass of apple juice (that I had not ordered, but which nonetheless arrived) served as the perfect meal on a cold January morning. I believe that the weather is never too cold to eat ice-cream. During the treatment, Abhi's mum and I chatted on video for an hour, and then I called a friend. Her little brother had been diagnosed with Hodgkin's disease[23] at a very young age. Thanks to the right treatment, support from family, and enormous self-resilience, he had fought and survived. He had been through chemotherapy and radiation therapy. She and I had come in contact with each other when he was on treatment. But unfortunately, I could not at the time understand what he was going through. The treatment for cancer was not as advanced as today, eight years ago. After the chat with her, I came back home and read about Hodgkin's disease. As I read, I could *feel* what he must have gone through. How difficult it must have been for him to face and fight such a deadly disease – at the age of only twenty! When his friends and peers were working hard, pursuing higher education, and having fun in life, he had to face cancer. How unfair life had been to him. But he had fought back, and was a survivor. I was suddenly filled with admiration for this young man whom I had never met or seen. And...I yearned to be where he was – in the category of the survivors!

Without ever speaking to him or even talking with my friend about his illness, I can understand it so much better now. Unfortunately, I had

---

[23]   Hodgkin's disease: Hodgkin lymphoma or Hodgkin disease is a cancer of the lymphatic system. The cause of Hodgkin lymphoma remains unknown. Its treatment is usually very successful even if it is in several different areas of the body.
Macmillan Cancer Support. "What is Hodgkin lymphoma?" Last modified August 2014. http://www.macmillan.org.uk/information-and-support/lymphoma/lymphoma-hodgkin/understanding-cancer/what-is-hodgkin-lymphoma.html. Last accessed April 09, 2015.

to experience cancer to be able to develop this level of empathy. This is the kind of empathy I had when I was a child. When I started growing up and joined in the rat race of life, I gained many important things, but I lost many priceless things too. I think this experience of cancer has helped me to regain some of those lost parts of myself. It is strange that I needed to go through such a deadly disease to be reminded of something so basic and so intrinsic to us all. As I had these thoughts, my body was hurting due to the toxic chemotherapy drugs that had been injected into my system the previous day – but my heart had a flutter of happiness, and the feeling of doing the right thing.

The journey towards becoming a better person had started three months and three weeks ago, with the diagnosis on the 17th of September. I just hope that it continues even after this is all over. *Insha'Allah!*

The first three days of Cycle VI passed rather uneventfully. We were excited and hoped that the last cycle would be easier – then on the fourth day, I started feeling unwell. As the morning progressed, I kept feeling worse. Weakness and fatigue overcame me. I managed to eat some breakfast, and went back to lie in bed. I felt too tired to even get out for a quick shower. I ultimately heaved myself out of bed and had a shower around noon. After getting dressed, I went to the dining room to have some lunch. I sat down at the table, but felt weird. The sense of an impending blackout began to overpower me, and so I moved towards my bed to lie down. I took a few steps, but I passed out at the door to the bedroom. My tiny flat had suddenly become *huge* for me. I did not have enough strength to move from one room to another. After a few moments, I regained consciousness and my mum helped me to my feet. When I felt a little better, she fed me lunch in bed, and I felt blessed to have her by my side. By afternoon, the side effects of the chemotherapy drugs had set in. The muscular pain had begun, and it had come back with a vengeance. With every movement, my muscles hurt. With every turn on the bed, I squirmed with pain. I spent the rest of the day in bed, feeling too weak to budge. Mum had pulled a chair next to the bed and she stayed there to look after me, just in case I needed anything. Even after I dozed off in the evening, she kept her vigil there, exhausted but determined to look after me.

Mum pressed my arms, my legs and my back, to relieve me of the pain. It helped, but only temporarily, and the pain would always return. Although giving me those massages was exhausting for my mum, she did it four times. In the evening, I felt no better and had a temperature. We called up the hospital for advice, and they asked us to come in. It was 9:15 pm and we were eating dinner. We finished the meal and decided to split the tasks among ourselves; I packed our bags for the hospital stay, while Abhi cleared up the kitchen and put on the dishwasher. By 10:05 pm, we had left home for Cambridge. The weather was very cold, and although the real feel of the weather was -2°C, it felt like -20°C to me. I was weak, and the cold air cut right through my body like a scalpel. We managed to reach the hospital by 11:15 pm, and there was a gentleman waiting for us at the door. That was a new experience; we had never had someone waiting for us at the hospital before. They took us in immediately. A series of blood tests and general check-up followed. Dr Charles came to see me in the middle of the night. It was amazing how reassured Abhi and I felt each time we met him. Our faith in him was deep – and of course, it is no mean task to trust someone with your life. The basic blood test result came out OK. Dr Charles didn't think that I was in any danger, and therefore, after two hours with a saline drip and a portable commode in the room, we settled in for the night. We asked for bedding for Abhi – they provided us with a big reclining chair and some blankets, and we called it a day.

We both slept for a few hours. The next day began at 6 am with the nurses coming in to check on me. Blood pressure, check; temperature, check – all normal. We ate breakfast and waited for Dr Charles to come for the morning round. He came, checked on me, and said that he was happy with my health. What a relief! Within the next ten minutes, the nurse came and removed the appendages from my port and we were ready to leave for home. ☺

I had ended up missing my Zoladex injection because of this emergency hospitalisation. I was supposed to meet Dr Peter, my GP, at the surgery that morning but thanks to the emergency hospitalisation, I was unable to attend the appointment. But Dr Peter was very kind and accommodated the injection at the end of the first half of the day. By afternoon, we were able to board the train to Hitchin and come back home.

During the sixth cycle, the dryness of my hands and feet had started improving. Mum had massaged my hands and feet twice a day with mustard oil, since the fifth cycle had started. E45 had become totally ineffective and would disappear from the skin in no time. It was exhausting for Mum to do so much, but she did it without fail, and thanks to her efforts my skin started showing signs of recovery.

My burnt hands still hurt a lot and I could neither write nor type. Since the fourth cycle, my diary had come to a halt. It was only after quite some time that I was able to write again, and I have tried my best to keep these time lapses from reflecting in my writing.

Chemotherapy had affected my work life drastically. In fact, the diagnosis was practically synonymous with 'getting irregular at work'. Before I started chemotherapy on the 27th of September 2012, I had hoped to be able to keep working. As per the doctor's advice, I had requested leave for the first week of each chemotherapy cycle. During the second week of each cycle, I decided to work from home. This was because my WBC and RBC were at their lowest in week two, putting me at an increased risk of contracting infections.

But as the chemotherapy sessions continued, I became progressively more and more tired. My project at work was at a critical stage, and so I did not take any time off except for two days for Diwali, which I spent with the terrible gastrointestinal tract spasm. I was putting in about ten to eleven hours at work every day. By the time the third cycle approached its end, I was knackered.

So my body was exhausted when I began the fourth cycle. The change of drugs in the fourth cycle only made the situation worse. My body revolted, and I had to take two weeks off at a critical time in the project. Obviously, this put our team on the spot, as the deliverables were affected, but the situation was out of my control. Thankfully, right after the fifth cycle, the Christmas break commenced and I was saved the consequences of having to take more time off from work. The fifth cycle passed without any major hiccups. Therefore, I expected the sixth cycle to be easy too. During the sixth cycle, while the side effects due to chemotherapy were less (the sheer reason being that my system had become increasingly accustomed to the toxicity of the drugs), the tiredness that had progressively built up overpowered me. Again, I had to take two weeks off. Over my six chemotherapy cycles of eighteen weeks, I had taken six weeks off! This could have been eight weeks, without the Christmas break. I wanted to work, but was unable to.

During chemotherapy, my colleagues helped me out enormously. They covered for me when I was on leave. Liz, my manager, gave me all the support I needed to accommodate my hospital appointments. Many times I could not work normal hours, but I was given leeway to work as per my convenience. I also worked quite a lot from home, especially in the second week of my chemotherapy cycle, due to the possibility of catching an infection. Instead of working for eight straight hours, I worked intermittently. So I began work early in the morning, worked for a few hours, and then rested. I resumed work after lunch, and would take rest breaks as required. I worked really odd hours at times. There were days when I worked until late in the night, if I was not able to sleep, or if there was more work that needed extra hours, or if I had had a bad day and had been unable to complete much work. I also had full support from the management team for the project and the organisation. They continued to trust me and never doubted me because I didn't compromise deliverables. It was I who said that I could not continue working after the fourth cycle, and took a back seat. I believe that I was really lucky to have been working at an organisation that has employee care as one of its topmost priorities. Thank you to each one of you.

I was frail from months of weakness built up through the six chemotherapy cycles, but I was free. The sweet taste of freedom felt incredible.

Deep vein thrombosis strikes

The three weeks of the last chemotherapy cycle finished on the 31st of January. The very next day, I noticed that my right forearm was swollen. It was Friday evening and I decided to observe my arm over the weekend, and call the hospital on Monday. On Monday 4th February, I called the hospital and told them about the swelling. It was in my right arm, the side on which the port was implanted. I was worried that my swelling and my port might be related. I spoke to the chemotherapy nurse, Lorraine, who in turn consulted Dr Charles. They asked me to come to the hospital for an ultrasound scan. I rushed to Cambridge. Thankfully, it was one of the relatively free mornings for the radiology department. They took me in immediately. I underwent the scan, which confirmed that there were a couple of clots in the vein, due to the port.

Now, there are two things that can possibly go wrong with the ports: one, they don't bleed back, and two, a clot or thrombosis happens. Both had now happened. Lorraine explained the options to me. I would have to take an anticoagulant injection, Clexane, for as long as the port was inside me. That would be until December 2013, for eleven more months. 'What is the frequency of the injections?' I asked. She said, 'Daily.' That made me nervous. *Daily injections for eleven months! Crazy!* Said a voice inside my head, and my face said the same. 'What are the alternatives?' I asked. 'Have the port removed, and take injections for three months,' she replied. Three months sounded better than eleven. That would be ninety-two injections in total – to be administered in the stomach. Lorraine suggested that I administer the injections on my own. I got more nervous. Lorraine could arrange for a district nurse to visit me and administer the injections, but I did not want to depend on a nurse for three months. I decided that I would do it on my own, or ask Abhi to do it for me. After a while, with Catherine's help, I tried to administer an injection on my own. I held it in my hand and I pulled it towards my stomach. But automatically, my hand stopped as soon as I reached close to the skin. After some effort, I shoved it inside myself and injected the fluid. Catherine told me that it might sting and leave the skin bruised. Well, I got both. I felt like jumping around for twenty minutes because of stinging, and had a big bruise on my stomach.

I shared the experience with Abhi, and he agreed to administer the injections. I set the dose while he took the injection and shoved it in – Bingo! Our teamwork was perfect. More stinging and jumping around followed. Gradually, over a period of days, the duration for which the stinging occurred lessened. My body was getting used to Clexane (heparin).

I had lost count of the number of times my body had been subjected to needles and punctured during this treatment.

Dr Charles asked me to come and see him on the 8th of February. During our discussion, it was decided that we should let the port remain inside and that I should be on Clexane injections for three months. He also mentioned that he would now like to rethink putting me on Tamoxifen[24]. Tamoxifen increases the risk of blood clots and therefore, the drug might be unsuitable for me. He was also considering Zoladex as hormonal therapy for me. But I knew that decision would be taken later, when I moved to London, and some other doctor would finalise it for me.

---

[24]   Tamoxifen: Tamoxifen is an anti-oestrogen drug used to treat breast cancer. It is occasionally used to treat a few other cancers.
Macmillan Cancer Support. "Tamoxifen." Last modified January 2013. http://www.macmillan.org.uk/Cancerinformation/Cancertreatment/Treatmenttypes/Hormonaltherapies/Individualhormonaltherapies/Tamoxifen.aspx. Last accessed December 05, 2014.

Abhi administered the injections to me for most of the three-month period. My mum did it for me once when he was travelling for work. Julia did them several times for me, when I stayed at her place to complete the radiation therapy.

Clexane increases the body's tendency to bruise. As we progressed through the three-month course of Clexane, I became more prone to bruises. The injections had to be administered in the tummy, preferably under the belly button. This gave us a space of just a few inches. For the first time ever, I was happy that there was extra flab on my stomach, because it gave me some more surface area for the injections! By the time the two months were over, there were blue patches all over the lower half of my stomach. Getting an injection in there every single day became a difficult task – as the area was already bruised and painful. But what needed to be done, had to be done. The 4th of May would definitely be a day to celebrate, when the last Clexane injection would finally be used up.

My work contract was coming to an end in February, and I was scared that it would not be renewed because of my irregularity at work. Moreover, with an arm affected by thrombosis, it was almost impossible to type or do much. But it was time that I stopped worrying about my job, and whether the contract would get renewed or not. This was one more thing that I had to 'let go'. Once I stopped worrying about the loss of my job, it became easy for me. The ambitious *me* had *chosen* to let go of work and my career. I had come to terms with not being part of the corporate rat race, at least not until my health had been restored. I found myself not spending innumerable hours trying to find another job. Again I thought, 'Weird that it took cancer for me to understand something so simple.' As I said before, the journey to becoming a better and wiser person had started – on the 17th of September 2012.

But the old me had a little confusion, and some doubt – was this really letting go, or just a loss of focus? If only moving out of rat race was so easy! ☺

And now, something strange happened. I had more free time as I was working less, and so I could have spent lots of time looking for a job. But my primary focus was upon recuperating. I would, once in a while, apply for a job or look for vacancies. This was completely different from how I had been a couple of years ago. Then, if my contract were coming to an end, I would have utilised all my free time to eagerly look for another job. For me, my work had not just been a means to earn money. It had always defined my identity and self-worth. It was important for me to be a top performer at work, because the recognition and success were important to me. Then, I had loved taking up those challenges, seeing work as the key thing that made me self-dependent. But now, after cancer, *I had begun to change.*

The day was the 13th of February, and this was an important day for two reasons:

One: I was due to undergo the cancer surgery the next day, the 14th of February. We would find out how well the chemotherapy had worked on me. After today, I would be in severe pain, for several weeks.

Two: It was the day I finished work at Cambridge University Press. My work contract had come to an end, and it had been a brilliant association of about two and a half years with the organisation.

I had a little Raleigh bike that I kept in Cambridge. It helped me get about the city whenever I needed to. I also used it to bicycle from the train station to office. When I finished work at the Press on the 13th of February, I had to carry the bike back home. At the end of the work day, I went to the bike shed, unlocked the bike like always, and rode it. I had to cover a distance of 0.8 miles. I am not much of a biker, but I had formerly been able to comfortably manage fifteen miles at a go, and about twenty miles with effort. I started riding my bike and by the time I covered half that short distance home, I was out of breath. I was getting more and more uncomfortable and by the time I had covered about three-quarters of the distance, I was about to fall off the bike with fatigue. My leg muscles ached badly. I could walk the bike; that was always an option. But if I did that, I would miss the train, and there would be a thirty-minute wait for the next train in the severe English winter. I decided to carry on. It felt strange that I was struggling to bicycle to the station, an activity that I used to do every day without any conscious effort. Now, things were different. I was a cancer patient, and it showed in everything I did. Somehow, I managed to reach the train station. I had to change the platform to board the train. Thankfully there was a lift at the Cambridge station, and I managed to load the bike onto the train. It felt as if I had run a marathon (not that I have ever actually run a marathon, yet, but I reckon that it must be a *huge* task). I crashed on a window seat. I was still out of breath, and it took me a good twenty-five minutes to get back to normal breathing. *Chemotherapy has completely messed up my stamina*, I thought. I felt a little miserable, in fact sad. The train was completely jam-packed with people. There were children who were excitedly discussing school. There was a group of working professionals sitting close to me, and they were talking about cracking some ambitious business deals in the corporate world.

I let out a breath. Everyone around me looked happy and seemed to be getting on with their lives, and I wondered if their lives were really as perfect as they looked. Maybe, or maybe not – I had no way to find out. What I did know was that my life was less than perfect. I realised that my eyes had grown wet while I looked around. It was dark outside, and the train pulled into a station. There was another train on the adjacent platform. As I glanced out of the window, I happened to see my reflection in the glass window of the other train. I kept looking at it for a few seconds... long enough to set my perspective right... I was still here, and that is what mattered. The lives of the other people looked perfect, but who knew what really lay beneath their smiling faces? I had a loving family, and I was going home to them; who knew whom the other passengers were going home to? Who knew if they had a real home? Who knew if anyone cared for them? But yet, at the same time, here I was – not even sure if I would survive cancer now, and if I did, no one knew if the cancer would come back and claim me later. The train had started crawling, and I saw my reflection disappearing fast. In the flash of a second, it was dark again.

While the outside world looked dark, I had seen my own reflection in the glass. It may have been fleeting, but it was there, as certainly as there was a moon in the sky above me. I was still here. Once again, I decided I would not give up and do everything I was required to do to kick cancer out of my body. No more trespassing!

> *In the fell clutch of circumstance*
> *I have not winced nor cried aloud.*
> *Under the bludgeonings of chance*
> *My head is bloody, but unbowed.*
> - William Ernest Henley, *Invictus*

I felt better after making this decision. It was time for me to get off the train at Hitchin. To get out of the station, I was required to change the platform, but there was a little problem. Hitchin is a small station and has no lift. There is a small subway, which I had to take to move across the platforms. I lifted the bike and walked down the stairs (about fifteen in number). It was not very difficult, but to get to the other side, I would now have to walk up an equal number of stairs! I tried to lift the bike and take the first stair, but my arm did not move. I am a right-hander, and I naturally use my right arm. I tried again, but the arm did not budge with the bike; it felt completely jammed! I knew that the DVT (deep vein thrombosis – in simple terms, the blood clot in my right arm) was preventing me from moving it properly. My arm was achy, swollen, and had very limited mobility. A young boy behind me noticed, and offered to carry the bike for me. I was grateful for his kindness. He lifted the bike with what looked like zero effort and carried it for me. The difference between what a normal person could do and what a cancer patient could not do was walking up the stairs in front of me.

I thanked the young boy, walked the bike to get out of the train station, and stood in the queue for a taxi. The weather had worsened. The sleet had started falling. Thankfully, I got a taxi large enough to accommodate my bike (my bike was little but it did not fold, and so I needed a large taxi). I gave the address to the driver. Home was only 1.75 miles away from the station. The driver commented, 'The weather still isn't too bad. You can ride that distance; shouldn't take you too long, you may reach home before it starts snowing.'

It was a simple comment to which I simply responded, 'I have cancer. I can't ride a bike for even this short distance.' The taxi driver was stunned with what he heard. He grew uncomfortable, said sorry, and a cancerous silence filled the taxi.

Cancer does make people very uncomfortable. I had become quite familiar with this silence, as I had encountered it repeatedly from family and friends. I knew that it would not go away unless I made an effort. I asked the taxi driver how his day had been, and saw him recover from the discomfort that I had put him in a few seconds ago. He looked almost relieved at the opportunity to talk about something else. I listened patiently while he talked about his day, and later his family. Soon, we reached our destination. The bike and I were home.

I am not buying today

It was a cold winter morning in the third week of February. The day looked deceptively bright. Abhi and I were still drowsy, having a lie-in. There was a soft but determined knock on the door. Now, this was strange! Any visitors should have had to call the residence from outside the building. A resident has to open the door to the main building, before any visitors can step in. Reaching a specific apartment is the second step. A direct knock on the flat door comes only in particular circumstances, when the visitor has special permission. Like when I'd had two visitors some time ago who were from a charity. They had special permission from the police to access flats directly, without having to depend on the residents to let them inside the building.

My mind made the connection with this memory. A salesman, so early in the morning! Grudgingly, I slipped out of bed to answer the knock on the door. I opened the door and saw a tall, broad, and dark man, probably in his late 50s. His attire was very English and he wore an old English hat, almost in the cowboy style. He inspired awe, but he also bore a calm countenance. His half-smile intrigued me. I mumbled, 'Hello, good morning... how can I help you?' in the regular local polite way. His smile broadened and he took a step closer to me. Somehow, that one step sent a chill down my spine and yet, bafflingly, it gave me a rather comforting, silent feeling. It was almost like a déjà vu. The tangled wires in my brain tried to make the connection – when and where had I felt this way before? And then my mind flashed to the year 1998, to the day when I was in a large swimming pool in college. My friend and I were swimming in parallel, and then her hand accidentally hit my head, hard. I was a novice swimmer and as soon as her hand hit me, I lost balance. I remember sinking into the water, steadily going deeper and deeper. I thought I was going to die. But with that intimidating thought in my head, strangely I felt calm, deep inside me. *That* man at the door reminded me of that feeling. Intriguing, terrifying, but strangely – soothing. I repeated my question, more firmly, 'How can I help you?'

He looked into my eyes and said, 'I am a salesman and... I am selling death.'

'Excuse me! What do you mean?'

He said, 'You can call me the old English ruffian salesman, or you can use a more familiar term. You have another name for me in your language – *Yama*[25].' I understood what looked familiar to me in the salesman's calm, chilling face. He reminded me of descriptions of the God of Death from Indian mythology. I took a deep breath and said, 'Sorry, Mr Salesman, but I am not buying. Consider coming back some other day.' I gave him a hard look, and then I closed the door. Through the eye on the door, I watched the ruffian walk away with the same intriguing smile on his face, and when he was out of my sight, I came back to the bedroom where Abhi was still lying. I climbed back into bed, ran my hand through his thick hair, and murmured to myself, '*No Mr Salesman, I am not buying from you. Not yet. Come back later. I don't know when, thirty or forty years feels like the right amount of time. Could be ten, maybe fifteen years too, but – NOT TODAY!*'

---

[25] Yama: Yama is the lord of death in Hinduism. Yama often is considered as '*Kala*' or time, for Yama comes in a particular time and that time is naturally selected; nobody can stop his coming and change the timing. He is usually depicted as dark and fierce looking.
Wikipedia. "Yama (Hinduism)." Last modified November 2014. http://en.wikipedia.org/wiki/Yama_(Hinduism). Last accessed December 05, 2014.

I have vivid dreams often, and this was just one of them. But what this dream reaffirmed was my determination to get through cancer. I had not given up hope and courage, not even in my dreams. When I woke up, it was already 8 am. A cuddle from Abhi to Andu (with a little fur on the head now) seemed the perfect way to start the week before the imminent surgery.

The surgery

The 14th of February was the day of my surgery. Just before the surgery, my father travelled from India to the UK to be with us. He wanted to be around when I went into surgery. Abhi had accompanied me to all the six chemotherapy cycles and the first Herceptin treatment. It was such a big support to have him around.

I was supposed to report at the hospital at 12:00 noon, and I could eat in the morning, but only before 6 am. It was difficult to get up in the morning, make toast and eat it at 5:30 am. But Abhi got up and ensured that I was up too. I made toast and tea, finished eating by 6 am, and went back to bed.

The morning was busy with regular chores. All of us seemed to be continuously occupied, probably intentionally, to keep ourselves from getting too worked up and talking about the imminent surgery. I remember that Abhi and I prepared *pooris*[26] for his and Papa's lunch at the hospital. Mum had already prepared curry the night before. We offered prayers, and left for the hospital at the designated time of 10:20 am. We reached the hospital by 12 noon and were shown to our room soon after. In about an hour's time, the preparations for the operation began. Blood pressure – check, pulse – check, temperature – check, change of clothes – check, pre-op medication – check, explanation of the next few steps by the nurse – check, red (for allergies) and white (for personal details) bands being put around the wrists – check, visit by Dr Parto for the consent form – check, explanation of the entire procedure

---

[26] Poori – A type of Indian bread, eaten with vegetable or curry.

by Dr Parto – check, visit by the anaesthetist, Dr Rakesh, to explain how he would knock me out – check. I was all set for the surgery.

I asked Dr Rakesh if he would use the port to administer the anaesthetic to me. He said, 'The port would give me direct access to your heart, and I certainly would not like that to happen to you on Valentine's Day.' We all laughed; amidst the anxiety of imminent cancer surgery, he was able to dissipate some of the tension.

At 2 pm, two nurses came and wheeled me away to the operation theatre. Abhi tried to click some pictures of me (at my insistence) to make a pre- and post-operation comparison. He and Papa accompanied me up to the door of the operating theatre. Abhi looked at me with enormous love and concern at the same time. He looked uncomfortable with the fact that in just a few seconds, I would be taken away into the operation theatre, parts of me would be sliced and diced, and God only knew what the doctors would find inside.

It was report card time for us. We were going to find out how well the chemotherapy treatment had worked for me. We were anxious like school-going children.

Dr Rakesh and Dr Parto came in as soon as I was wheeled into the operation theatre. Dr Rakesh explained to me that he would inject the anaesthetic through a cannula in my arm. There came a sharp prick and the cannula was set in. He said that the anaesthetic would make me sleepy. I asked, 'Do I get to choose my dreams?' He responded, 'You better do that fast.' Before I could process this statement, I was knocked out.

In the operating theatre, I underwent surgery for the removal of whatever remained of the cancerous lump after chemotherapy, and they did something called a sentinel lymph node[27] biopsy. A blue dye was injected close to the site of the cancer. Dr Parto looked for the lymph nodes that were stained blue, and removed them. The dye would give me a bright blue boob for a few days after the procedure, I had been told. The results of the sentinel lymph node biopsy would contribute to the decision about whether I needed further surgery.

I remember waking up in the recovery room and speaking to someone. I am not sure what I said and to whom I spoke but there was some conversation. I was then brought back into my room. I was falling in and out of consciousness. Papa left the hospital in the evening to get back home. Abhi sat with me while I blabbered on and off. By 6:30 pm I was hungry; I hadn't eaten for over twelve hours. I asked for some soup, which was brought in instantly. I devoured it. The vegetable cheese sandwich came next. It was *huge*. I knew that it was too big for me to consume. I asked Abhi to finish off whatever I was unable to eat. I was still delirious with the effect of anaesthesia. Abhi started feeding it to me, as I could not sit properly. Gradually I finished it all, and still felt hungry. I called up the catering service and they told me that the kitchen was closed already, but the lady kindly fixed another sandwich for me. I was grateful and ate half of that too! I think this was the biggest portion of sandwich I have ever eaten in one go. ☺

The rest of the evening was uneventful, except for a bout of sickness. For the sickness, the nurse decided to give me an injection. She rather unceremoniously picked up the syringe and thrust it into the muscle of my thigh. Ouchhh! That really hurt and I carried a huge blue mark around in the spot for the next three weeks. At around 10 pm, Abhi left for our friends' place to spend the night there, and I went off to sleep.

---

27   Cancer Research UK. "Types of breast cancer surgery." Last modified July 2014. http://www.cancerresearchuk.org/about-cancer/type/breast-cancer/treatment/surgery/types-of-breast-cancer-surgery#sentinel. Last accessed April 09, 2015.

I kept wandering in and out of sleep until 5 am. I lay in for an hour and eventually got up. I didn't feel too sore, as I was still under the effect of painkillers. Breakfast came and it was devoured quickly, despite my single functioning arm.

At 9 am, it was time to take a shower while making sure that I did not wet the operated area. With very limited mobility, I could hardly manage washing myself properly. I asked for help from the nurse on duty. A tall and lanky nurse came in. She checked on the towels and got me a fresh supply. Then she helped me wash, by lathering the soap on my back, patting it dry, and applying moisturiser, gently and with a lot of love. I was touched with the love that she put into an activity that was a regular task for her. I felt grateful and mentioned that she was doing it amazingly well. She responded, 'I think that it could be me some day.' She also went on to tell me that one of her daughters had had cancer of the vulva a few years ago. *Goodness! Breast cancer sounds so much less complicated than vulva cancer*, I told myself. She told me that the surgeons had had to remove half of the labia majora of her daughter and she'd had to get reconstruction done. Now *that* must have hurt really badly. She also mentioned that the cancer had already recurred once, and that her daughter could not go beyond six months without a check-up. This was how it would be for rest of her life. The nurse was so calm while she said all this. There was no sign of regret or annoyance or the question that many people facing cancer ask: 'Why me? Why us?'

In such a short exchange, the nurse said quite a lot. She reached out to me with so many things that day: Here was a woman who was aware that she was puny before the Higher Forces. She knew that it could be *her* some day! It is not often that we *Homo sapiens* are humble and realistic enough to realise this. And because she had accepted that the patient could be herself someday, she was committed to doing even her day-to-day tasks with full dedication and humility. She was a nurse taking care of cancer patients, but she did not let that drain her positivity – she was warm, and put so much effort into a demanding job which can also be emotionally draining. And then, she was a mother, and must have been so shattered to see her daughter in such agony. Yet she knew that they must continue doing what they should, and intended to persevere until the last moment.

After she had finished helping me with the wash, she asked the plastic surgery nurse to come and have a chat with me. Lynn came in and gave me advice on bras. She also got me a freebie, and there, I had a fabulous bra that I would wear for several days after the operation. I was touched by the level of effort everyone was putting in just to make me comfortable – the nurse, the plastic surgery nurse, the doctors, and the rest of the healthcare team.

I was discharged from the hospital the following day. My stay had been comfortable except for the food. Breakfast was fine, but somehow rest of the meals were difficult to consume. I remember that we ordered stir-fried vegetables with rice for dinner and could hardly eat any of it. I did not quite understand how they got stir-fried vegetables wrong – or maybe I was still groggy from all the anaesthetic that had been injected into me! Thankfully, I was discharged right after dinner (which was served before 6 pm) and we were able to call home and tell Mum that we would eat at home. The taxi ride back home was uneventful, and there was lovely ginger tea waiting when we got home. Eating rice and dal felt like such a blessing!

The next day onwards, the ordeal with physical pain began. My upper back and the region close to the operated area were sore and very painful. My back was stiff, as I could only lie down straight on my back. I could not lie on my right side, as I found the implanted port restrictive, and I obviously could not lie on my left side, as that was the region of the operation. To make it worse, as per Dr Parto's instructions, I was required to wear a well-fitting bra all the time, even while sleeping. Such a tight bra further stiffened my back. It was only when I loosened it slightly after a couple of days that I realised why this instruction had been given to me. Without 100% support, the slightest movement in the breast caused severe pain. Having a stiff back was far better than such severe pain.

There was one patch in particular that was relatively more painful. Mum massaged my back and neck every morning, to alleviate some stiffness. It worked but only temporarily, and soon, I would have the same level of pain.

Nine days passed and the much-awaited 25th of February arrived.

Hallelujah!

It was time for the biopsy results to be declared. Abhi took the day off and accompanied me to the hospital. He wanted to be there with me *just in case* it was bad news. And he also wanted to receive the news first-hand, if it was good! I immensely appreciated his being around. Unfortunately, when I had been given that heads-up for cancer, I had been alone in the hospital. A week later, receiving the confirmation of the cancer diagnosis had been easier in Abhi's company. I was grateful that he was coming with me to the hospital for the results: I wanted to share the much-awaited moment of happiness with him, or feel strong with his support, if things went otherwise.

We were going to the hospital to collect the results. After some waiting, we were called into Dr Parto's consultation room. He looked rather serious. He delivered the much-awaited results to us. He said, 'We found just one cancerous cell, which has been removed, and we also found some pre-cancerous cells that have been removed.' Abhi and I panicked. Did this mean that these pre-cancerous cells would turn into cancerous cells later, and that I would be back to square one? Would I have to go through cancer treatment again? We seemed to completely ignore that part of report that said the 'cancer was removed'! The doctor looked rather surprised that I was panicking. It was after a couple of minutes that he realised that we had misinterpreted the results. He explained again – this time slowly! The fact that no cancer had been found in the biopsy report was brilliant. This meant that my body had responded amazingly well to chemotherapy, and chemotherapy had succeeded in doing what it needed to do – killing cancer! And all the four sentinel lymph nodes were clear of malignancy.

This meant that no further rounds of surgery would be required. Breast reduction surgery or a mastectomy was something that I been dreading over last five and a half months. You know that during the entire treatment, I just could not come to terms with a potential mastectomy. As soon as Dr Parto said that no further surgery was required, we both heaved such a sigh of relief!

Abhi asked Dr Parto if there was something that we could do to prevent cancer from coming back – anything at all, like lifestyle changes or changes in food habits. He responded, 'No. If it has to come back, it will come back, and there is nothing that you can do to stop it.' It felt like a rather demotivating but matter-of-fact statement. We both appreciated that we were being kept apprised of reality, so that we knew what was possible. Abhi and I decided to leave this discussion for another day, and celebrate what we had today: a body that was free of cancer. Suddenly, all the pain, the hard work, the stress and the perseverance seemed to have paid off!

Dr Parto further asked me to go to the check-up room, so that he could examine how well I was healing. 'You seem to be doing well,' he said. I mentioned the severe pain and stiffness near the site of the operation. He investigated this under the ultrasound machine, and found that some fluid had collected in the region, causing severe pain. The fluid needed to be sucked out with a syringe, he explained. He asked the nurse for a syringe and when I saw its size, I was nervous. Thankfully, the operated region was almost dead and I did not feel any pain. As soon as the fluid was sucked into the syringe, I felt better.

While I was with the doctor, Abhi called home to inform my parents that the cancer was gone! My father received the call and almost choked with happiness. While still holding the phone in hand, he called out to my mum and gave her the news. Oh what a moment of happiness and relief it was. Abhi delivered the news and quickly put down the phone. Next he called up his mum and shared the news! She knew that our appointment was in the evening, and had been eagerly waiting for our call all day. It was another moment of miraculous happiness. Hers, my mum's, and several other people's prayers had been answered. We were fully aware that I still had to go through radiation therapy, but after the good news that Dr Parto had 'got it all', we decided to treat radiation therapy as only a mop-up treatment to kill any rogue cell that might have escaped the chemo and the surgery.

When we reached home, we found that my parents were tearful with joy. Mum had cooked delicious potato-*halwa*²⁸ to celebrate the special day. We chatted excitedly and spent the evening together.

Hallelujah! I was finally cancer-free! Thank you God, thank you family, thank you friends, thank you everyone who kept me in their prayers!

They say that a normal person wants many things in their life, but a cancer patient wants just one – being told that they are cancer-free. How true! It felt amazing to be told that my doctor had 'got it all' during the surgery. Suddenly, my spirits rose, and I felt as if a massive weight had been lifted off my chest. I felt on top of the world as I went through my routine. My arm was still very sore, and I could not lift anything with it. The bra felt too tight but I must continue wearing it. I still could not sleep well because of pain. I still woke up with terrible stiffness in the mornings, and the hot flushes were equally bad. I still looked (almost) like a boiled egg, with no eyebrows or eye lashes and a little fur on my head. My mum still massaged my back every day, and sickness and tiredness got the better of me every now and then. I still could not sit up for more than a couple of hours. I was unemployed, and had no idea when I would be able to return to work. Our earnings and financial planning had gone for a toss. I had no idea if I would ever be able to have a baby. And still – I felt great. I was no longer a cancer patient; the cancer was probably meeting its nemesis somewhere in a pathology lab!

---

²⁸   Halwa: Halwa is a sweet dish, which can be made of different types of flour or vegetables. This one was made with potatoes.

After coming back from the hospital with the brilliant news, I had written to all my friends and family, informing them that I was cancer-free. Most of them responded with beautiful messages. Some messages moved me deeply. I could clearly see how excited they were with my news. We revelled in my happiness together. I have put together some of my favourite messages below.

From Julia:

Hi Parul,

Thank you for your message – I am so very happy for you! You are a brave, strong woman, and there is no doubt that you have many happy times ahead of you. I hope that having gone through this difficult time, you have come out the other end wiser, stronger and happier than before. I think of you often and am sending you all my best wishes and lots of love,

Julia

From Sachin, my brother:

I am really happy.

Got goose bumps :)

From GF (GF's birthday was two days later):

Heyyyy this is the best birthday gift for me!!!!

May god bless u with lots of happiness and my sincere prayers that you should never ever get into any such thing in life again.

Luv u ....longing to hear more from you

GF

I was so pleased when I received this email. I felt as if a burden had been lifted off my chest.

GF was my best friend, and she had been so shocked to hear the news of my cancer diagnosis that apart from two initial mails, she had gone silent. She'd said that she was uncomfortable writing or talking to me about it, even when I said that I really needed to talk to her, and that I needed her to be with me during this difficult time. Later, if she did write, it was only every couple of months. She said that she would pray for my speedy recovery.

I felt that GF had cut herself off from me after the cancer diagnosis and I had been very deeply hurt because of this. At a time when I needed her most, she was just not there. Other than being angry, deep inside me I was scared of losing her as a friend. I was scared that I probably did not mean as much to her as I had before. And now, in her email, she had written that she was longing to hear my voice and speak to me. I was still angry, afraid, and very hurt, but I decided to stand up to my feelings. I made the phone call.

That conversation turned out to be one of the most important conversations of my life. I realised that she had been in shock after my diagnosis. The fact that she could not see me, or be with me, made her feel worse. She went into a very negative frame of mind, as she felt helpless. Here I was, in a different country battling a terrible disease, and there she was – so far away and unable to do anything to help me recuperate. This helplessness frustrated her.

111

When she felt low because she was concerned about me, she decided to stay away from me, as she did not want her negativity to brush off on me. She did not want me to find her in such low spirits. She wanted to be my strength, and when she realised that she felt too weak to be able to do that, she stepped away. She thought that she was protecting me – from negative thoughts, from worrisome questions, and from sadness. She knows me better than most other people. She was aware that I tend to get impatient with negative people who complain about situations all the time. She did not want to be one of those people. If only she had communicated this to me properly, I would not have been so hurt. I would have kept her abreast of my progress, as I would not have felt so isolated and uncared-for. She would have been comfortable knowing what was happening to me. I am sure she understood that I was hurt, but found it difficult to change anything. I realised how incorrect I was in my judgement of her. Thank you, GF, for holding that mirror up to my face, and helping me understand how judgemental I can be.

But then, who said that communication was simple?

(How ironic that in the real life, two Toastmasters did such a terrible job at communicating!)

Ruks had an interesting explanation for this situation. She said that the conflict arose due to the poor alignment of our needs. The cancer triggered in me a need to be accepted and nurtured, and it triggered in GF a need to protect and heal. Because our needs were different, the communication broke down. We, human beings, often end up communicating at the level of emotion – expressing happiness, anger, sadness, etc. If we could go deeper and communicate at the level of needs, we would perhaps find unity in an instant, and there would be little scope for such misunderstandings. This line of thought definitely made lot of sense.

Looking back, I am so glad that I picked up the phone and made that phone call to GF.

If you are a friend who is finding it difficult to talk to someone who has recently been diagnosed with cancer, please remember that they need you, now more than ever. Relationships can be more complicated than we think they are, and being there in solidarity for your loved ones is incredibly important. It may also be useful to align your needs as suggested by Ruks.

By the end of February, I had also stopped using the baby toothbrush and baby toothpaste, and was back to using a toothbrush and toothpaste meant for adults. Such a tiny change also felt like good progress. It remained to be seen when my mouth would cope with the swift movements of an electric toothbrush.

Soon it was March, and my arm had started recovering from the operation. The area around the operated site felt dead – it had no sensation at all. Dr Parto said that this was expected, as during the operation the nerves must have been severed. The sensation should come back in a few months, he said.

Indeed, it did start coming back soon after. It made its presence felt with shooting pains, like electric shocks. I was eating breakfast when I suddenly jumped with pain. I felt as if an electric current had shot through me. It started at the chest, went through the breast and slowly terminated in the armpit. The effect remained for a few seconds. But then it came back with greater intensity, and lasted longer. Each time it happened, I writhed in pain. But this pain was a good sign. It indicated that my body was recovering, and that the sensation was coming back. Over the next two weeks, the pain worsened and each time it hit me, I tried to cheer myself up under the pretext of recovery.

For about a month and a half after the operation, I was unable to do any typing. Apart from my quasi-burnt hands, the slightest movement or the rubbing of the arm against the breast caused severe pain. The diary would have to wait for a few more weeks at least. Maybe I would be able to pick it up again during radiation therapy.

The girl with three tattoos

Radiation therapy was expected to begin in the last week of March or at the beginning of April. In simple terms, radiation therapy[29] is a treatment that uses high-energy radiation to kill cancerous and pre-cancerous cells by damaging their DNA. The radiation can be administered externally through a machine, or internally through a radioactive substance placed or injected in the body. In my case, it would be the external kind. The intention to give me radiation therapy was curative. This meant that the intention was to cure me – by killing any stubborn cancerous cells that may have survived chemotherapy, and by killing the precancerous cells so that they didn't make babies in future.

On the 11th of March, I went to the hospital for a planning session for my radiation therapy. This comprised a CT scan and lots of imaging, so that the radiographers and the physicist could plan my treatment. They needed to determine the exact site to target with the radiation. Radiation therapy does not discriminate between cancerous cells and normal cells; it damages both alike. So it needs to be administered accurately.

Jim was one of the technicians, and he asked me if I was comfortable with him carrying out my treatment. I smiled wryly: After letting so many men (doctors) see my boobs, how would it matter if he saw them too? But I was polite, and I responded with a simple 'yes'. There was

---

[29]   Macmillan Cancer Support. "What is radiotherapy?" Last modified May 2013. http://www.macmillan.org.uk/information-and-support/treating/radiotherapy/radiotherapy-explained/what-is-radiotherapy.html. Last accessed April 09, 2015.

no need for him to know what was going on in my head. I think there comes a time during the long cancer treatment when you stop feeling squeamish about these things!

There were, in total, three people in the planning room for the radiation therapy. They placed me carefully on the table under a big machine. I was instructed to lie down with as little motion as possible. If I could play dead, it would be perfect. I was playing dead for the machine, so that I would not be dead in real life!

The objective was to take lots of pictures and do a scan of the breast, to determine exactly where the radiation should be directed. I had to lift my arms and place them above my head, but the operated arm was sore and wouldn't move properly. I was not able to lift it and place it above my head, which prevented me from getting into the right position to start the scan, obstructing the planning. The radiographers were extremely patient. Each time they tried to manoeuvre my arm, I let out a scream and they would stop immediately. They told me that I was required to raise my arms to a minimum distance, failing which the planning was not possible. Instead, I would be sent to the physiotherapy department, and would need to take a few sessions before we could resume planning for radiation therapy.

I did not want my radiation therapy to be delayed. I knew that even if we were on schedule, April would easily be consumed in the treatment. I couldn't wait for the whole thing to get over. In my head, I decided that even if my arm hurt, I would hold myself in that position to enable the scan. Thankfully, my arm got positioned correctly at the lowest spot that was allowed, and the scan began. The wrenching pain was dragging my arm down, but I was determined to lie still to get the scan done.

Once the scan was done, it was time for the tattoos. They told me that I would be given three tattoos. 'How exciting!' I exclaimed. 'Do I get to choose the design?'

'They are going to be very small dots, I'm afraid,' said one of the radiographers. It was time for me to get the first three tattoos (possibly also the last three) of my life, and she wouldn't let me choose the design. *Cruel!*

'OK – do I get to choose the colour?' I asked, not to be deterred.

'It is going to be the basic green colour, sorry.'

Cruel, cruel! I thought.

'This is going to hurt,' she said.

'Hmmm... I have heard that getting tattoos done is painful.'

'No, you will be fine with the remaining two. Just this one will hurt. We'll be doing it just above your chest bone. That will hurt, as there is minimal fat on this area to provide cushioning. Ready?'

You got to be kidding me. After giving me all that information on how badly it will hurt, you ask me if I am ready? Not only that, you also expect yes for an answer! But as before, I smiled and gave a short response, 'Yes'. But then I interjected: 'Wait. I am allowed to scream, or am I not?'

I think she looked a little sad, as if saying, 'I am sorry to be inflicting this pain on you.' She did not answer. I closed my eyes in anticipation of the pain. I was ready to scream.

I heard the tattoo machine growl. From the slanted angle of my eyes, I saw that it was closing in on me. It appeared to get bigger and bigger.

As it touched my chest, I screamed as loud as I could, without moving even a tiny bit. I knew how to play dead for the scan machines. The innumerable scans that I had been through during my cancer treatment had given me enough practice. Thankfully, the pain was short-lived and the dot was done. I had my first real tattoo. The machine was growling and getting ready to give me the second tattoo.

Actually, the second one did not hurt much. It was placed on my right side. I was apprehensive about getting the tattoo done on the operated side. I was scared that it would hurt badly, as I still had lot of pain in my arm after the operation. But surprisingly, it did not hurt at all. The nerve endings had been severed at the time of operation, and this ensured that I didn't feel any pain.

I was the girl with three tattoos now. Yippee! I was all set for the radiation therapy.

Radiation Therapy

If I choose a few adjectives or phrases to define radiation therapy, they will be: a doddle – as compared to chemotherapy; and time consuming.

Radiation therapy indeed turned out to be a doddle when compared to chemotherapy, just as Dr Charles had said. But my fair guess is that most treatments must be a doddle when compared to chemotherapy.

I had gone to Cambridge for a follow-up consultation with Dr Charles. Since I was in the hospital, I went to the radiation therapy department, and asked if my treatment schedule was ready. Indeed, it was. The receptionist very kindly printed out a copy for me. This is how I interpreted it:

- Radiation therapy would begin on the 26th of March, about five weeks after the operation.
- Nineteen treatments would be spread over four weeks. This meant that I would make a visit to the hospital everyday from 26th March until 23rd April.
- The appointments would be spread from 7:50 am to 5:52 pm. The schedule was interesting, as the appointment times were extremely precise: 9:18 am or 11:52 am or 2:27 pm.
- I would receive treatment for three days from 26 to 28 March, followed by an Easter break.
- The actual treatment would be about ten minutes each day. To get those ten minutes of treatment, I would travel for more than three hours every day. There would also be an enormous waiting

time at the hospital (which, of course, I would only discover when the radiation therapy had started).

On day one of the radiation therapy, one of the radiographers called me in for a briefing session before the actual treatment. Essentially, I was not supposed to use any soap or moisturiser with colour or fragrance on the left breast, and keep the area well moisturised. I was given the names of the brands that I could use.

After the briefing session, I went back to the waiting area and waited my turn. I was called in later and the first few minutes were spent in further instructions. The most interesting instruction was when they said they would need to get me in the exact position for the treatment, and I must *not* help them out. Sorry, did I hear that correctly? Apparently, it is easier for them to position people when the manoeuvring is fully in their control. What was I supposed to do, I asked. Lie still – as still as possible and do nothing, was the reply.

It was time to play dead again. The slightest movement in my body would change the target position for the radiation, and it would do great damage to the surrounding tissues. Over the next nineteen days, I would master the art of keeping still. No matter whether I got the urge to cough or sneeze, or whether I got itchy, I would learn to control it. In short, I would master the art of playing dead while placed under a machine.

My favourite part during radiation therapy was at the beginning of the treatment. I would lie down under the machines, and two radiographers would position me, with an accuracy down to millimetres. They stood on my either side, and physically moved me or the bed to get me in the right position. They called out the desired measurements, and confirmed to each other when they had got it right. The numbers were the same every day (at least they appeared that way). I tried to remember them when they were called out. I always thought that I had memorised the numbers, but before I left the room, I would forget them all. I never succeeded in remembering them. Another thing I did while lying still during the treatment was to count the rings in the design on the ceiling, like counting sheep when there were no sheep around.

The radiation therapy treatment in itself was OK, a doddle, just like Dr Charles had said. But it was the effort of getting to the hospital every day that got to me. At the hospital, there was always lot of waiting time. I noticed that many people there were accompanied by a friend or someone in the family. It alleviated the drudgery of coming to the hospital every day. Since radiation therapy runs over several weeks, we saw the same people in the waiting area, time and again. We would share our stories, talk about the cancer, the treatment, the hair loss, and the hope of getting back to work soon. Many of us in that waiting area had been off work; some people for a few weeks, others for several months. There was a lady who had been off work for as long as eighteen months. My time off work had just started. Hopefully it would not be for too long, I thought. (As it turns out, my time off work eventually exceeded eighteen months.)

Here are a couple of tips for the family and friends of those undergoing radiation therapy:

First, the effort of getting to the hospital every day for radiation therapy wears people out. Therefore, if you are able to accompany the person undergoing treatment, it will be great. My father used to come to the hospital with me every day during radiotherapy, and that took away a lot of the boredom.

Second, the machines for radiotherapy are expensive, which prevents many hospitals from offering this treatment. Therefore, a lot of the time, people have to travel long distances to get to a hospital for radiotherapy. If you are able to help out with daily chores, like taking care of the kids during the hospital visit, or fixing a meal, or doing the laundry, it will be immensely helpful. If you are a colleague, then you could help out by sharing the patient's work load, to accommodate the hospital visits. The fact that the treatment often runs over several weeks, five days a week, adds to the complexity of managing family, work and treatment concurrently.

While radiation therapy was going on in April, my taste buds had improved significantly. My sense of smell was still heightened. I could also use my hands slightly more than before. Although the skin felt burnt and the touch of my arm against the breast caused pain, I started to use the laptop again. It had been a very long time since I had written anything, and I felt all bottled up. While the anti-cancer drugs exhausted my body, the forced menopause made me feel low. I felt my spirits to be in the doldrums time and again. While my parents and Abhi were with me and were doing everything possible to look after me, I did not always share how I had been feeling. I didn't want to bother them sometimes about how low I really felt. There were several moments when I wanted to share my fears with them, but didn't. I needed to vent my emotions and my diary came in handy.

During the second week of radiation therapy, I happened to meet a lady at the hospital who had finished undergoing radiation therapy a couple of months earlier. I mentioned to her that my radiation therapy was on-going, and that I felt great. She warned me that I may have gotten too excited too soon. In her case, the side effects had set in after the four-week treatment had finished. She had been expecting them during the treatment, and when they did not appear, she was exhilarated. But one week after the radiation therapy finished, her skin looked burnt and it hurt. Also there came the flu-like feeling of running a temperature along with a severe body ache. As time progressed, her skin got completely burnt. It was raw, and every single brush of the cloth she was wearing or the lightest physical touch had her screaming with pain. Imagine having a breast and underarm severely burnt. How bad will it make you feel? *Ouch!* I had to see how it would be in my case.

Tiredness was a prominent side effect of radiation. In fact, there was still lot of sickness from the chemotherapy, but it had started getting better as the radiotherapy progressed. It appeared as if I was having an easy time during radiation therapy. I had started hoping that the remaining sessions would be uneventful too. How wrong I was!

I finished twelve treatments of radiation therapy while we were still living in Hitchin. It was time for my parents to return to India, as their visas were coming to an end. Mum had been at our place for five and a half months and Papa for a little over two months. They both seemed so heartbroken when they boarded the taxi to get to the airport. My mum couldn't stop herself from crying. She didn't want to go back while my treatment was still going on. I still struggled while doing basic chores, and Mum wasn't sure how I would manage everything on my own. But they had to leave. What a huge support they had been!

The lease for our flat was coming to an end, and we had decided to move to London. On Saturday, the 13th of April, we moved house. On the 15th of April, I travelled from London to Cambridge for my radiation therapy session. The plan was to stay with Julia at her place at Fen Ditton, which is a small village just outside Cambridge. From Monday until Friday, I stayed at Julia's. She took care of me, cooked healthy meals for me, spent time talking to me and entertaining me, and did the Clexane injections for me in the evening. She completely understood that I was unwell and did not let me do much, lest I should get tired. I happily spent time with her and her family, and felt blessed to have such caring friends. I came back home on Friday after the radiation therapy treatment. Seventeen radiation therapy sessions were over. The last two remained, for the following Monday and Tuesday. I had to travel all the way back to Cambridge for the remaining sessions. Monday morning, I boarded the train, travelled for about three hours, and reached Addenbrooke's Hospital by afternoon. I finished the eighteenth treatment just after lunch time and left for Julia's place.

A flu-like feeling came upon me when I was on my way to Julia's place. By evening, my body ached and I felt feverish. A sniffling nose made me feel worse. I went to bed early, and hoped that sleep might partially or wholly cure the problem. But I woke up at 1:30 am, with a terrible ache in my leg. I have never had such pain in the leg before. It was so severe that it kept me awake for three hours. Eventually, I fell asleep out of sheer exhaustion. When I got up in the morning to go to the hospital, I felt worse than the previous day. I needed to see a doctor as soon as possible.

I reached the hospital and went to the Oncology Unit straight away, to bawl about how terrible I was feeling. One of the benefits of being a cancer patient is that you get attention everywhere, and really fast. A nurse and a doctor checked me and they deduced that the radiation therapy was responsible for my condition. I was allowed to take paracetamol for the pain and fever. As far as my leg was concerned, it looked fine, medically (read as: no cancer or nothing major). I was able to make whatever movements I was asked to, and therefore no remedy was given to me. This meant that I came out of the Oncology Unit as ill as I was going in, and with a bad limp due to severe pain. Every step that I took felt like a colossal task.

I finished the final session of radiation therapy. It was the day when I should have felt elated – but instead I felt like absolute rubbish.

The side effects of radiation had set in.

The next two weeks were spent in agony. I constantly felt feverish; my skin turned red, and then black. The skin was burnt and the slightest touch made me scream. It ruptured in the armpit, which only made my situation worse. Now I had to be careful to not pick up an infection. Almost the final nail in the coffin came in the form of insomnia. Due to severe pain in my leg, fever, a burnt breast, and a wounded armpit, I could hardly manage to sleep. Twelve days of remaining awake at night worked wonders in transforming me into a zombie. All I yearned for was a good night's sleep.

The side effects of radiation therapy were accompanied by the heart scare. I woke up to chest pain on a Saturday morning. It was mid-May. For some unknown reason, all these severe troubles happened over the weekend. Because I had been on Herceptin, which causes cardiac toxicity, for about six months, our first worry was that my heart was in trouble.

The pain subsided in about fifteen minutes, but I continued feeling poorly for the rest of the day. On Monday, I went in to see the GP, and he sent me for some tests – A blood test, an ECG and a chest X-ray. When it is about the heart, they can't take any risk, they said. I spent several hours in the hospital in the following week, as I got appointments on different days for all these tests. When the reports came back a week later, we found that the results were normal. The blood report was fine, and so were the chest X-ray and ECG. Thank goodness for that! However, the chest pain kept coming back, on and off, and it bothered me several times all through May. While it was good news that there was no visible problem with the heart, we couldn't diagnose the reason for the chest pains. We just hoped that they would settle down on their own. Eventually, after a plight of about six weeks, they went away for good.

May was a difficult month. I struggled with the side effects of radiation therapy and the chest pains. It would be several weeks before the skin started healing from the radiation therapy.

But in May, my eyebrows had begun to grow back, and so had the eye lashes. The former were thinner than before the cancer treatment, while the latter were definitely prettier and longer. *There is always a silver lining in the dark clouds; the question is, are we always ready to appreciate the silver lining in our circumstances?*

SECTION II

We can grow strong at the broken places.
- Rachel Naomi Remen, *Stories of the Spirit, Stories of the Heart*

(Dedicated to that phase of cancer treatment when I made several choices and reclaimed (some) control over my life!)

SECTION II

A note about Section II

Cancer had ensured that several things were 'done to' me, whether I wanted them or not. However, when the main aggressive treatment (chemotherapy, surgery, and radiation therapy) was finished, I had some time to breathe, to process what I had been through, and to take stock of my new life.

This section of the book talks about how I approached my life after cancer – my struggles at the physical, emotional and physiological level, how I coped with the stress, and how I changed with the experience of cancer in important and valuable ways. Some of these changes were as beautiful as others were painful. The whole experience brought me a sense of meaning, knowledge, and a kind of wisdom that I might otherwise have taken much longer to attain.

I am very happy to share this phase of my experience, because even though I struggled badly, I succeeded in moving on from cancer and learning immensely from my experience. I hope that you find my story inspirational, and that it helps you too.

Words of Wisdom

I had gone to see Dr Charles to plan the transfer of my care to London hospital. I was moving house and taking treatment locally made obvious sense. I was apprehensive about being transferred to the care of another oncologist, but it had to be done.

We went through the usual routine of discussing how I was doing. I talked about the side effects of the treatment, and he documented what I was saying. After a while I said, loud and clear, 'Doc, I am scared.' He continued typing for a while, and then looked up at me without saying anything. It was his way of saying, 'Go on.'

I continued, 'I'm scared that the cancer will come back and get me.'

'It's OK to be scared; it is only natural that you feel so. But I cannot *not* tell you that there is a risk that the cancer may come back.'

'I appreciate the information you give me, because it gives me the correct picture of my situation. I know that the cancer is gone, but I do worry at times that it will come back. Is there anything I can do to minimize its recurrence?'

'You should eat healthy food, exercise, and maintain a healthy lifestyle.'

'I will do that. But is there something in particular that I can do?'

'No.'

I grew silent. After a short pause, I said, 'I am also worried about the ten years thing, Doc. What is my chance of making it for ten years or more?'

Dr Charles leaned forward and shifted the screen of his computer towards me. After a few clicks, he said, 'Let's see what the statistical tools say.'

I did not know that there were statistical tools to predict specific cancer patients' survival and life expectancy rates! My Statistics professor in college had said that we would eventually use statistics everywhere, and therefore we should all learn it well. I should have listened to him when there was time!

As I looked at the screen, Dr Charles punched in data specific to my case – the size of the tumour, my age, the treatments that I had gone through (chemotherapy, surgery and radiation therapy), the results of the treatment – and clicked 'Go'. A fancy-looking chart popped up, and it showed that I had an 80% chance of making it for ten years. It also showed what the probability would have been if I had undergone just chemotherapy, or surgery, or radiation therapy. Since I had had all the three, my chances were really good, at 80%. This tool predicted survival probabilities according to research done in the US.

I was conscious that I was taking too much of Dr Charles' time. I felt embarrassed about it but he, like always, wanted to give me as much time as I needed. With loads of patience, he explained the whole chart to me, and then said, 'Let me show you another tool.' It was similar to the previous tool, but the research had been done in the UK. Again, in went my data, and out came a pretty chart. This time the number was not 80%, but a whopping 86%. *That* is a very high number, just 14% less than 100%.

'You know something? You are a good horse in this race.'

He went on to say something I hadn't expected him to say, 'We grow when we face adverse situations. We are like trees and shrubs; we need to be pruned in order to flower. Every tough situation that we go through makes us strong. We learn through adversity.' He added, 'I have seen so many people go through cancer, and survive. Many of them come back and say that their lives changed forever after cancer, and not necessarily for the worse. Cancer is a life-changing experience. Let it be an experience that changes things for the better for you. And… it's OK to be scared about how many years you have, but more importantly, you are here today – that is what matters.'

My oncologist had just turned into my counsellor, and at a time when I needed his counselling the most. He was one of the key persons who had preserved my health and my life. I left the hospital feeling reassured. I was a good horse in the race of cancer. There were no bets placed on this good horse, but I left with a resolve to look beyond the trauma that cancer had caused and the loss that I had incurred because of it.

I requested Dr Charles to find another good oncologist for me in London. Surely, finding someone as wonderful as he is must have been very difficult, but he managed to do it for me.

I share a very special bond with both my doctors, Dr Parto and Dr Charles. I trusted them with my life – and it is a serious matter to trust someone with your life. I am grateful that my trust was justified every time, during our association of over seven and a half months.

My care was transferred to St George's Hospital in Tooting, London.

Transition to St George's Hospital, London

I was scared – a bit like children are, when they change schools – about moving to a new hospital. However, my fears proved to be unfounded. My transition to St George's was seamless, and the new hospital and my healthcare team were excellent.

At St George's, we went through my case history. They wanted me to go through some tests, to sort out some of the troubles I was having with the side effects. An urgent leg X-ray was done, because my leg pain would not subside. It was especially bad when I tried to move from a sedentary position. The first few steps, when I tried to move, were very painful. However, the X-ray was clear. We couldn't find what was bothering my leg so badly.

There remained several such unexplained pains and glitches in my body. I had been suffering from a strange pain in the upper back region. The pain had set in when we started chemotherapy. It showed up the moment there was the slightest discomfort in my body, be it breathlessness, fatigue, nausea, or even a high temperature.

The only explanation that we had for all these problems was that my body had been through the mill – chemotherapy, surgery, and radiation therapy, all separated by a gap of a mere six weeks each. The body needed time to get back its equilibrium. There was no way that I could rush through the recovery process. I must give myself time, and patience was the name of the game now. For someone who always liked to be occupied, it was a different experience to try and not do anything, and just recuperate. For someone who got awfully impatient with doing nothing or not doing enough, this was a sea change.

The five-year course of tamoxifen had also started. Because of our recent experiences, Abhi and I felt that we should probably explore parenthood. I contemplated stopping the course of tamoxifen after two years, put an end to the cancer saga, and move on with a normal life. However, my oncologist thought that it was too early to make this decision. I had started taking tamoxifen in May 2013, and we had quite some time before we needed to make this decision. I was aware that the probability of a recurrence was lower after taking tamoxifen for five years than it is when tamoxifen is taken for only two years. Abhi was certain that I should complete the course, but I was not sure. I finally decided we should cross the bridge when we came to it – after two years.

I was gradually adjusting to my new life. My main tasks now were to take care of the home, and to look after myself. I was doing everything possible to get better. Gradually, I started enjoying the peace that my new life brought. I indeed began to appreciate that what mattered the most was the present – today.

At St George's Hospital, I continue to be very well supported by my breast care nurse, Charmaine Case. She immediately acts on anything that I report – and I report an awful lot of things. I have been a happy patient there.

If only I could take a break from the routine life and get away, it would be perfect! How about a short holiday?

The beautiful Edinburgh

Since being diagnosed with cancer, I had not taken any holiday at all. It had been eight months since the diagnosis, and Abhi and I longed for a break. Therefore, at the end of May, we planned a short holiday to Edinburgh. A vacation away from the city where I was undergoing treatment meant preparation – I packed a large bag of medicines, and my case history papers related to cancer. I also collated information about the nearest hospital from our hotel that had an oncology department.

This was our second trip to Edinburgh. When we had visited Edinburgh during the Easter holidays in 2012, we had fallen in love with the city. After thirteen months, on our second visit, the city looked equally charming. Once we were there, I had to be very disciplined with food and physical activity. I couldn't devour hash browns like before. I ate small portions of healthy food at regular intervals, and ensured that I walked as much as possible every day for exercise. I think discipline becomes an important aspect of life after cancer. Healthy lifestyle choices are no longer just things that are 'nice to do'; instead they become things you 'need to do'.

On our previous trip, we had really enjoyed walking up to Arthur's Seat. While I was apprehensive of whether I could walk so much right after going through the treatment, I decided to give it a try. Walking up several miles to almost reach the top of Arthur's Seat was awesome. I was knackered by the time we came down, but happy.

Being away from London and from home helped us to take our minds off the treatment. It was a good change, and thankfully, there were no major surprises or emergency hospital visits. During the trip, I could not help but compare how my life had changed (forever) since the last time I had visited Edinburgh – all in a span of just thirteen months.

Cancer and my relationships

It is indeed a sad thing that I was diagnosed with cancer. But, if cancer had to happen to me, I am glad that it happened when I had the most amazing team of doctors and healthcare professionals to look after me.

I am immensely grateful to my doctors, Dr Parto and Dr Charles. I like calling Dr Parto 'the magician'. His hands are so skilled at surgery that there seems to be magic in them. The surgical knife, in his hand, is as close to a magic wand as anything can be. It is not just his skill, but also the high level of concern that he had for me as a doctor, for which I am grateful.

Dr Charles is a doctor who was there for me, day or night, during the treatment. I had the leeway to call him up at anytime that I needed help. If he was busy, he ensured that he returned my call. I remember that I was significantly unwell on one of the days during chemotherapy. I had spoken to him, and had been reassured that all the side effects I was experiencing were as expected, and that there was no imminent danger to my health. After speaking to him, I went off to sleep. I was woken up by the ringing of my cell phone at 10:45 pm. It was a call from Dr Charles. He had just finished work and before leaving for home, he wanted to know how I had been doing. What amazing commitment!

The most precious thing about both my doctors was that while they always showed me the truth, even if it wasn't pretty, they ensured that they kept the hope ignited in me. They never gave me false hope, but at the same time, they made me feel in control of my situation by giving me the right information. I am so thankful that they treated me like a person, and not as another number or a cancer statistic.

Similarly, when the cancer diagnosis was confirmed, my GP Dr Peter called me up and expressed how sorry he was to hear about the diagnosis.

I have never seen doctors who proactively call their patients to find out how they have been, or to say how sorry they are about a bad diagnosis. I am astonished and touched that these doctors have such a high level of concern and empathy for every patient, despite the fact that they have been doing this work for so many years.

I am grateful to the nurses who administered the treatment to me or looked after me. They played an indispensable role in my recovery.

I am also thankful to the rest of the healthcare team (the radiographers, the technicians, the housekeeping staff, the caterer, and everyone else whom I may not have met but who played a role in my treatment), for having looked after me so well. Some of them may say that they were just doing their job. But they did their jobs so well that they made a real difference to the lives of others, including mine.

My special thanks go to the cook at Nuffield Hospital, Cambridge for preparing the most awesome jacket potato and beans.

Thank you to all these lovely people who helped me beat the hell out of cancer!

And thank you, cancer, because it is owing to you, and you alone, that I met these incredible people.

But it was not just my healthcare team who prompted me to think more about relationships. It was time to re-look at the way I interpreted relationships in general. I had always had a sense of conflict between the relationships that we get by virtue of birth, and the ones that we make. I always wondered if people would do what they did if they were not obligated by their relationships.

What my experience of going through cancer revealed about relationships was interesting, to say the least. A close friend said that since they could not do anything for me, they had decided to stay away from even writing or calling, and just pray for me. They found it saddening to listen to the difficult facts, when they asked how I was doing. But then, saying that I was doing great would have been an utter lie. What do you expect to hear from someone who is battling cancer and who is expected to be truthful to you? If I could not sound sad before my best friends, where would I express my deepest thoughts? If my best friends could not bear to hear my sad talk in times of extreme stress, who else would?

Another friend took ages to find the time to respond to my initial email wherein I had just been trying to reconnect. Later when he finally got to know about the illness, he was shocked and (I think) sad, but nonetheless, could not find the time to speak to me over the phone or write to me during the entire cancer experience (twenty-seven months since the diagnosis as this manuscript goes into publishing) – nor was he willing to ask how I was, when I called him a few times!

Another friend did not connect with me because he didn't realise that cancer was a bad disease (not that any disease is good, but I think some diseases are worse than others). I happened to speak to him after several months and he told me that he didn't know that cancer was a malignant condition. I must confess that I didn't quite believe him; I couldn't accept that he did not know about cancer being a malignant condition. I thought that he was just pretending to be ignorant, to take the easy way out for not having kept in touch during a difficult phase in my life. After all, he is well-read and well-educated. It hurt me deeply. But now I realise that I may have been judging him. Clearly, he had not watched many movies – certainly not the ones in which cancer is portrayed as a condition that kills. I had definitely seen at least one Spanish movie and several Hindi and English movies where cancer had killed characters and made me cry. It looks like some serious work needs to be done to build awareness about cancer!

139

After my hair loss had happened, I remember I was speaking to someone in the family on Skype, someone to whom I had been very close. I was telling them about how I was, and about the hair loss. But not even once did they ask me how I was. They behaved as if the cancer didn't exist, that I had been saying something incomprehensible over the last five minutes, that they didn't need to respond to or even acknowledge my words. I understand that cancer can be a difficult topic to discuss. But I could not understand why people found it so difficult to talk about, if I was venturing out the information on my own? Clearly, there was something that I was missing.

I was very hurt by this behaviour and felt angry. Angry because they could not find time or the willingness to support me, or even talk to me! Maybe I was judging them, but when cancer struck, this is genuinely how I felt.

I felt very alone because of this anger. I lived through this isolation over and over again in my head, until I realised that no explanation really satisfied me, there was no right answer. Abhi told me that the trouble was not that they did not give me time; the trouble was that I expected them to give me their time and emotional bandwidth. Theoretically, I agreed with him, but a part of me did not agree with him at an emotional level.

I logged into Facebook one day and a friend pinged me. She and I had studied together during our MBA programme, and we had been in touch, on and off. In response to one of her questions, I happened to tell her about the cancer. She was stunned. She knew about cancer and its treatment fairly well, as she had closely seen someone go through it. She wished me well, and even though we were just chatting on Facebook, I had faith in everything she was saying. No judgements, no doubts whatsoever. I knew that she was really sad with the news of my illness, and wanted me to get well as soon as possible. Was this faith that had not been betrayed, or had trust existed here at all, when there were no expectations in the first place?

I thought often about why people get so uncomfortable while talking about cancer. Some people tend to feel uncomfortable at the mere mention of it. As my experience illustrates, this discomfort shows at various levels: disappearing after the diagnosis, not keeping in touch, not bringing up the topic of cancer as if it were a sacrilege, or failing to even acknowledge that there is cancer and that you have just been diagnosed!

Cancer is a condition that has the word 'death' associated with it. It is true that far more people survive cancer today than before, but it still remains a tough battle. Why are people so scared to talk about cancer? Is it because when they look at someone who has or has had cancer, all they can think is that the person will probably die? Or is it because when they see someone with cancer, they are reminded of *their own* mortality, which causes discomfort? Or is it because when they see someone with cancer, their worst fears about their loved ones surface?

I remember talking to a young, educated lady about a smear test – how it is essential for diagnosing cervical cancer, and why all women in the susceptible age group should regularly get it done. She got awfully uncomfortable, and said that she did not feel the need to get *such* a test done. I was surprised at how brusque her response was, and how annoyed she became with this discussion.

For God's sake, getting a test done because you are aware does not mean that you are expecting a disease, and it certainly doesn't mean you will get it! I am certain that in my case, it was my awareness that helped me get diagnosed crucially early. All I'd emphasise again is: Stay aware – Stay healthy – Stay alive.

But as I said, it was time to re-look at my relationships and start letting go. This change began when I was at the hospital for my treatment, and leafed through a book kept there. The title of the book was *The Cancer*

Journey: Positive steps to help yourself heal. It was written by three cancer survivors – Dr Pam Evans, Polly Noble, and Nicholas Hull-Malham. A section of the book was dedicated to people and our relationships with them. There was one particular point that held my attention. They said that when your loved ones found out about your condition, they would all behave differently. Some would come forward, while others would recoil. The latter category of people typically did not know what to say and how to say it, but that did not mean that they did not care. I pondered this statement, and realised this was how my folks had behaved. There I was sitting in the hospital chair undergoing treatment, and rethinking and revalidating my relationships. And as Nikhil said, the 'undying optimist' was back again. I thought, maybe my friends fell under this category too... maybe I was in their prayers... maybe they really did care.

It is true that some friendships waned off during the cancer experience. But it is equally true that many new ones developed. I was lucky to receive a lot of support from friends at work. There were three people who made it a point to take extra care of me. Liz, who was my manager, sent me treats at home...fragrant bath gels, to pamper me. She also provided me tremendous support at work. Right from the time I had found the lump in my body, Liz had been supportive. She knew a lot about cancer and what it could do, and she helped me with information and emotional support at all stages of my treatment. She helped me understand how the healthcare system, both NHS as well as private through insurance, works in the UK. I missed several days of work while on chemotherapy, and Liz and I worked out the schedule for when I would work and how much I would work. She also picked up medicines for me from the hospital, and sent them to me by post during the first crazy chemo cycle.

There was Sarah, who bought me aromatherapy oils to keep any infection at bay. Sarah was also my confidante and my sounding board. Whether it was for advice on where to buy trainers, or to share my most intimate fears about cancer, I always went to Sarah. She also helped to fill in for me when I missed work. Because of my deteriorating health, I could not bicycle anymore. She took me for a much-needed shopping trip, and willingly waited while I ambivalently took forever to decide on what I wanted to buy. Cancer or no cancer, Sarah is the kind of friend who is an absolute blessing to have.

There was Julia, who knitted a pretty purple set with a hat, a pair of mittens and a long scarf, to keep me warm during winters. She chose the colours very carefully, each with a special significance related to positivity and healing. While she knitted, she wove in lots of healing thoughts for me, to help me fight cancer. Later, during the radiation therapy, I stayed with Julia for eight days to complete my treatment.

There was Clara, who kept track of my treatment schedule and made it a point to ask for an update after various appointments. On a particular day, when I was extremely unwell and needed a supply of medicines, Clara went to the hospital, picked up the medicines, and ensured that I got them before my stock finished.

The rest of my colleagues and the management at work gave me great support. My HR Director, Cathy, gave me a piece of her mind when she found out that I was putting in long hours at work during chemotherapy. I am thankful to her for putting some sense into me. Apparently, many times I just don't happen to learn things the easy way or through common sense. I am so glad that I listened to her and stopped before harming myself badly. She was the one who strongly suggested that I take a break from work to recuperate. Taking a break had not occurred to me at all. But later, when I stayed off work for a long time, I was able to get the required rest and recover well. Thank you, Cathy.

Hema and Vallabh made sure that they kept in touch and enquired regularly about how I was. Hema, in particular, spent a lot of time chatting with me. In fact, I felt I came closer to the both of them during the treatment than I had been before.

Rashid wrote to me often, to be apprised of how I was getting on with the treatment. His emails clearly showed how concerned he was for me, and how keen he was to be kept informed.

Ruks did distance energy healing for me, and she and Madhura kept me in their prayers.

Neha Achrekar perked me up innumerable times with logic and love, as the only doctor friend I have. The other Neha checked on me from time to time.

Puja, the only friend with whom I have managed to be in contact after leaving college, stayed in touch to know how I was doing. So did Sumita, my friend from Mumbai.

Shubhra, my friend from the University, wrote regularly to find out about my health. I remember that I mentioned my deteriorated looks to her, and she said that I must still be the most beautiful woman in the world to Abhi! Muah!

A few cousins called, and so did many aunts and uncles, to share their concern.

Lorraine Smillie, my homeopath, performed energy healing for me with her meditation group to help me get through chemotherapy with fewer side effects. Later, she played a crucial role in helping me to recover from the side effects of the treatment.

I do not even have a count of all the people who prayed for me. Abhi's mum and my mum, both of whom are devout pray-ers, must have spent hundreds of hours praying for me. Abhi prayed for me every single day too. Their prayers worked for me magically. I believe that they played an important role in my recovery, along with the skill of my healthcare team and the care of the rest of my family and friends.

While some of my friends and some family members chose to take the back seat, there were others in the family who simply did not have a choice, or rather, I would say, they did not exercise that choice.

There was Abhi, who had been my rock of support from day one. He did not say even once that he was too shocked to assimilate this news, or that he could not speak to me as it was too difficult to talk or listen. There were my parents and my brothers, who spoke to me every single day. They all have busy lives, and yet they always had time to speak to me. My brother, Sachin, who works in the US in the corporate world in a senior position, travelled to the UK at one day's notice to be with us for my first chemotherapy treatment. He was here because he wanted to be here. He was here because it was important for him to be here. He was here because he wanted to ensure that Abhi and I did not have to start this scary journey all by ourselves.

The same way, my mum travelled to the UK all alone to take care of me. We have always had our differences as parent and child, but in this instance, Mum simply buried the hatchet and looked after me like a mother would do. She gave me the support I had always yearned for. It was so important for her to come and help me get well that she let go of everything else.

My father came to the UK just before the surgery and stayed with us for two months. He accompanied me for a walk every day, and came to the hospital for every single appointment. The radiation therapy started while he was still in the UK, and he came to the hospital everyday with me. He wanted to keep me company, so that the long hours that I spent in the hospital didn't get to me. Whenever I got impatient, he would always calm me down. It was through him that I learnt that I was always in a hurry. If the bus got delayed by five minutes, I would get impatient. He, on the contrary, remained calm, as the arrival of the bus really wasn't in our control. Gradually, in his company, I started getting less anxious in situations where I had no control.

Dinesh ensured that he got an update from me after every hospital visit or scan or consultation. We talked very often on Skype and he frequently told me that I looked pretty; and being told that you are pretty never hurts, does it?

Sachin called me up at least once every day over the next eighteen months, to talk to me and find out how I was doing. He invested an incredible amount of time and effort with me. He and Abhi were so familiar with what I was going through that when this book was written, they seemed to know almost all its contents. It clearly shows that I had discussed my cancer experience with them at length.

Abhi's sister, Manisha, wrote to me often and enquired about my well-being. Her emails were full of concern and care for me.

If I look at all these facts objectively, I clearly see the difference in the support that I received from various people. It is true that I did not expect all the people I knew to take care of me, nor did I think that they should drop their lives for me – but I didn't expect that they would not have even couple of minutes to speak to me or write to me. My sceptical mind came to the conclusion that if someone matters to you, you will find time for them. Your real commitment towards a relationship shows up in times of crisis.

In an ideal world, I would not want the cancer to exist at all. I would wish that no one should ever have to go through cancer. But unfortunately, it is not an ideal world that we live in. I am thankful to each of those people who made me feel isolated – because they eventually contributed to my growth as an individual. If anyone important to me ever has to go through this horrid experience, I will try and act differently. I have experienced how it feels to be abandoned and isolated. If everyone had cared for me, I may not have been equally appreciative of the effort that some specific people took for me. Of course, I will treasure the latter category of people for the rest of my life.

I understand that I was very lucky to have enormous support from my family. The way my mum came over to look after me is more of an exception rather than the norm. Because I had such fabulous support, I didn't really think that I needed a cancer support centre, and I didn't visit one until the end of radiation therapy. My perception of support centres was influenced by their portrayal in Hollywood movies. I had never thought of myself as a 'group' person, nor did I think that I would benefit from talking to some people who I didn't know very well at a support centre. To me, talking to family and friends was enough, and the key ownership for my situation lay with me.

How wrong I was! I realised that once I started visiting a cancer support centre – I healed faster. When I shared my emotions with fellow cancer patients, I felt understood. The guilt of burdening my family with sob-stories never raised its head, as all of us were in a similar state. We may have been at different stages of treatment, or inflicted with different types of cancer, but we could all relate to each other. At the same time, it was never about wallowing in each other's misery. There was always a fantastic mix of empathy and objectivity. I'd say that no matter what kind of support you have from your loved ones, support centres have an important role to play in your healing. I really wish that I had visited them earlier. I have written more about them later in this book.

Rediscovering myself

Ruks, my dear friend, also practices complementary healing. She had advised me start letting go right at the beginning, during that unforgettable week between the heads-up about cancer and its confirmation. I had called her up to explore if complementary healing could help me.

I am not a person who holds onto things too strongly. Yes, I do like to hold on to the people I love, because they really matter to me. But that is necessarily not a bad thing, is it? I asked Ruks about what I could do to let go – if she had any suggestions. She asked me to travel to India, and let go of all the old possessions I had kept there. She suggested that I could do it mentally to start with, and actually do it when I really got there.

I agreed, and did it mentally. The idea was to reduce my attachment to perishable things. I also decided (something I had been thinking of doing anyway) that the next time I went to India, I would give away lot of the possessions I had left there.

But in the entire cancer experience, I did not have to let go of only my attachment to household belongings. I had always been possessive of Abhi, through the time I had known him, because I loved him most of all. When I was diagnosed with cancer, I knew there was a small chance that I would not make it through. So, it was time to let go of the one thing I wanted all to myself. With all my courage, I told Abhi, 'If I don't make it through this, I want you to move on.' Abhi was livid, but I had made him promise that he would listen. So I went on to add,

'And... I want you to get over me first, before you move into another relationship.' It took me enormous courage to say that. But once I had said it, I felt so relieved. I knew I would not be holding him back, if it came to that. I do think that I was a little selfish when I said this, because Abhi must have been very hurt when he heard it. If I were in his place, I would have hated it too. But I felt that it had to be done, and that it was the right thing to do. I may not have the time and courage to say all this later. Time had ceased to be a limitless commodity!

My looks were the next thing. I received a few glances and stares when I didn't have hair. It felt weird to see how some people looked shocked when they didn't see any hair on my head. But thankfully I understood that losing hair was part of the immensely important cure, and therefore I took the hair loss in my stride.

The change in my looks continued, as the chemotherapy progressed. I had always been conscious about putting on weight. I struggled with weight issues, and was careful about my diet. During cancer treatment, I had to let go of my fear of putting on weight. The last three cycles of chemotherapy were accompanied with heavy doses of steroids, which caused water retention, and I piled on pounds. Later, tamoxifen could do similar things (and it did).

My nails looked awful due to the discoloration, ridges, and brittleness.

I had to accept that the cancer treatment would mess up my looks, and rediscover my comfort about the new me.

Cancer gave me the impetus to work on things that I had wanted to do for a long time, but hadn't got around to doing. I used the 'cancer time' as an opportunity to forgive and seek forgiveness. There were certain relationships from the past in which I had not achieved closure. Either I had been hurt about things, or I had hurt others. I was able to get in touch with some of these people, and come to what can be closest to closure for incidents that have already happened and cannot be changed. I also used this time to let go of my hurt and forgive many people with whom I had been angry or disappointed. And I invested energy in forgiving myself, for things I had done in the past and was not proud of. There are many relationships that I cannot heal now, as it is too late for doing so. But it is never too late to come to terms with what has happened, grieve, forgive, and move on. Some of these people are no more; I have lost contact with many others. I realised that at times, I had been too hard on others, and on myself. Therefore, the best thing was to face what had happened, let it go, and move on. It was like 'closing the loop' with people who had mattered to me at least once in my lifetime. Cancer as a medical condition showed me the futility of holding angst in my heart. I now understand that it is possible to lose your life, people, meaningful relationships, work, and peace of mind, in a single all-changing moment.

Of course, this remains a constant process and I continue to work on relationships and closing the loop with people in my life.

Ruks was the first person who brought to my attention how awfully goal-oriented I had always been. After cancer, I let go of the need to set timelines for everything in life. My work contract was coming to an end in February, and I had planned to resume work a couple of months after that. A couple of months was the goal that I had set for myself. However, as I progressed through the treatment, I realised that my strength was too low and that I needed to give my body more time to recover. There was no point in setting a goal for returning to work. But developing that new attitude needed some conscious work. Thankfully, I was sensible enough to not set up a timeline for inculcating this attitude!

Letting go indeed!

This illness gave me lot of time for introspection. Before, I would introspect once in a while, but never so deeply. Ever since Dr Parto had said, 'Sorry, Mrs Banka, but I have to confirm that you have cancer,' I had wondered where my *Karma* fit in the picture. I was a believer in the philosophy of *Karma* which, simply put, means, 'As you sow, so shall you reap'. I spent a long time wondering which deeds of mine had caused this. Ten months after the diagnosis, I was still unable to understand what exactly I had sowed that I was now reaping in the form of cancer. While it might be a natural question to ask, the reality is that the world of cancer is more complicated than that. There is definitely more information about cancer, its causes, and its cure now than there was a few years ago; but a lot about cancer is still difficult to understand. Eventually, I came to the conclusion that I had not planted the seed of cancer in my life. But through this introspection, I did find several other traits that I needed to work hard on and change. I received feedback from my immediate family about undesirable aspects of my personality that they had been putting up with for several years. I found out (unfortunately, this was not a surprise, but it was the intensity that startled me for sure) that I always chose to be right, rather than kind. If there was a situation where I had to choose to say either what was right (and hurtful) or something that was kind, I always chose the former. I don't know why I had such a deep need to say the right thing. What would happen if I didn't tell another adult mature person that they were being stupid, or tell them the right thing to do? I am sure they could figure it out for themselves, just the way I did.

I also found out that I had lot of anger in me. By angry, I don't mean being the kind of angry person who throws plates across the kitchen or vases across the living room. By angry, I mean the emotion that rises deep within you, when someone says hurtful things and you hold on to that pain as if your own life depended on it. By angry, I mean how you see people through that filter of angry emotions, whenever you interact with them. I knew that I had always found it difficult to let go of resentment, but had not realised that I could seriously do better with anger management. When things do not go as I desire or are against my value system, I get rude and hurtful. I have hurt many people like this. I have hurt friends and my family, who care about me and love me.

When you hurt the people whom you love like crazy and who love you like crazy, it usually turns out OK. It's not perfect, but they are willing to let go and accept you, despite the tantrums. You vent your feelings to them because you know you can do it and get away with it; they give in, because it is you. And when you do this to people who are strangers, or the ones who you don't care much about, that's always OK too, because whatever is said or done does not really matter much. But it is in between these two categories that things get complicated. You are not so close to this category of people that you would condone everything, but you are not so far from them that you would not care. This is the category where I mess up, because here, handling relationships requires real hard work. It requires empathy, sympathy, and the ability to let go and keep your ego in check. It also requires a great deal of forgiveness, for the times when things do not go as you wish.

As I thought about these qualities in myself, I often found myself feeling conflicted. Were these really moments of truth, or were they just moments of self-doubt? Were these realisations brought by honest feedback and introspection, or were they just born of my low confidence in difficult times? Did I doubt the truth of these insights only because I was too scared or unprepared to accept them?

When I started writing this book, I was angry. I was not angry because I was chosen for cancer; but I was definitely angry with all the pain it had caused. I was angry with the loss of control over my life. I was angry at how even the smallest decision in my life suddenly had to be made with cancer as the main consideration. I was exhausted and consequently angry at the number of hours I spent in bed. I was angry because I had to stop working. I was angry because I found it difficult to cope with the 30°C heat in the summer, when I had spent 32 years of my life in the hot tropical climate of India. I was angry because I lost some meaningful relationships during cancer, and I felt frustrated at discovering that these people let go of me at a difficult time in my life. I was angry because no matter how well I was supported by my family and friends, I still felt alone. I rationalised this feeling of isolation time and again, but it chose not to go away, and that angered me more. It was a vicious circle of being angry and then feeling angrier because I found the anger overpowering. I was in a constant battle with myself – I knew what I had to do, rationally, but was unable to do it. And that exhausted me and made me angrier. But gradually, as time passed, I started to heal and less anger reflected in my writing. This is how I wanted it to be: the anger to diminish until it was all gone.

I took up the issue of anger and my need to be in control later during the treatment. What use was self-discovery if I didn't do anything to change myself for the better? In exploring the difficult and the painful, there can be great rewards.

Cancer has made me accept things I can't change. A simple example is blood donation: I have always strongly believed in donating blood, as it can save lives. But now, as someone who has had cancer, I may not be allowed to donate blood. Different countries have different eligibility criteria for blood donation. The UK, with the exception of a few types of cancer, does not allow people to donate blood if they have had cancer[30]. In India[31], eligibility depends on the type of cancer and treatment history. Other countries, like Australia or the US, suggest

---

[30]   Cancer research UK. "Can I donate blood if I have had cancer?" Last modified April 2013. http://www.cancerresearchuk.org/about-cancer/cancers-in-general/cancer-questions/can-i-donate-blood-if-i-have-had-cancer. Last accessed December 05, 2014.

[31]   Blood Bank India. "DOs and DON'Ts of blood donation." http://www.bloodbankindia.net/eligibility.php. Last accessed December 05, 2014.
And
Sankalp India Foundation. "Eligibility as per red cross." http://www.sankalpindia.net/drupal/eligibility-red-cross. Last accessed December 05, 2014.

a hiatus of a few years between finishing the treatment and donating blood. It is sad that I may now have to let go of something that I so strongly believe in.

Similarly, being able to get a medical insurance cover or a life insurance cover at an affordable price would be very challenging now. It is all right in the UK, thanks to the NHS. But in a different country, where all healthcare treatment is private, it will be stressful and definitely fairly expensive.

I knew I couldn't possibly fight these things; I must learn to accept them as they were. As it turned out, I would get to explore 'acceptance' in detail, at a later stage in my cancer journey. I would spend the larger part of the summer of 2013 introspecting and working on acceptance.

It was during this phase of introspection that I attended a seminar about disfigurement and the challenges faced by people affected by disfigurement in the workplace, particularly when it came to the perceptions of other people. After a discussion about where the law stood on the issue of disfigurement, there was a presentation by a lady who had worked for about twenty years helping people with disfigurement. It was an eye-opener that taught me about the challenges and stigma faced by these people. Cancer, and the change in people's looks due to cancer, were mentioned as well. Of course, the discussion revolved around several other conditions, like burns and congenital diseases, which cause far more severe and often permanent changes in one's looks.

After this presentation, there was a brief talk by a visitor who looked different from the rest of us. I guess that he must have looked like most of us until the fateful day in 2007 when he was on vacation in the US, learning how to fly an aircraft. He had been flying his tiny aircraft for about three weeks without an instructor, and was happy that he was getting better at it. An ex-policeman and currently an army man, he had always enjoyed outdoor activities that demanded physical fitness. So on that day, he was in the aircraft; all was well until the aircraft engine suddenly caught fire. He was still a thousand feet above the ground, and needed to make an emergency landing. The fire was furious and gripped him by the feet, moving upwards. Despite the emergency landing, by the time he was near the ground, the fire had reached his neck. He had been burning for about thirty seconds. He let the aircraft come to an abrupt halt by running on the grass. The fire had now reached his face. Somehow, he managed to switch off the controls of the engine and scramble out of the cockpit. He landed with a huge impact on the ground, which caused severe injuries to his burnt face.

He was rushed to a hospital in the city, with 60% third degree burns; he spent six months there, in the intensive care unit. When his condition was a little more stable, he returned to England. He spent another two months in the ICU, followed by about sixteen months in the hospital as an inpatient. The number of reconstructive surgeries that he had gone through was phenomenal, and yet, the final result made him look extremely different from others. Imagine the experience of living in the hospital for two years – its impact on the psyche, work, life, everything else.

Honestly, I can't even imagine this level of trauma. I was looking at a man who must have been good-looking, a fitness enthusiast, just like rest of us, until a vacation went wrong. The life that had *happened* to him was so unfair. Yet he wasn't complaining. He was there to build awareness about how things can change without our choice, and how we need to be sensitive when such things happen. I was shaken by his story. I was aghast at how his life had changed. For a moment, I felt puny, and berated myself about feeling *low* after a hospital visit. I suddenly found that my ugliness due to cancer was no big deal. The curious looks that I had received due to cancer and its treatment suddenly felt less painful.

I am not patronising him, nor am I saying that the suffering of cancer patients (me included) is belittled because someone went through a terrible accident in their life. But what I am definitely saying is that it is so important to count our blessings every day. As I sat in the seminar hall listening to this man, I was inspired by his courage and his zest for life. It also reinforced my knowledge that life can change at any moment, and we may have no control over it. However, what we can control is how we respond to the change.

A maelstrom of emotions arose inside me in that seminar hall. I felt empathy for that man, for his suffering, and I felt extreme admiration for his courage. I want to dedicate these beautiful lines to him and every person who has shown resilience in the face of adversity:

> *Beyond this place of wrath and tears*
> *Looms but the Horror of the shade,*
> *And yet the menace of the years*
> *Finds, and shall find, me unafraid.*
>
> *It matters not how strait the gate,*
> *How charged with punishments the scroll,*
> *I am the master of my fate:*
> *I am the captain of my soul.*
>
> - William Ernest Henley, *Invictus*

I continue to become more thankful and more empathic as I go through the cancer experience.

Cancer has been about rediscovering myself as a person, as a wife, as a daughter, as a sister, as a friend, as a colleague, as a relative, and as an employee. Who says that cancer causes only those changes that aren't pretty? Thankfully, I also have time to savour these new changes in my life.

Life continues in the slow traffic lane

The year 2012 had been different because of the two major illnesses that I told you about right at the beginning of this book. Just when I thought I was all fixed up after the first illness, in less than a week, I was diagnosed with cancer. Yup, I had spent an awful lot of time in the hospital over the last three years. Until illness engulfed me, my life had been busy with work, home, hobbies, and Abhi. After cancer, I had to take time off work, and had lot of free time to think, as I could not do much else. Life suddenly moved from the fast lane to the slow lane. There was time to look out of the bedroom window and appreciate the autumn colours; there was time to listen to my own thoughts; and there was time to just stare at nothing and appreciate nothingness.

There is more to life than increasing its speed.
- Mahatma Gandhi

As I began to shift into the slow lane, one day, I came across a picture of some of my good friends on Facebook. The title of the picture was 'Happy Family'. Had it been any other day, I would have smiled at the photo, clicked on the 'Like' button, may have posted a nice comment, and moved on. But this did not happen on that particular day. I was suddenly reminded that the people in the picture were not really family. They knew each other socially. Some of these people did not get along with their real families. I could not but help think that a lot of times, instead of mending relationships, it is so much easier to drop them.

What is it that keeps us from investing enough effort in our own relationships, while we run helter-skelter to develop new ones? My thoughts were not a criticism of the picture or the people in it. Nor am I suggesting that these particular people didn't do what they needed to do to sort out their relationships. This was a more general chain of thoughts that was triggered by a simple picture. It was also a realisation that I had taken this easy route in the past myself. I determined that at least with the key people in my life, I wouldn't take shortcuts.

As I have said before, my brother Sachin came to the UK to be with us for my first session of chemotherapy. He stayed with us for three weeks, and it was wonderful to have him there. I noticed that while he was with us, he was happy during the first week. In the second week he started getting restless, and in the third week, I could see he was unhappy. He was missing his family, and could not stay away from them for much longer. I saw him cheer up when he spoke to his kids over the phone. He, for reasons known only to him, had never used Skype before. We had insisted quite a few times, but he would always evade using Skype and prefer to use the phone. But while he was here, he missed his family so much that he began using Skype; he just needed to see his children. I saw his happiness change into impatience to get back home. When it was time for him to go back, I noticed how excitedly he shopped for chocolates and toys for the children, and how keenly he packed his bags. All this eagerness was not because he did not want to stay with us, but because he wanted to be with his children.

Seeing his eagerness and impatience build up every day got me thinking. Sachin is a successful man in the corporate world. He has travelled across countries and lived in many of them. Several years ago, when he left home to go to university, his parents (who are, of course, my parents too) had to let go of him. As he moved away from home for his education, and subsequently out of the country for work, our parents had to let him go; and he expected them to do so. If they hadn't, they would probably have run the risk of being called 'helicopter parents'. I also clearly recollect how eager we had all been to step out of home, to experience living on our own at university, and then to travel around the world.

I went on thinking that when Sachin's kids grew up, they would also want to explore the world, and want to move away from home. Would he not have trouble staying away from them? The conflict here is: While we expect our parents to let go of us, we want to hold on to our own children! The cycle seems to go on with every generation; I reckon this is how it is. Some people may say that I should not be making this statement, as I don't have children. I could be wrong, but I have a feeling that I am not – it is true that I have not experienced this dilemma as a parent, but I have definitely experienced it as a child. I must say that people have to have big hearts, if they want to let go. I think I appreciate our parents' letting go of us better now.

Remember the benign lump (fibroadenoma) that Dr Parto had removed for me before the two major illnesses hit me? Like with any standard procedure, the samples after excision of the fibroadenoma were sent for biopsy. Now, the result of the biopsy could either be benign or malignant. There was a 50% chance of getting either result.

I remember that I was telling someone about the biopsy report when I said, 'Thank God, the results were all fine.' They were shocked when they heard this and asked, 'What else could the results be?' I was a little surprised but said, 'Well, the report could have brought bad news too. But it didn't. I am glad that the tumour was benign, I thank the Almighty for that.'

Later, when the cancer was diagnosed, I was repeatedly told that I had got cancer because I'd thought that I could get it. Those who said this strongly believed that I had *invited* cancer upon myself, because I had worried that my earlier biopsy report could bring the bad news. I'd like to clarify here that such beliefs are more prevalent in some cultures than they are in others. Reflecting on this, I am awed at how much our cultures, faiths, environments, or families impact how we understand anything – in this case, how we interpret cancer and its diagnosis, how we cope with such a disease, and how we behave with someone who has been diagnosed with cancer. I am also wondering how these people would cope, had the cancer diagnosis been handed over to them.

I think such judgement is unfair. Believe me, no one wants cancer, and no one wants to invite it upon themselves. If such thinking could invite diseases, all pre-emptive medical tests would enable us to attract diseases, instead of being instrumental in stopping them. People get vaccinated because they expect to be protected from diseases. Taking a vaccine does not mean that they will invite that particular illness – just because their awareness tells them that a particular disease could happen to them!

It is so easy to judge others and their situations – but that's not how it should be. Telling someone that they invited such a difficult medical condition upon themselves, or that they deserved such a thing because of their expectation or *Karma*, is inappropriate to say the least.

As human beings, we need to be more sensitive when dealing with others. It is not rocket science, but unfortunately, so many people fail to understand something so basic. I am aware that I am also guilty of passing unfair judgments on others. It is true that I have never blamed anyone for inviting cancer, or cardiac arrest, or similar critical medical conditions, upon themselves. But I have passed judgements about other things, some of which I am sure were hurtful. There were times when I may not have said anything upfront, but I passed a judgment in my head. Having gone through cancer, and after having so much time to reflect, I decided to be less judgemental. The ideal situation would be to not judge at all. I hope to get there someday.

And so, don't let anyone, including yourself, tell you that they know the reason behind your cancer. Don't take it to heart (as much as possible, although if you feel mad each time you are reminded of it, that is understandable) if they tell you that you got cancer because of your acts or intentions or emotions or lifestyle choices. There are several factors that increase the risk of cancer, and it is difficult to say what is responsible for making normal cells cancerous. You can't say for sure whether the continued over-usage of disposable bottles caused it, or the extra-browned barbeque food contributed to it. There is no telling whether you got cancer at an early age because you happen to be one of those women who decided not to bear children, or chose to not have children at a young age. Therefore, do not let others make you believe that God, or some human being, or you, are to be blamed for your condition. Blame will not help with the cure of cancer, and you need to always remember that. Hopefully, before people make insensitive remarks, they will remember that the shoes could have been on the other feet.

What could have been a regular incident assumed bigger proportions for me after cancer. Just to give you a perspective, there are some communities in India where menstruation is considered sordid. People do not visit temples, or offer prayers, or cook food while they are menstruating, as they consider themselves to be unclean. I have never bought into such theories, as for me, menstruation is an important physiological process of a female body. And so, during cancer, I occasionally found myself in situations where people bemoaned menstruation, or discussed how they had to work around it to accommodate important tasks like cooking while entertaining guests. Listening to these discussions, I couldn't help wondering how things that are so dirty to some people could be so precious to others. As a woman who had been made menopausal twenty years before the normal age for menopause, and who had less than a 100% chance of getting her periods back, it was sad to hear this. Something that was so important to me was dispensable for these other women. But isn't that the way it is for most things? People have different priorities in life, which often change with the experiences they go through. In my case, cancer had definitely made me revaluate my priorities and choices.

Some wonderful books I read

There were several books that I read during my cancer journey. Some of them stayed with me, while others did not. I would like to tell you about the books that impacted me.

The first book, *Chicken Soup for the Soul: The Cancer Book: 101 Stories of Courage, Support & Love*[32] is a collection of 101 stories about people whose lives were impacted by cancer. There are stories by patients, survivors, people who have survived cancer multiple times, parents, children, doctors, nurses, carers and friends. There were stories that made me laugh, there were stories that made me cry and there were the ones that stunned me with their pathos and suffering. They were stories of battle, loss, victory, despair, bereavement, hope, learning and spirituality.

I was particularly moved by an anecdote in the Foreword to the book. Bonnie had cancer and had lost more than one of the parts of her body that are said to define a woman. One day she overheard her teenage daughter telling her boyfriend, 'My mom has no breasts, no uterus and no hair, and my dad still loves her. That's the kind of love I want.' I cried when I read this story. I cried at the struggle, the loss, the despair, the empathy, and finally, the love that this story evoked. I cried because it was the story of a man whose love for his wife was not defined by her body or her hair.

---

[32]   Canfield, Jack, and Hansen, Mark V, and Tabatsky, David. 2013. *Chicken Soup for the Soul: The Cancer Book: 101 Stories of Courage, Support & Love*. United States of America: Chicken Soup for the Soul Publishing, LLC.

When I stopped crying, I realised that was the kind of love I had. Not many people are lucky enough to have this kind of love. Further, most of the people who have this kind of love are not lucky enough to realise it. It was double luck for me. Although I had never taken Abhi's love for granted, cancer helped me realise the intensity of this love. *And I was lucky enough to realise all of this at the age of 34.* Now, how many people really understand the precious love they have, at such an early age?

Story number 26, 'Marry me', is one of my favourites too. It is the story of Victoria and Charles. They were in a relationship; Victoria was 34 years old and 8½ months pregnant with their daughter, when she felt a mass under her left breast. Their daughter was delivered, and a week later, Victoria had a biopsy. It was confirmed to be a Stage 3b invasive ductal carcinoma. She lost a breast, and a few days later, Charles proposed marriage to Victoria. Victoria was amazed. She could not understand why someone would wish to marry a person who could die. She endured surgery, chemotherapy, and radiation therapy to recover from the cancer. The doctors thought that she could never conceive again, but she did. Their miracle boy, Sidney, was born. Four months later, Victoria had another discovery – one that froze her with fear. She found a lump in her right arm! The cancer was back, and this time it was bigger and stronger. Stage IV breast cancer. The second breast went away too, and chemotherapy restarted. Once again, she lost her hair. But she hung in there. Months later, when she was better, Charles proposed marriage again, and she said what he had been longing to hear for months: 'Yes.' As they were united as man and wife for eternity, they lingered over a long kiss. Their love embodied the beautiful message, *Every day is a good day to be alive.*

Another favourite is story number 41, 'In the Ring'. The author, Ali Zidel Meyers, gives a wonderful account of the battle with cancer – in the boxing ring. It is a vivid description of the fight of a lifetime – between the heavy weight champion, Colon Cancer (CC), and the up-and-coming lightweight competitor, Ali Zidel Meyers. While reading this two and a half page story, I cheered for Ali, I booed CC, and I clapped. I know that Ali eventually won this battle and more significantly, her spirit and her humour won against fear and despair.

A champion shows who he is when he's tested. When a person
gets up and says, 'I can still do it,' he's a champion.

- Evander Holyfield,
American professional boxer and World Champion

There were several other stories that I loved in this book. They covered the entire gamut of emotions. There was one particular emotion that flowed seamlessly almost through all of them – the gratitude for being alive – *today*.

I must say that I am in general a very big fan of the *Chicken Soup for the Soul* series. I find their stories brilliant. The only trouble with them is that with all the crying, they really increase my consumption of Kleenex – but I'm not complaining! Stories that make me cry are not the only kind they publish; most of their stories are as heart-warming as hot, thick butternut squash soup with a generous dollop of double cream on a winter evening. Absolute bliss!

John Diamond's book, *C: Because Cowards Get Cancer Too*[33] is a powerful narration of John's battle with cancer. John goes into deep and sometimes gory detail about his cancer and how his life changed as cancer gradually took over him. I marvelled at how he managed to maintain a sense of humour, while writing about an illness that he was scared of. His situation was so ironic: he was a TV show broadcaster, who had lost his tongue to the illness. He was a man who couldn't eat when throat cancer attacked his body, while his wife was the author of best-seller cook-books and host of a TV cooking show. An absolutely

---

[33] Diamond, John. 1998. *C: Because Cowards Get Cancer Too*. Great Britain: Vermilion.

brilliant and yet sad narration of a man's cancer journey; I greatly appreciated the literary aspect of the book, but I also felt extremely sad about what John had to go through. And how I counted my blessings, as I read through one page after the other!

The Cancer Journey: Positive steps to help yourself heal[34] is a simple and readable book. This was the book that helped me see beyond my anger, and I am immensely thankful to the authors for that. I read this book during all the long hospital hours. I felt an instant connection with what was written in the book. There was nothing preachy about the book; the tips were easy to implement, and the experience was sensitive and easy to share.

The support that we gain by learning about others' experiences is not only uplifting, but often also lends us a useful perspective.

I also enjoyed reading the following books:

Anni's cancer companion[35], by Anni Mathews – This is a comprehensive book covering every possible aspect of cancer treatment. It is a shame that I read this book about a year after the diagnosis. This is a book that should be read right after the cancer diagnosis, as the wealth of knowledge it contains is priceless.

Thrive: The Bah! Guide to Wellness After cancer[36], by Stephanie Butland – This is simply an awesome book. If you need some pepping up and want to actively help yourself to get better, then this is the book to read.

---

[34]   Evans, Pam, and Noble, Polly, and Hull-Malham Nicholas. 2011. *The Cancer Journey: Positive Steps to Help Yourself Heal.* UK: Antony Rowe Publishing Services.

[35]   Matthews, Anni. 2011. *Anni's Cancer Companion: An A-Z of Treatments, Therapies and Healing.* UK: Singing Dragon.

[36]   Butland, Stephanie. 2012. *Thrive: The Bah! Guide to Wellness After cancer.* UK: Hay House.

But it is not just pepping up that this book provides. It succinctly and clearly provides several self-help tools that you can employ to say 'bah' to cancer, and thrive. I was so filled with admiration for the author when I read this book. In fact, it does not feel like a book on cancer at all. It is so full of life and humour that you will thrive when you read it. It is again one of those books which require you to keep a box of Kleenex handy. You will have tears streaming down your face – because of laughter!

Cancer as a Turning Point: A Handbook for People with Cancer[37], by Lawrence LeShan – This is a great book that talks about the changes we can make in our lives to keep illness (and cancer) away from us. The author says that when we do what we truly enjoy, we attain meaning and good health in our lives. I share with you one of my favourite quotes from the book below:

When we are actively singing our own song, we realise that it is only philosophers and depressives who ask what is the meaning of life. When we are using ourselves in the way we are built for, we know (page 148).

This book strongly advocates that we must all 'sing our song'. When we sing our song, what follows is the melody of happiness, satisfaction and good health.

Fear No Evil: A Personal Struggle with Cancer[38], by David Watson – I found this book interesting because it explores the relationship between faith and cancer. What hooked my attention is how the author came to terms with his terminal illness and felt ready to go, by finding strength in his faith, prayer, and God.

---

[37]   LeShan, Lawrence. 1994. *Cancer as a Turning Point: A Handbook for People with Cancer, Their Families, and Health Professionals.* United States of America: Plume.

[38]   Watson, David. 1984. *Fear No Evil: A Personal Struggle with Cancer.* UK: Hodder & Stoughton Religious.

Complementary Therapies and Cancer Support Centres

I am reminded of the time when I had the last radiation therapy treatment on the 23rd of April, and after two days, I had Herceptin on the 26th of April. From the time I had been diagnosed with cancer, I had spent innumerable hours in the hospital. April had been especially difficult, as I had to be in the hospital every day for radiation therapy. I was hugely looking forward to the 26th of April, because I knew that I would get a break for a few days before I was required to make the next visit to the hospital.

The 26th of April came and went. I was elated – no more hospital visits for a week. After that, I was supposed to go and meet my new oncologist at the London hospital. No needle pricks, no intravenous treatment, for another two weeks. I thought that the happy times had begun.

How far from truth I was! While I was on the cancer treatment (chemotherapy, surgery, and radiation therapy), I had to put up a brave face. I knew I couldn't afford to give up or fall weak, as I had to get through the grind of the treatment, and get better. But when I had more time on my hands, after the 26th of April, the devastating cancer experience came back to haunt me. I suddenly felt scared. I would get teary-eyed at the drop of a hat, or for no apparent reason. I felt as if I was shutting down, and the world was closing in on me. The brave and 'I will get there' attitude was suddenly disappearing. While maintaining a positive face, I had not had the time to get in touch with my darkest fears. But now that I had some free time to process all the information, those fears were coming to the surface, and I had nowhere to run. I decided to ask for help, before my fear consumed me completely. I was clearly crumbling under the psychological stress that cancer had brought into my life.

I went to see my GP in the first week of May (where I registered after moving to London), and she asked me how I was coping with all the stress that cancer must have brought. I honestly confessed to her how I had been brave for over seven months, and how I had been struggling over the last seven days. She suggested that I speak to a counsellor. She very kindly handed me a card and asked me to call them up when I felt ready. She seemed to understand very well that I might need help, and had therefore touched upon this topic herself.

I thanked her and came back home. I decided that I would see how I felt for a week or so. If after a week, I still felt anxious and in the doldrums, I would call the number on that card.

The next week, I had an appointment to see a senior therapist, Nadia, at a cancer support centre called The Haven, which is a charity organisation providing support to breast cancer patients, survivors, and their families. In that first meeting at The Haven, I shared with Nadia how I was reeling under an emotional meltdown at a time when I expected to be relieved. I had expected that she would be surprised at my condition; but on the contrary, she understood me completely. In fact, she assured me that what I was feeling was absolutely normal, and that many people who have been through cancer treatment go through such feelings. She told me that people feel most scared at two moments in the cancer journey: at the time of the diagnosis, and when a major chunk of the treatment gets over.

All this time, I had been rushing to the hospital several times a week, and undergoing difficult treatment, which required courage; and now suddenly it was over (well, not so suddenly). I now had time to breathe, and process what had happened to me. Over the last few months, whenever there had been the slightest trouble, I had got in touch with my oncologist and the rest of the healthcare team, knowing that they would take care of me. Now they had handed my life back to me, and had asked me to get on with it; they would only check on me once in a while. I was scared and newly diffident, as I started to rebuild my life after cancer. It was a bit like learning to walk, as if I had had a terrible accident and had been on crutches all these months; letting go of the crutches was intimidating. Together, Nadia and I chalked out a plan that would help me recover from the physical, emotional, and psychological scars of cancer.

The cancer treatment had done what it was supposed to do – kill cancer. But in the process of killing malignant cells, it had killed lot of good cells too. This had badly depleted my energy levels and stamina. Now I could just wait, and let my body flush out the drugs gradually. But the expected timeline for that to happen was anywhere between six months to two years. I did not want to sit around, doing nothing (which was at times a good thing in my situation). I decided to expedite my recovery process. I wanted to get back to normal life again, as soon as possible.

I tried a variety of things at The Haven, at the Maggie's Wallace Care Centre, and the Paul's Cancer Support Centre, and I feel that I benefited immensely from them. They are listed below for your reference:

Look Good Feel Better (LGFB): I went through a fabulous programme called 'Look Good Feel Better'[39] at The Haven. LGFB is an independent cancer support charity, and they organise make-up workshops at various hospitals and cancer support centres. That is how I got to know about them at The Haven.

---

[39]   Look Good Feel Better. "Who we are." http://www.lookgoodfeelbetter.co.uk/about. Last accessed December 05, 2014.

It was a two-hour workshop, which was attended by about twelve participants. We were given a make-up kit, with lots of goodies from some of the best cosmetic brands. The objective of the workshop was to teach us how to do make-up, so that we could tackle the visible side effects of cancer treatment. There was lots of advice on skin care, and tips on products suitable to our skin tones. I also met some wonderful people in the workshop. For a change, being marked by cancer was not an uncomfortable sight – we were all learning to apply make-up and look prettier. I wish I had attended this workshop soon after the diagnosis but as they say, better late than never.

Take it from a person who had almost never worn make-up before: this workshop and what they teach you is really useful. What makes it special is that it is fun! And oh the goody bag – who doesn't love freebies? I certainly do!

Acupuncture: Acupuncture is an ancient system of healing from traditional Chinese medicine, and involves the insertion of fine, sterile needles into specific points located on the body. The needles are left in the body for a short time (from a few minutes to up to thirty minutes) and then removed.

Acupuncture is based on the theory that 'chi', a form of electro-magnetic energy, flows along a network of channels, called meridians. If chi is flowing freely through the body, there is wellness. However, if chi gets obstructed, the blockage manifests itself in the form of an ailment. When needles are inserted into the body, they help the chi flow, and bring the body back into equilibrium.

I took several sessions of acupuncture at The Haven to help me recover from the side effects of the cancer treatment. It helped me enormously in treating nausea, fatigue, insomnia, hot flushes, and night sweats. Later, when I started taking Tamoxifen, my appetite increased as a side effect of the drug. Acupuncture helped me manage this. The benefit of the acupuncture sessions seemed small in the beginning, but as we progressed, the effect cumulatively increased. The only trouble was that typically after the treatment, for about a day, I felt unwell. It could be either flu-like symptoms, or sickness. It felt as if the body was reacting when shaken out of its comfort zone of illness. Typically, a new state of equilibrium would soon follow this unsettled, ill period.

During my treatment (as well as throughout life), I always asked lots of questions. I like to be aware of what is happening to me, why the doctors or therapists think they should do what they are doing, and what comes next. I think this feeds the rational need of my brain. But my acupuncturist, Chris, was a man of few words. He hardly spoke, let alone explaining the details of the treatment. I was uncomfortable in going ahead with the treatment when I knew so little about what was happening. It probably made me feel as if I was not in control of the situation, or that I didn't know what to expect. But with Chris I learnt to simply trust and carry on, without asking too many questions or feeding the rational side of the brain. I knew that he knew what he was doing; he knew what I wanted to achieve; and for a change, it was so nice to let go of the steering wheel, not trying to be in control of the situation. Thank you, Chris.

Reiki: Throughout cancer and afterwards, I practiced Reiki on myself, to expedite the healing and to manage the side effects of the treatment. Reiki is the universal life force energy, which flows freely throughout the universe. Reiki or the healing energy can be tapped by every human being through a process called attunement, which needs to be done by a Reiki teacher. Once attunement has been completed, the person becomes capable of tapping this universal life force energy. I have been a Reiki practitioner for over ten years. I have always benefitted from Reiki, and it proved to be very useful during cancer treatment too.

Biodynamic massage: Biodynamic massage is a form of massage that addresses both the body and the mind. It affects all aspects of our being – mental, physical, emotional and spiritual – using a wide range of techniques. The underlying theory of biodynamic massage is that we digest unexpressed emotions and the after-effects of stress through the digestive organs; a process called psycho-peristalsis. The therapist uses a tiny stethoscope to listen to the client's peristalsis, for feedback on how they are responding to the massage.

My therapist, Daniel, worked with me based on my physical and emotional needs, and used touch as an invitation to engage in a deeper relationship with myself. This massage recognises the connection between repressed emotions or energy and physical health. Stresses, strains, and traumas held in the body can, over time, give rise to problems and illness. The effects can manifest in physical troubles or emotional issues. In this massage, the relationship and trust with the therapist is of paramount importance. If during the massage, my mind wandered, Daniel was able to figure it out immediately and bring me back to the present moment.

After the biodynamic massage, I always felt at peace. The constant chatter that seemed to otherwise go on in my head calmed down. Daniel encouraged me to listen to what my body told me. For instance, if I felt the need to rest, I must stop watching TV and lie down. I must say that I felt little change after the first session; I felt relaxed, for sure, but nothing more. But like acupuncture, the benefit of biodynamic massage also builds up gradually. I remember that after the fourth session, I was so much at peace that I came back home and slept for several hours. My contentment with the self increased more and more, and my need to depend on external distractions reduced, as I progressed with the biodynamic massage.

Healthy eating: For me, cancer treatment was synonymous with healthy eating. I ate healthy soups (spinach and watercress being the most regular one) frequently. My mum ensured that the food was very low on fat and high on good ingredients like protein. We also became used to eating food without spices.

Abhi and Mum supported me diligently when I was on a diet that was not really tasty (applicable for the times when I could taste food). I was completely off spices and fats. Simple food that met my health needs was cooked, and everyone ate the same food. There never was a situation when I ate boring food and they ate delicious food. It was a simple but strong gesture of solidarity from them.

Later on, as I recovered, I attended various workshops on raw foods, juices, smoothies, and other health foods at The Haven. Moving away from sugar still seems to be the biggest challenge for me. I do know that with all the hormonal treatment that I am going through, sugar would just contribute to weight gain, which is not good. But as I write this, my battle to give up sugar completely is on-going, and sugar remains my poison.

Walking: During chemotherapy, I was mostly unable to go for regular walks. The weather was very cold too. However, I tried to incorporate walking in my routine whenever I went to the hospital (and you know that I went there an awful lot). The hospital was over a mile away from the train station, and I always made it a point to walk both ways. I did this without exception: whether I was there for a consultation or a scan or chemotherapy or Herceptin – although I must admit that I needed to walk more than I actually did. I picked up walking as a mode of exercise after chemotherapy got over. Gradually, I made sure to walk if I had to go to any place within the radius of two miles. I reduced my dependence on buses for local trips like going to the High Street or the town centre. Walking helped to keep me healthy.

Swimming: It had been ten years since I stepped into a swimming pool. I had forgotten whatever little I knew of swimming. My new oncologist had suggested that I take up swimming as an exercise. And so I enrolled for weekly swimming lessons.

When I entered the pool, I was afraid to put my face under water. As soon as I went under water, I would start gasping for air. I shared my fear of water with the instructor. She was considerate. She said that there was no hurry, and that I could start putting my head under the water when I felt ready to. She did caution that I must not leave it for too long, otherwise I would find it challenging later.

I was given the floating muscles, and I swam and floated in the first session. I did not feel ready to get my face underwater, and so I didn't. Next week, I went back to swimming class, tried to get underwater, and again I panicked and stood up. I was scared. As I stood in the shallow end of the pool, gathering my breath after the initial panic, I thought of my life over last eight months. My previous life flashed before me, followed by the one with cancer. A wry smile appeared on my face as I realised that life does not give you unlimited time to continue being scared. If I wanted to battle my fear of getting underwater, it had to be right then. I took a deep breath, shaped my body into a streamlined position, and plunged into the water.

Swimming helped me to gradually build stamina. The happy hormones released with all the swimming and other modes of exercise helped too. It turned out to be very effective in managing lymphoedema.

Homeopathy: Soon after the diagnosis, someone had suggested that I consider homeopathy as the mainstream treatment. However, I had chosen not to. Maybe homeopathy can cure cancer, I have no idea; but I felt safer with conventional medicine. I didn't want to take any chances with cancer.

I used homeopathy to recover from the side effects of cancer treatment, after all the six chemotherapy sessions were over. It helped me immensely in recovering from side effects such as insomnia, weakness, fatigue, and sickness.

The surgery had left a patch on my arm where I had lost sensation. I also felt shooting pains, like electric shocks, in the operated area. I developed a lot of scar tissue after the surgery, which was painful. Homeopathy helped to alleviate these symptoms. Similarly, when the side effects of radiation therapy set in, homeopathy helped me recover. It was especially good in healing the burnt skin and tackling insomnia.

As more time passed, Lorraine Smillie, my homeopath, began to give me remedies that would try to bring my body back into equilibrium. Later, when I was feeling low, Lorraine gave me other remedies that helped me emotionally. With her support, I started healing and putting the trauma of cancer behind me.

Reflexology: Reflexology, or foot massage, helped to ease the fatigue in my legs. While acupuncture and homeopathy helped to ease the severe pain in my legs that had developed when the radiation therapy was coming to an end, they didn't cure it. Later, I used reflexology along with EFT tapping (described later in this section) to further alleviate the pain. It was a reflexologist who thought that the pain was actually sciatica[40], while another one thought that it was probably tendonitis[41] that had been triggered due to radiation therapy.

---

[40] Sciatica pain: Sciatica is pain associated with the sciatic nerve which runs from the back of pelvis through buttocks, down the legs and ends at the feet.
NHS Choices. "Sciatica." Last modified August 2014. http://www.nhs.uk/conditions/sciatica/Pages/Introduction.aspx. Last accessed December 05, 2014.

[41] Tendonitis: Tendonitis refers to inflammation of a tendon, the tissue that attaches a bone to a muscle.
Patient.co.uk. "Tendonitis and Tenosynovitis." Last modified June 2013. http://www.patient.co.uk/health/tendonitis-and-tenosynovitis. Last accessed December 05, 2014.

After suffering from this pain for over six months, I had myself checked for vitamin D. Guess what? The results showed that the vitamin D in my blood was extremely low; it fell within the lowest range that is picked up in the blood test. The vitamin D must have dropped so low because I had spent the larger part of the last fourteen months staying at home, and my vegetarian diet did not supply much of this nutrient. We had a gorgeous summer in the UK in 2013, but I found it difficult to step out that season because the heat aggravated the side effects from cancer. Lack of vitamin D is responsible for aches and pains in the body. Watch out for vitamin D, if your illness is preventing you from getting enough sunlight.

After chemotherapy, the body loves to react to almost everything. I became excited rather early about the discovery of my vitamin D deficiency. I thought it was time for the resolution of the pain in my leg. I was given the highest dose of vitamin D (20,000 units of vitamin D$_3$, three times a week), to tackle this deficiency. I benefitted within a week after I began taking the supplements. However, after two weeks, I developed symptoms[42] of excessive thirst, increased trips to the loo, nausea and vomiting, dizziness and headaches. I felt as if lots of the side effects from chemotherapy times were back. My reflexologist brought to my attention that it was probably the vitamin D supplements that were causing these chemo-like symptoms. An immediate Google search suggested that she was probably right. I had to stop the supplements immediately. The symptoms settled, but this meant that my initial problem of vitamin D deficiency still remained to be dealt with. Nadia, the fabulous therapist and nutritionist at The Haven, advised me on how I could tackle the vitamin D deficiency through nutrition. Her advice worked, and in two months' time, my vitamin D levels changed

---

[42] Side effects of vitamin D supplements: Side effects from Vitamin D supplements are extremely rare but possible.
Patient.co.uk. "Vitamin D Deficiency including Osteomalacia and Rickets." Last modified July 2012. http://www.patient.co.uk/health/vitamin-d-deficiency-including-osteomalacia-and-rickets-leaflet. Last accessed December 05, 2014.

from non-existent to good. The leg pain reduced, but still remained unresolved.

Through further consultations, I was referred to a podiatrist, who figured out that my foot had developed something called a neuroma. An ultrasound scan confirmed that it was the inflammation of a neuroma[43] as well as of a bursa[44]. Finally, I seemed to know what was going on with the foot, after enduring the pain for fourteen months. Now was the time to get rid of the neuroma and bursa, with targeted treatment. I went for the treatment (read: ultrasound guided anti-inflammatory steroidal injection). The injection was extremely painful, as it was put in at the exact spot that hurt. I limped and suffered with a swollen foot for a week, but it really helped to alleviate the leg and foot pain.

Counselling: I never saw myself as a person who would benefit from counselling. I always thought that the support from family and friends was sufficient to take care of my emotional needs. Maybe somewhere deep inside me I also associated counselling with therapy for the weak. Therefore, going for something like counselling just did not agree with my self-image of a strong person. But cancer turned out to be an exception.

I remember meeting my counsellor, Emma, and asking for some tools that I could use as self-help techniques. Emma didn't say no; she indulged me and said that we would eventually get there. In the beginning, I felt that I was not benefitting at all from the sessions. What I hadn't yet understood was that counselling was not a quick-fix solution to problems.

---

[43] NHS Choices. "Morton's neuroma." Last modified December 2014. http://www.nhs.uk/conditions/mortonsneuroma/pages/introduction.aspx. Last accessed April 13, 2015.

[44] NHS Choices. "Bursitis – Treatment." Last modified January 2013. http://www.nhs.uk/Conditions/Bursitis/Pages/Treatment.aspx. Last accessed December 05, 2014.

So one day, I asked Emma if she could give me some tools to manage my anxiety. I had been a problem-solver all my life, and I was in my 'I have got to fix this myself' mode. She responded, 'Before we do that, let us try and explore why you get anxious.' By the end of the session, she had directed my thoughts to help me figure out the reason for the anxiety. What I had been asking for was a solution, like taking paracetamol when there was fever. But what she had done was to look at the reason that was causing the fever, instead of merely treating the symptom, a temperature. That was the first session in which I understood the value that I was getting through counselling.

As we progressed through the sessions, the discussions became more contemplative. With Emma's help, I was able to explore some patterns in my thinking. She also helped me understand the traits of my personality, based on my upbringing. When we finished the sessions, there was a clear shift within me, from an angry person to a more contemplative person, who got in touch with her inner self more deeply.

Believe me: counselling is not just for people who have insufficient support from family and friends. Working with a trained psychotherapist or a counsellor can help you see patterns in your thinking, or explore the reasons behind your behaviour, or even dive into those aspects of your personality that you did not know existed. It is not a solution that can bring in changes overnight. But it worked for me, because I was willing to put in an effort to work with myself.

Hypnotherapy: I checked out hypnotherapy, not only as a therapy to recover from side effects of cancer treatment, but also because of the sheer fascination of what it can do (or what I thought it could do).

In simple terms, hypnotherapy enables the therapist to access the client's subconscious mind. It can be used to achieve various changes in health, psychology, or behaviour. The therapist makes suggestions to the client who is in the state of trance, which is essentially a state of extreme relaxation. You feel heaviness in the arms and legs; you can still move them, but you would rather not.

When I met my hypnotherapist, Patrick, for the first time, I had been plagued with insomnia – I had been able to sleep well only for two nights in the last two weeks. Out of the various changes that I imagined myself achieving through hypnotherapy, being able to sleep well was the most immediate concern. Patrick and I discussed my needs and we arrived at some goals. Subsequently, he induced the state of trance, and when I came out of the trance, I felt relaxed and calm. He also 'planted' the suggestion that I should find sleeping easy when I go to bed at night. Indeed, I did. It was such a relief to be able to sleep well. Anyone who has been on cancer treatment knows how precious sleep becomes!

Subsequently, I used self-hypnosis to work on insomnia and for relaxation, through Patrick's Apple apps.

Mind and body therapy: 'Thoughts become things' is the philosophy based on which many complementary therapies work. Ruks suggested there might be something that I was doing (consciously or unconsciously) which was causing all my illnesses. I had noticed that my body had a tendency to grow lumps: fibroadenoma, fibroid, and then cancer. These were growths that were unwanted and undesired in my body. Most of these were fast-growing and they grew larger than what was typically expected of such masses.

With cancer behind me (but with the possibility of a recurrence), I wanted to do everything that was within my reach to get better. Mind-body therapy was one of the initiatives I undertook to achieve this.

As a person who would always assign a rational explanation to every situation and move on, I had not really explored the correlation between mind and body. But we know better than to expect or assume that rationality works everywhere in life, don't we? So, while I thought I was handling a few things (read: emotions) rationally, I was not. Over the last two years, I had been introspecting to try and figure out why I had been ill so often all my life. Why should I catch a cold if someone only sneezed in my vicinity, and why should I take weeks to recover from it afterwards, when most people recovered from it more quickly? Let me tell you that I could not find answers to my questions. Some ideas were presented to me from a complementary healing point of view, but I could not relate to them. I believed in the concept of complementary healing, but perhaps I was not reaching deep enough within myself to understand what I needed to do.

Therefore, after battling serious illnesses for about two years, I was ready to let go of whatever had been causing misery in my life. It sounds only logical – we must get rid of what is detrimental to our well-being. But is it all that easy to implement? How easy is it to throw away the cloak of misery under which we have become accustomed to living, and start all over again? Do we even know that there is such misery? Are we aware that we can choose to throw it away, and let the fresh air ventilate our system and clear the cobwebs? I'd say that we know this only at a cognitive level, where we rationalize and assign pragmatic explanations to everything – but it takes a deeper knowledge to do something about it. And so, after a great deal of introspection, I found myself sitting in a room called 'Jade' with the transformational coach, Gosia, from Poland.

Gosia asked me to think of the emotions that I wanted to get rid of. She said that she would ask me specific questions, and I must respond without thinking too much, a bit like a rapid-fire game. She also asked me to just go with the flow, and participate in the entire session as if we were playing a game. Thanks to the introspection I had been doing, I knew to a large extent what was going on inside my head. This is how the session progressed:

'What are the negative emotions that you experience?' Gosia asked.

'Anger. And hurt.'

'Why do you feel angry?'

Among other kinds of anger, I had realised that I had been angry about something that someone had said to me seven years ago. They had said it multiple times, and I just hadn't been able to let go of it. The anger got to me so badly that it almost consumed me. I was always angry with the person who said that hurtful thing. You may call it irrationality; but that is what happened. I could not let go of this anger.

My logical side was not helping either. I was mad over something that someone else had said and in the process I was letting them decide whether I should be happy or not. Also, the fact that I had not really stood up to them, or told them how they were impacting me, made me feel terrible. I was angry with myself, as I had just taken the victim's position and hadn't really done anything about my pain. This worsened the situation, as I wanted to have accountability for my happiness and my life. But there I was: livid that someone had said bad things about something very precious to me, that I had taken no action. It became a deadlock: I tried to battle that anger and when I could not, it aggravated my annoyance. As a person, I don't usually get bogged down by what others have to say, save for a few things that are key to my value system. It was one of those things – and I couldn't give it up, even if the anger was detrimental to me.

I have been told repeatedly that my illnesses (a huge uterine fibroid, and later cancer) were products of this hurt and anger. All the negative energy that developed inside me had to be channelled somewhere. So, my body harboured it in the form of unwanted growths inside me. Although I worried that anger might have caused the stress and subsequently these illnesses, the current evidence[45] points to a different truth. According to current research, there is very little correlation between anger or stress and cancer. Anger and stress definitely damage the quality of your life, but they do not increase the risk of cancer. Thinking back, I realise that for about two and a half years before the cancer was diagnosed, I had been unwell. There had been several inexplicable symptoms in my body, and the diagnostic tests could not confirm anything. There was this terrible cough that shook my body each time it came. There were changes in my skin. I was achy all the time, and felt low on energy. There were days when just a normal routine exhausted me, and I found it difficult to even move because of exhaustion. I wasn't sure why this was happening. But after I finished the cancer treatment, all these weird unexplained symptoms disappeared too. Perhaps it was my body telling me that some changes had set in, and that it was time to sit up and take notice.

Honestly, I do not know if my anger caused the cancer or other illnesses. It is possible that such an opinion was just a judgement that was being passed on my condition. But what I do know is that I had been angry for many years, and that day when I sat opposite Gosia, I was ready to let go. I wanted to let go of this anger and hurt – not because I had come to terms with the awful things that had been said to me, but because I deserved happiness. I was ready to let go and move beyond what they had said. I was ready to move beyond my inability to prevent that statement and its memory from affecting me. I was exhausted, I needed help, and I was open to taking the help I needed.

---

[45]   Breastcancer.org. "October 2000: Feelings About Breast Cancer." Last modified September 2012. http://www.breastcancer.org/tips/ask_expert/2000_10#qdoes-anger-or-sadness-cause-cancer. Last accessed December 05, 2014.
And
National Cancer Institute. "Psychological Stress and Cancer." Last modified October 2012. http://www.cancer.gov/cancertopics/factsheet/Risk/stress. Last accessed December 05, 2014.

Gosia went on to ask, 'On a scale of 1 to 10, 10 being the worst, how angry are you?'

'I'd say 9. I am very angry about it,' I confessed.

Gosia came up with a very interesting explanation of why I was so angry. She summarized it in a simple sentence, 'You are a control freak.'

I was indignant. 'Huh! I am sorry. How can you say that? And... anyhow, what does being angry have to do with being a control freak?'

'I say that you are a control freak because you have been trying to control what others should think, and what is appropriate for them to say. You have been busy thinking that it was wrong on their part to say what they said.'

'Yes, and I still believe that such an act or saying something like this is atrocious.' Period.

She replied, 'I agree that it is wrong; but why do you want to control how they think? In simpler words, your expectation that people should not have said what they said is misplaced. Did you ever make it clear to them how this statement was affecting you?'

'No, I didn't. If they cared enough, they probably would not have thought of or suggested such a horrendous thing.'

'But it is possible that they are not even aware that you are hurt. Do you think that it is possible?'

There was a pause. A long pause. A strange pause.

'Yes, I think it is possible,' I said.

'I am not asking you to agree with what they said. I am not asking you to accept their way of thinking. And I am not asking you to condone their behaviour. What I am asking you to do is to stop battling it. Look at this wall. What will happen if I push against it for two hours?'

'You will hurt yourself.'

'Yes, I will probably have a dislocated shoulder. In your case, you are battling that wall – the wall of negativity and expectation. It is pushing you back, and hurting you.'

'I know that the person who said all this is, otherwise, a very loving person. But I have not been able to move on – even after they stopped saying this.'

'You don't need to qualify anything here,' Gosia said gently.

'I want to – because I want you to know that we are talking about a person who is good at heart. But they have said bad things, or things that I perceive as bad or wrong. I have tried to get over it, but I have not been able to. I am sure that this hurt and anger are hurting me not only emotionally but also physically. I don't quite understand how thoughts manifest as various conditions in the body, but I believe that they do.'

She replied, 'That is why we will work at letting go. I will help you to get rid of this anger and hurt. Let us get started. I want you to take this as a game, and just do it, and not read too much into it.'

'OK – let us give it a try. Although I must admit that my rational mind is sceptical about whether someone else can help me with this. It is not that I don't know what I need to do, but I have not been able to achieve it.'

'Answer one more question. Why are you hurt and how badly are you hurt?'

'When I was diagnosed with cancer, there were family and friends who completely withdrew from me. Some of them did not even ask me how I was. They could not find even five minutes to speak to me, over the last eight months. I am badly hurt at this behaviour. I'd say it is a 5 on the scale now, but it was definitely 9 when it happened.'

Gosia said that she had met some cancer patients and survivors whose families had withdrawn from them during their illness. Some of them were OK with that behaviour, while others were not. I was in the latter category, primarily because I had a pre-defined idea how people should have behaved during my illness. When they didn't do what I thought was appropriate, I was hurt.

Gosia asked me, the newly discovered control freak, to repeat whatever she said, while tapping at specific points on my hand. How would that help? The rational, pragmatic monster started raising its head inside me, and I had to beat it to a pulp to keep up with what Gosia was saying. The only thing she explained to me was that tapping would help to clear out the blocked energy channels in my body, removing the negative emotions.

It was time to start tapping. We did it in three steps.

Step one: I rated my distress at about 9 on a scale of 10 – here we tackled the anger that I had been harbouring inside me.

Step two: Affirmation and acceptance time.

- Even if I am very angry with this person (I said the name of the person) for saying something so horrendous (I actually mentioned what was said), I deeply and completely accept myself.

- Even if I am very angry with this person (name of the person) for saying something so horrendous (actual mention of what was said), I deeply and completely accept myself.
- Even if I am very angry with this person (name of the person) for saying something so horrendous (actual mention of what was said), I deeply and completely accept myself.

Step three: The actual tapping.

Gosia asked me to repeat the reminder phrase of the problem (naming the anger that I had), while tapping seven or eight times on various spots on my body – the top of my head, the beginning of my eyebrow, the bone at the side of the eye, the bone just under the eye, the spot between the nose and the upper lip, the spot between the bottom lip and the chin, just under the collarbone, and about four inches under the armpit.

We continued repeating this, while I said the two phrases: in the first, I acknowledged my deep-seated anger and accepted myself, and in the second, I repeated that I was angry.

After this, she asked me to hold the door stopper in my hand, and imagine that all the anger in my heart was being sucked into it. Once all the anger had been sucked in, she asked me to drop that door stopper on the floor. We repeated this a few more times.

When we had finished tapping and dropping the door stopper on the floor, she asked me how angry I felt. I looked deep within and was surprised to find that the anger had decreased. From a 9, it had moved to maybe a 5. In fact, my rational mind was telling me that I should be angry. How could I not be angry towards that person, just after spending ten minutes or so on tapping? I looked within myself again, and was surprised to find little anger. Acknowledging my anger was the first step towards resolving it. I was not pushing against the wall anymore.

I was sceptical, and shared my concern with Gosia. She explained that she could work with me only in the present moment. I might need to do the tapping exercise to clear the energy within me, time and again. Gradually, the anger would be resolved.

I said, 'But I don't really remember much of what you said. I was concentrating on repeating what you said, and didn't register enough to be able to do the exercise at home by myself.'

'Don't worry. I will send you some tools by email that will help you practice what we just did.'

Gosia helped me visualise what I wanted in my life about seven years from now: a happy relationship with Abhi, a successful career, a healthy body, and a lovely healthy daughter. The to-be life felt perfect.

My session had come to an end. I felt lighter. I was not sure if my head and heart would continue to be at peace, but I felt light at that moment. I thanked Gosia and left.

Gosia sent me a couple of documents by email the following day. When I went through them, I found out that the tapping we were doing was a technique called the EFT[46] – the Emotional Freedom Technique. It is an emotional healing technique that also relieves many physical symptoms. More than twenty hours had passed since my session with Gosia. I took a break from reading to check if the memory we had dealt with yesterday triggered an angry reaction. Poof! While the memory was there, there was no charge or anger. I was clearly experiencing something new and

---

[46]   For Dummies. "Emotional Freedom Technique For Dummies (UK Edition)." http://www.dummies.com/how-to/content/emotional-freedom-technique-for-dummies-cheat-shee.html. Last accessed December 05, 2014.
And
The EFT Centre. "What is EFT and Why is Everyone Talking about It?" http://www.theeftcentre.com/eft.html. Last accessed February 14, 2015.

miraculous. I decided to try it on other things, to clear out the negative energy in me, and also to reinforce the absence of anger.

I felt free. I was letting open the gates of the prison that I had trapped myself in over the past several years. To use Ruks' language, I was letting go.

A few weeks later, I saw Gosia again. The day was the 7th of July, a special day. Before I left home for my appointment with Gosia, I picked up the hair brush from the dressing table and used it – after more than eight and a half months! It didn't do much, but it helped to settle some stubborn hair that had chosen to poke out of my head. It felt good to hold the brush in my hand and comb my hair.

This time I worked on two other negative feelings. Incidentally, while I felt better during the second session, the negative emotions came back after a while. So I had to repeat the techniques that Gosia had taught me, to move beyond the negativity.

As I write about my experience with Gosia, I suddenly feel aware of a pattern in me. Gosia had told me that I had a need to be in control of things. I also had expectations of situations or people. When I felt that things were not in my control, or they didn't meet my expectations, I would get stressed. When I look back at my cancer journey, I realise that this pattern showed up time and again. There are so many examples.

When the hair loss didn't set in for the first two weeks after chemotherapy started, I started hoping that it would not happen to me. I had been told that it would happen for sure, but a part of me wanted to be in control of the situation. In this case, I did lose my hair.

When there was a likelihood that I would lose my nails, I again started hoping that it wouldn't happen to me. I could have just gone with the flow, and waited for things to unfold. It was not in my control – and wasting breath over it was useless.

When I was taking acupuncture sessions, I wanted to know what exactly we were doing, what we were aiming for, and how long we expected to take to reach the goal. Thankfully, with Chris, I learnt to trust and not feed the rational side of the mind all the time.

Similarly, as Gosia said, I expected certain people to keep in touch with me when I was unwell. When this need was not met, I felt hurt. I also hoped that people would be more sensitive and stop passing negative remarks, during or after the treatment. Gosia thought that I was trying to control how they should view my situation and how they should behave. In reality, my situation (of undergoing cancer) had nothing much to do with the expectations that I had of people. I was no one to decide how they should behave. What was in my control was to choose how I would behave if someone I loved was going through a similar situation.

During cancer, there were so many times when I wanted to perform simple tasks, like fixing a quick meal for myself, but was unable to do so. I felt under-utilised, useless, and most of all, not in control of my life. I was not really used to having others do things for me, and it felt weird to depend on them for most of my needs. It was a blow to my ego. I also like to utilise my time as much as possible. Doing nothing was sacrilege to me. Here I was, forced into a situation where fighting fatigue was becoming impossible. I had to learn what Ruks had told me umpteen times – that I should let others take care of me, and not have the need to do everything myself. She said that it was also a journey for them, which would help them evolve. Indeed it was a journey.

It was now time to let go of being in control, and learn to move with the flow of life.

In the end, only three things matter: how much you loved, how gently you lived, and how gracefully you let go of things not meant for you.
- Buddha

The day I cried in public

I was at St George's Hospital for the Herceptin treatment. I had left home at 9 am and it was about 2:30 pm when my treatment finished. Based on my very limited stamina, it had been a pretty long day for me. I was tired and hungry, and I wanted to reach home as soon as possible.

There was a direct bus that I could take from the hospital to home. So I got on the bus and sat quietly with my head resting against the window. It was a weekday and there were only three passengers onboard. The fatigue overtook me and I tried to doze off. Suddenly I awoke with a start when I sensed some commotion in the bus. I turned back and saw the man sitting a few seats away from me was having a severe fit. It was a scary moment. His body convulsed, and his hands were turned inside out. The other girl on the bus and I called out to the driver, and he responded immediately. He pulled the bus into the closest bus stop. The vehicle came to a halt. Before the three of us (two co-passengers and the driver) could say anything, we saw a lady knock at the door violently. The driver opened the door.

When the bus pulled in at the bus stop, this lady was standing there. She had been waiting for another bus. She had a friend who suffered from a medical condition in which he got fits. When she saw the man having fits from outside the bus, she knocked on the door to help out. She knew the first aid he needed! It was the month of May, and the weather was still cold in London. So the bus had the heater on and all the windows were closed. She walked into the bus and threw open all the windows where the man was sitting...and behold! He started taking deeper breaths and his face began to return to normal. All this happened within the span of less than a minute.

I pulled out my phone and called the emergency helpline. It was my first call to any emergency number, and I was making it for a co-passenger on the bus. I now realise that I did not do a brilliant job of giving the details to the emergency helpline team. Never mind – it was an emergency and I was allowed to be confused! Simultaneously, the driver went back to his cabin and he placed a call to the emergency helpline too. For some reason, I was still speaking to the emergency rescue team when help arrived, thanks to the call made by the driver. The experts hopped out of the NHS ambulance and boarded our bus to look after the man. His fits had stopped, and he was in safe hands. Relieved, I stepped out of the bus into the open and cold bus stop.

I had tears in my eyes. I was crying because it had hurt me to see that man have such terrible fits on the bus. He had no company, and I did not know how much lag time was permitted in his condition before getting help. I was reminded of my chemotherapy days, when I would travel on the bus and train alone for multiple appointments. There was always the fear that I might not be able to cope with the stress and fatigue of travel. Therefore, I carried my treatment plan book in my bag all the time. If I crashed someday during travel, and if someone looked into my bag, they would easily find the relevant details about my cancer treatment.

Looking at that man, I was reminded of the pain that I had been through and that he potentially might be going through. I heard a lady comment that when people have such terrible diseases, they must always be accompanied by someone. Very logical, thank you. But isn't it rather impractical? Not everyone is blessed to have company each time they need to step out of home. It is just not feasible. Having lived through a difficult treatment and attended most of the appointments alone, I knew that having someone accompany you all the time is not realistic. If I had expected Abhi to come with me for every appointment, he would have missed work for a good six months. Somebody needed to go and earn for the family; I wasn't working, and if I'd stopped Abhi from working, there would have been enormous financial pressure upon us. But of course, you tend to know these things only when you have first-hand experience of such a situation. People judge all the time, and we can't expect them to understand what we are going through.

I was crying not only because I was reminded of the pain that I had been through because of cancer, but also because I was happy to see that help had arrived for the man on time. Cancer had brought back the empathy that I had lost under the pretext of growing up and becoming pragmatic.

Thank you, cancer!

When I look back, I do realise that while I was busy making rational choices and taking all the right steps to sort things out, I hardly got in touch with my feelings. What I was *feeling* had been swept under the carpet (by me). I was not really processing much, on an emotional level. That is the reason why I felt calm most of the time. There were so many feelings, especially of fear, that were left to be explored. The fear of being a burden on my family, fear of losing control over my life, fear of the uncertainty of what lay ahead, fear of physical and emotional dependence, fear of my worsening physical appearance, fear of the loss of a breast, fear of immeasurable physical and emotional pain, fear of the inability to work and its impact on my career, fear of financial instability, fear of the cancer recurring after being cured, and the biggest fear of all – the fear of mortality. I was afraid of dying, and along with it came the fear that I might have to leave Abhi behind. I am someone who worries about his every meal and every mood fluctuation, and the thought that I might not be there to look after him and to love him was shattering and intimidating. Although I did not take the time to explore my feelings, inside, I was on a rollercoaster ride of emotions.

I did not give myself a chance to grieve or be sad, because I jumped into the 'I need to act now to get rid of cancer' mode. This was not a bad thing to do. It did more good than harm (I believe so) and helped me immensely in getting through the treatment. However, all those bottled up feelings came back to haunt me, later, when I had some time to breathe. And so I felt low on energy for several months.

Time passed; it was now August 2013, and I still felt low often. I was still rationally taking care of myself and of our home, and doing whatever I must do to recover from the side effects of the treatment; but I was not like I had been before – effervescent and always full of energy. There were several days when I didn't feel like speaking to people. I no longer called up my friends or wrote to them regularly. At times, I called up my parents, once every several days. Often I needed time alone. My current mood (and it had been this way since April) didn't agree with the self-image of a strong person. I had changed. I was not 'me from the pre-cancer days'. Cancer had left me with several scars that could be seen, and many others that couldn't. They said in the movie *Trial by Fire Lives Re-forged*, 'Scars are like tattoos - but with better stories.' I was struggling to find the stories in my scars, to view them as tattoos.

Cancer had made me feel vulnerable.

I visited a cancer support centre, and was reassured by the therapist – again – that it was normal to feel low after cancer treatment. Really, was it OK to not feel OK? There were times when I wanted to cry, and I wanted to cry alone. During the entire cancer experience, I had hardly cried, because I had to be strong – for myself, for Abhi, and to get through the treatment. Now that the worst was over, most of the people had gone back to their lives, while mine was still moving slowly. I felt misunderstood many times. I felt that people did not really understand what was going on with me. All the hormonal treatment definitely had a role to play in making me feel this way. I had expected that I would pick up my life and get on with it, once I was cancer-free. But this was not how things went.

I used acupuncture and homeopathy to tackle my depleted energy levels and enthusiasm. They definitely helped. If you have been going through a similar phase of feeling low, seek help – either in conventional medicine or alternate medicine, whichever works for you. I can tell you from experience that you will need to be at your 100% (or whatever best is feasible) to battle this illness. Therefore, do everything possible to keep psychologically and physically fit.

How could you help someone going through cancer treatment?

The world of cancer is complicated. From understanding the reason why it happens to people, to the difficulties of treatment, to the variations in how different people respond to the same treatment, to the physiological scarring, the physical and emotional vulnerability caused by it, and why it comes back in some people and does not in others – it is all challenging to understand. Likewise, another complicated matter to understand is how a cancer diagnosis impacts relationships. I now understand that people find it difficult to talk to someone with cancer, and they have good reasons. However, this understanding came once I had crossed the bridge to being a cancer survivor.

If you know someone who has received a cancer diagnosis, I hope these tips will be useful to you and them. These tips are based on the literature that I have read and on my own experiences; they also describe how I would have felt better supported during my cancer journey. I promise I'll try my best not to be preachy.

1. **Day to day chores:** Cancer takes a toll on your physical health, and doing the most basic tasks becomes impossible. Can you help out with some shopping or washing? My friend, Sarah, once took me out for a shopping trip, and it was so helpful. When my father was visiting, he took care of all the shopping for two months, and it was such a relief for Abhi and for me. When our energy was limited, we didn't want to spend it buying

groceries and fruits. Online shopping was a life saver, as it took away the physical effort of going out and shopping.

2. **Talking and listening:** There are some people who connect by talking. I fall into this category. The only support that I need from most people in my life is that they remain connected with me – talking and listening is enough. It is extremely rare that I expect others to do anything else for me. Therefore, when some of my folks pulled away, I felt that my support system was adversely impacted.

However, if your friend who has been diagnosed happens to be among those people who prefer not to talk about difficult personal situations, then please back off. One of my friends was diagnosed with cancer a few weeks before I was. After the diagnosis, she spent a couple of days calling up everyone in her family and friends whom she felt close to. She shared the bad news with them, and also mentioned that she wanted to go through the experience only with her husband and daughters. She said that she would be in touch when the cancer was behind her and she felt ready to talk about it. I really appreciated her forthrightness, and also that her folks respected her request. They stayed out of touch, as was expected of them.

You may be worried that you may end up saying something inappropriate. If that is your fear, you can be there for the person by listening actively. Listening can be such a big support. Many times, what we want of others is just a listening ear. We don't really expect them to solve our problems for us. Also, the fact that you are there for your loved one will supersede what you will say. Of course, you must ensure that you follow the basic rules and avoid hurtful comments – for instance, I was actually told (more than once) that some people whom I loved and who loved me could die of shock and pain when they found out about my diagnosis. Somehow, the person who said this to me seemed completely sure that those people would die if they got to know about my cancer diagnosis. Each time I heard this, I felt rage in the pit of my stomach, in the deepest possible part. It quickly rose and engulfed my visceral organs – the gut, the intestines, the inner lining of my torso. It reached out for my heart and it hurt badly. I seriously think that it was a very unkind thing to say.

It is unfair to say how your life has been messed up because of someone's cancer. Cancer is a medical condition, and it can happen to anyone. When it happens, it is immensely painful for everyone involved. This, however, does not mean that the person who has this diagnosis needs to take responsibility for everyone else's agony - not because they don't or should not care, but because they neither have any role in getting cancer, nor any role in hurting people because they have the cancer diagnosis.

I felt scared because I had cancer. I was in pain because the treatment was very difficult, physically and psychologically. I was hurt because I was being held responsible for the misery and even the potential death of my loved ones.

I believe that it is not up to human beings to decide who should live or die, or stay happy or unhappy. It is not our prerogative to make such critical decisions. Such decisions are for the Higher Powers, whether you call them God, Nature, or Destiny.

If affecting a life was in the hands of a cancer patient, I am sure they would bargain for one specific life with the Powers above – *their own*!

We also need to understand that when someone is going through cancer, they are in a far more vulnerable place than usual. If I were told today that someone I love would die if the news of my cancer diagnosis reached them, I'd say, 'Are you crazy? Who do you think I am, that I have power to "cause" the death of other people?' I would still get irritated, but I think I would stand up to them. But things were different when I was going through cancer. By telling me and Abhi such things, these people were fuelling some of our worst fears – mine of causing pain and suffering to my loved ones; and Abhi's fear of losing still more people who mattered to him, even as he was dealing with the possibility of losing me. Through their own fears, these people were also adding weight to the whole concept of loss and bereavement.

I remained angry with these people for several months, but I later realised that I should give them the benefit of the doubt. Maybe each time they looked at me, all they saw was mortality and the transience of life. My illness probably forced them to face their darkest fears about losing their loved ones. While I think I understood their situation at an intellectual level, I took a long time to come to terms with it at an emotional level (and only after doing a lot of work at the spiritual level).

In short, please support your friend who has cancer by talking and listening to them; but please can you watch out if you tend to say the wrong things at the wrong time? Could you consider that maybe your feet are just too large and they might inadvertently trample on people's feelings?

3. **Offer help:** People like me want to be self-reliant, and find it difficult when they need others to take care of them. We like to continue doing our tasks like nothing has changed. But the fact is that cancer changes everything. Therefore, if you are close to someone who has cancer, then it may be useful to ask them how they want to be supported, and not go away when

the offer is initially turned down. I know you may ask why you should persist when refused. The bottom-line is that you want to help, and your friend needs help. Just as you don't know how to offer help, they may not know how to ask for it. It is a journey in which everyone is learning. Because cancer can make a person dependant on others, the patient may also feel guilty about asking for help. Both parties will need to look beyond their discomfort and guilt, to make the most of the support that is available.

4. **Respite for carers:** I realised that by the time I was through with chemotherapy, the stress to which my mum had been subjected was phenomenal. I really wished there was some way in which we could give her a respite, at least for a short while. Abhi had to put in long hours at work, while emotionally dealing with my illness. I was dealing with cancer and managing work whenever I could. My mum was looking after me, while she battled her fears and the agony of seeing me with cancer.

Over the weekends, Abhi tried to help her out with some chores. I helped her whenever I could. The objective was to give her a break from caring for me and from her other chores. I feel that it would have been more useful if she were able to get away from home (with its environment of illness), at least for a short while, which was not really feasible in our case due to her limited mobility and the severe winter.

Even though Mum was my primary carer, Abhi went through hell seeing me suffer. He also took care of me emotionally, and was therefore directly affected by what I went through. We often discussed the illness and its side effects. I am sure it must have been detrimental to his peace of mind to continue listening to such negative things. His long hours at work might have been a respite from the cancer environment, but unfortunately in our personal lives, we couldn't do away with these discussions, at least not for some time.

If you are in a similar position, I'd suggest that you look for some way to relieve the stress. In fact, you may not even realise that you are awfully stressed. But when cancer or its treatment are going on at home, stress is always within arm's reach, right close to our hearts. Better get rid of it, rather sooner than later. In the UK, cancer support centres provide support not just to patients but also to their immediate families, to help them cope with the stress of cancer. I think that it is a great idea to avail of their services. While I write this, I do appreciate that if you are working full-time, like Abhi is, you may not really get the opportunity to visit the support centres.

5. **Share your pain:** When you are in pain, please share with us what you are going through. Please remember that despite all the trouble we have been in ever since joining the Big C club, we'd like to help you. You don't need to protect us all the time. If you continue protecting us by not sharing, it can lead to frustration or guilt in us. I think it is very important for us to know what is going on with you. *Together we can survive this and we will.*

6. **Childcare:** If your friend who has been diagnosed with cancer has little children, can you help out with that aspect? It can be very difficult to manage an illness like cancer when there are little children at home. Occasionally, I have seen people in the hospital with their little children. I really think that it must be menacingly difficult to go through this treatment when they also have to look after toddlers or babies. Any support on this front will be gratefully accepted.

7. **Understanding the fears of the person who has been diagnosed:** Understanding what the other person is going

through is absolutely imperative in providing the right support. In fact, I'd say that this is the most critical thing. Most of the time, if you are sensitive and show empathy, you will be fine. But it is very easy to step on to the wrong side when dealing with someone facing cancer. Below, I have jotted down some critical things that scare a person going through cancer:

- **Poor health and the inability to take care of themselves:** This is applicable throughout the treatment, and only gets worse as the treatment progresses. Cancer is different from many other illnesses, because many people feel really ill due to the treatment and not so much due to the illness.
- **Fear of death:** It is true that more people survive cancer these days, but fear of death still remains strong. Even if a person is cured, there is always the fear of recurrence.

In my case, I must say that an 80% chance of survival looked brilliant on the 17th of September, as an initial reaction. I would be lying if I said that 80% looked good enough later. John Diamond wrote in his book *C: Because Cowards Get Cancer Too* that chances are never 80-20, or 40-60, or anything else that the doctors tell you. Chances are always 50-50: either you die of cancer, or you don't. As we progressed through treatment, there were ample times when this percentage of 80% felt like 50% or even less. During dark insomniac nights and long difficult days of treatment, many times I felt that I would not get through this illness. Sometimes I felt that even if I got cured now, cancer would come back and get me. When I went to see my consulting oncologist, Dr Charles, for follow-up appointments, there would be several breast cancer patients there. I would smile at them and even chat with a couple of them. But sometimes a little birdie inside my head would say, 'Out of the five of you in this room, there is a strong chance that one will die. Remember the chances of survival are 80%?' I would steal a look at them and wonder in my heart who it would be – one of them, or me, or probably none of us? After all, we were just talking numbers and probabilities, and nothing more!

I was told by my doctor that if people survive for ten years, then they are considered to be at the same risk as the normal population.

I understand that 'five years' or 'ten years' are just the terms used to explain the statistics. They relate to the number of people who were part of research and still alive after five or ten years. This does not mean that those people lived exactly for five or ten years and then died, nor does it mean that they were completely cured. Some may have been cured, some may have had recurrences of cancer and been alive at the end of the research, and some of the participants may have recurrences in the future and eventually die of cancer.

The statistics did not mean that I would live for just five or ten years. But when I was diagnosed with cancer, I could not put this data out of my head. The question that kept coming back to me was: Were ten years good enough? I had always been grateful to life for all the wonderful things it offers, and now I was scared that I might lose out on so much. While I was mostly optimistic about the prognosis, a part of me got scared now and then.

One of my favourite Hindi movies is *Anand*, in which the protagonist Anand is dying of lymphosarcoma of the intestines. The movie was released in 1971, when the fight against cancer was most often lost. The prognosis for cancer was not as good then as it is now. In the film, Anand says, '*Zindagi lambi nahin, badi honi chahiye.*' – Life needn't be long, but it should be fulfilled and grand. 'What a beautiful thing to say,' I'd always say! But how ironic and difficult it was to come to terms with this idea when I was put in Anand's shoes... and I was not even dying, like Anand was!

I remember that Abhi and I were once sharing my oesophagitis experience with some people. That was one of the days when we felt that I might not survive this illness. However, when we shared our apprehension about the 'dying' part, they responded with a seemingly careless 'Ah! That is OK,' and moved on to discussing something else. I thought that they probably hadn't heard me. So I repeated what I had said before. I received exactly the same response. I must admit that I found this response born of a lack of empathy, and even thought that it was very callous, when it happened. I am sure that my anger prevented me from being objective about the situation. But now that I am able to see beyond my anger, I feel that they must not have understood what the fear of death could be for me and for Abhi. With the latter understanding, their response looks more acceptable.

I was speaking to someone who played the role of primary carer for her father while he battled terminal cancer. She recounted her experience of having a particular visitor over at her place, who had 'cancer eyes'. 'Cancer eyes' is the expression she used because their eyes seemed to have only two expressions – pity and helplessness for the cancer patient and their family. The visitor didn't say anything while they quietly sipped their tea, and left without saying anything to the family they were visiting. What their cancer eyes showed was essentially a reflection of their own fears.

- **The loss of control:** I remember how I felt frustrated at not being able to do what I wanted to do. Such loss of control was difficult to cope with.
- **Having to face uncertainty:** Every cancer treatment will have some uncertainty. Will I survive or not, will the cancer

come back, if it does will it be curable, how soon will I be able to go back to work, will it be a mastectomy or a lumpectomy, will I have a normal life after cancer...? The list goes on.

• **Visible 'cancer' symptoms:** Cancer treatment has some typical side effects. I remember that I was in the pantry at the office making myself a cup of tea, when a colleague walked over and asked me if I was on chemotherapy. Sure thing, I was. I looked different. It was November and the weather was cold, but the number of layers I was wearing under my business suit looked crazy. Anyhow, the office was kept warm, and so it was not that the office interiors were cold. My nails were blue in colour and I was wearing a hat. Generally, I looked unwell. Specifically, that colleague was able to figure out that I was undergoing chemotherapy. I felt *marked* because of cancer.

She told me that her sister had been diagnosed with breast cancer, and would very soon start chemotherapy. I shared with her whatever tips I had (like shaving off the hair before hair loss sets in to prevent a painful scalp, massaging the skin and scalp with mustard or coconut or almond oil, etc.) to help out her sister, and that was the beginning of our friendship.

It is very helpful if you try and understand these changes, and how your friend or loved one going through cancer is affected by them. The best thing that you can do is neither to stare nor to look away when you witness these symptoms. Believe me, we notice! I noticed each time someone gave me a second look for my hair (or for the lack of it). Also, try not to make us feel different or ugly. I received a few comments or looks on my hair and weight, and it was not flattering at all. While I was trying to gather the smallest iota of strength to get through cancer treatment, passing a comment on my piled-up weight was important to someone! Some people may not find these comments to be very strong or hurtful. Probably these comments aren't strong on a stand-alone basis; but they quickly assume a different meaning in a larger and difficult context like cancer. Here's how such a comment could get processed in the mind of someone going through cancer:

As I catch a glimpse of myself – in the mirror hung in the bathroom, or in the glass of the window, or as I roll up the car window, I see a face that isn't as pretty as it used to be. The beautiful fringe that once adorned my forehead is long gone; my face looks weird, with no eyebrows and eyelashes. As I slip into my favourite pair of jeans, I find that they do not fit well anymore. The steroids and the rest of the treatment have made me put on so much flab. As I step on the weighing scale, the needle flickering towards a higher number makes my confidence dip in the other direction. As my fingers run over my body to apply moisturiser, they feel every scar etched out by the surgery or by the needles. My fingers gradually tend to every bit of scar tissue and all the skin burnt by radiation therapy. When I wear a low-cut dress, the scar caused by the insertion and removal of the port shows. Every time my confidence shatters into a million pieces, I pick myself up and try to move on to rebuild my life after cancer. No, I don't feel sorry for myself all the time, nor do I want you to feel sorry for me. But I have good days as well as bad days. And there are good moments in the bad days and bad moments in the good days. So while I struggle like this, a few or several times a day, you suddenly laugh and tell me that I am fat. Your lips curve in a smirk when you see my clothes bursting at the seams. You steal a glance at my head when I remove my hat and my hairless head gets exposed. Or you suggest that I should cover my head so that my mum does not feel shocked when she sees me! When you see me, you reckon that you should wait before you can let your folk see me, as 'cancer' is written all over me, and this is the news that you want to keep confined.

I don't know why you say or do these things; it may be an off-the cuff remark for you, but whenever you do it, believe me, you break my confidence.

Cancer is a difficult fight. Please try and understand the everyday struggles and trials that come with a cancer diagnosis. I request that you remember to be the friend or the family you would want, if you were the patient.

• **Social isolation:** During cancer, people tend to feel socially isolated. It maybe because they stop being fun, as they feel so poorly, and because friends and family do not know what to say or how to say it. There are some people who get ample support from their family. But not everyone is so lucky. An illness like cancer can make you feel isolated even when you have a supportive family. I remember that my friend, Sarah, visited me and it was so nice to have her. A few other friends kept in touch by email or phone or chat. All their concern and keeping in touch was gratefully received.

8. **Helping with body image:** Cancer patients have a difficult relationship with the mirror. At a cancer support group session, I once met up with several other women who had been through breast cancer. I found out that many of them hated to look at themselves in the mirror. The fact is that cancer was something none of us had chosen, and cancer had caused changes to our bodies – the loss of a part of breast, the loss of a complete breast,

the loss of both the breasts, unequal breasts, lots of scars, scar tissue after the operation, changes in the body after hormone therapy, chemotherapy and radiation therapy – many of those changes are permanent. A cancer patient has to learn to accept and love their new body, whether it consists of scars or has missing body parts. What level of effort and courage would be required to let go of your old self and embrace the new self?

I know of people whose suffering was compounded by the fact that their partners could not come to terms with cancer and the changes it caused. Imagine someone moving out of the bedroom after their spouse was diagnosed with cancer. Were they thinking that cancer is an infectious disease and that they were at risk of catching it? How shattered must the spouse have been? Someone who works at a cancer support centre told me how some people stood at a distance from cancer patients when they were in the same elevator! For God's sake, cancer is *not* contagious! Unfortunately, the stories of discomfort and ignorance about cancer are abundant.

As a partner, you can provide enormous support on the issues of self-image and sexuality. If you are not able to embrace the changes caused by cancer in your partner, it will be very difficult for your loved one to move on. If I get upset about the damage that cancer has done to me, Abhi remembers to reassure and comfort me.

9. **No pressure please:** Going through cancer treatment demands lot of courage. Since the treatment is usually long and difficult, there are abundant good days and bad days. It is natural for the patient to flip and lose optimism once in a while. During my treatment, not only did I have the expectation that I would hold myself together all the time, but I felt that others also expected this of me. At times, this pressurised me into feeling upbeat

about my situation, no matter how much pain I was in. But I now think that cancer patients will benefit if they don't have to carry the burden of being positive all the time. Please don't tell them that they ought to look after themselves, as everyone else is working hard to make them better. Such an attitude will only add to their sense of guilt and suffering. Once in a while if you just let them complain or rant, you may actually help them. Please understand that cancer makes them vulnerable.

10. **Our immediate circle:** These are the people before whom we can vent our emotions. If you fall in this circle, you can provide enormous support. Just be careful that while you are bucking someone up, you do not patronise them. The cancer patient may choose who the people in this category are. It can be someone with whom they can share everything, because they feel so close to them. Or it can be a good friend, who cares, but won't be bogged down when listening to their darkest fears.

In my case, while my mum was my primary carer, I never shared my fears about mortality with her. I felt that it would be difficult for her to listen to something like this. Maybe I was protecting her, although I am not sure if she needed any such protection. I did share everything with Abhi. I also found it useful to be able to talk about such things with a couple of my close friends (like Sarah). They were not involved in my life on a daily basis, and therefore, were able to bring an objective view to the situation.

Of course, there is nothing right or wrong about whom to choose. It simply depends on what works for whom.

11. **Work out whether your loved one wants to discuss it or not:** I was in a reflexology session with Nick, a fabulous reflexologist and an EFT practitioner. I was plugged to the

treatment machine at the hospital for Herceptin, and I was getting pampered simultaneously. It was my first session with him. He wanted to know about me and asked, 'Are you OK to talk about your condition or would you rather leave it where it belongs – in the past?' I loved his question, as it showed that he understood that some people might not be willing to discuss a painful topic. While I was open to discussing my condition, I respect the decision of those who choose not to discuss it. If the latter case applies to you, I'd humbly suggest that you be careful of not dealing with it or sweeping it under the carpet, as this will not help.

12. **Become informed:** Based on my experience, I believe that a lot of problems can be avoided or resolved by becoming more aware about cancer as a medical condition. Recently, a friend was asking us about the recurrence of cancer. I answered her questions when she said, 'It should not be very difficult if there is a recurrence. You can always undergo the treatment again and get rid of cancer.' Her husband definitely felt awkward when he heard her. He explained aloud that cancer treatment is so difficult that recurrence is an undesirable situation to be in. Moreover, at the time of recurrence, cancer may affect a different body part. It is not necessary that breast cancer will come back as breast cancer; it can show up as brain cancer, or bone cancer, or any other cancer. And not all cancers are curable – not yet. When I heard her remark, I didn't even feel angry. I could clearly see that she had no idea about cancer and its difficulties and uncertainties. If she were better informed, she would not have said what she did.

Thanks to the NHS, everyone in the UK has access to the same quality of treatment, irrespective of their economic status. If people have private medical insurance, it is a bonus; otherwise, the NHS is brilliant, especially for life-threatening conditions like cancer. The doctors are great, and so is the rest of the healthcare team. They listen to you emphatically and look after you really well. And all this is free.

Imagine having to go through cancer treatment again (in response to the comment that recurrence should not be a big problem) in countries where healthcare is not free, such as India. People plough in their savings to go through every single treatment. Something like Herceptin can be very difficult to afford. If such a statement is thrown at someone who is paying for the treatment, it will definitely lead to an awkward situation – because in these countries, if you can't pay, you don't get treatment. With life-threatening medical conditions, no treatment means that people die and lose their loved ones. A condition like cancer not only impacts the family's ability to earn while the patient is at home, it also destabilises the entire family, because their savings are used up in the treatment. Therefore, it is a good idea to be informed, at least about the basics of the medical condition.

While there are several great sources of information about cancer on the internet, my two favourite ones are: Macmillan Cancer Support (http://www.macmillan.org.uk/Home.aspx) and Cancer Research UK (http://www.cancerresearchuk.org). Both Macmillan Cancer Support and Cancer Research UK provide printed material, in addition to online resources, which can be found at various oncology units in hospitals and cancer support centres. Thanks to Macmillan and Cancer Research UK, our entire cancer experience was more informed and less painful than it would have been otherwise.

13. **Be kind:** Kindness is essentially an under-rated virtue. But honestly, it does wonders greater than the greatest of gifts. I think what I appreciated the most during my entire cancer

experience were the little instances of kindness that touched Abhi and me.

On the night of the oesophagitis episode, the taxi driver had not taken the full fare from us – not because he pitied us because of the cancer, but because he felt that taking money from someone in so much trouble was not right.

The hair dresser who had shaved off my hair during the chemotherapy treatment in October had also refused to take payment. He said that he had hardly taken thirty seconds to shave off my hair, whereas the fact really was that he had put in a considerable amount of time and care to ensure that my sensitive scalp was not hurt. I insisted on paying him, but he would not take any money.

I think all these people were doing whatever they could to help us out. Little savings in the taxi fare or at the barber shop did not make a huge difference to our finances, but their little acts of consideration and kindness definitely did affect our lives.

I remember an incident that took place when I was at the hospital for my three-weekly dose of Herceptin in October 2013. Some patients had come alone, while a few others had company. Most of us looked slightly bored while hooked to the machines. Undergoing intravenous treatment in the oncology ward is certainly not on the top of 'my most exciting things to do' list. Suddenly, the young woman next to me (who was accompanying her mum, who was undergoing treatment) asked the lady to her right, who was absent-mindedly staring at the bleeping machine, if she wanted tea. 'Sure thing,' was the hesitant response. Over the next half-hour, this woman went around asking every patient undergoing treatment in the chemo unit if they wanted tea, and made tea for them. I usually don't drink tea in the hospital, but I was so excited at her offer (yes, I get excited about little things in life!) that I promptly agreed to have a cuppa. The ambience in the room changed – suddenly everyone perked up. I had been visiting the hospital for the last thirteen months, and it was my first experience of this kind. It was a simple and genuine act of kindness. More than the tea, it was her consideration that warmed up the people on that cold morning.

During my cancer journey, whenever I was hurt, all I wished for was a little kindness from others, more than anything else. I do think that most of the 'inappropriate comments' could have been avoided if people were just kinder; they didn't necessarily need to know about the medical aspects of cancer. But overall, I was fortunate to have people around me who were kind and considerate.

14. **Help rebuild our confidence:** I know that it must be very difficult and frustrating for you to see us go through cancer and its painful treatment, and not be able to throw cancer out of our lives. I know that you want to protect us, but every time you doubt, 'Are you sure you can do this?' remember you are not any doing good to our confidence. Cancer has beaten us and robbed us of many things, including our confidence. Therefore, even if your intentions are great, please don't doubt us time and again – instead, help us regain our confidence. There is no need to be overprotective. We have come this far with your love and support, we will definitely get to the other side; just keep telling us that we can do it.

I have already shared with you that after my cancer diagnosis, my family took some time to come to terms with it. They were scared, not knowing what to expect. They were shocked – we have never had cancer before in our family. But about a week after the diagnosis, Dinesh said to his daughter Ananya, 'She is going to make it through this. She is a strong-willed woman. She *is* going to make it through this. I can feel it in my heart.'

And here I am, well and alive to share my story with you!

Thank you, Dinesh, for your confidence in me.

15. **Two steps forward and one step back or one step forward and two steps back:** There was a young woman, recently diagnosed with cancer, who had to make exactly the same choice as I had faced, with respect to preserving herself over her ability to have children. It would now be uncertain if she would get her fertility back. When I got to know about this, I was sad. It may be difficult for anyone else to understand why I would expose myself to the grimness of cancer and get affected by it. But the fact is that it is difficult to not think about what has happened. Also, cancer brings people together, and enables them to empathise with each other in solidarity. At times this means that we get emotionally perturbed, but being there for each other is something that comes naturally to many people who have been through cancer.

Cancer is a hideous medical condition, and people take time to heal from it, especially at the psychological level. It is important that you understand that after going through the treatment, it is difficult to turn off some kind of inner switch so we can move on completely.

Source: The pointers for this chapter have been borrowed from Macmillan and have been supplemented with anecdotes from my own experience.

I hope that I kept my promise of not being too preachy while writing this chapter. I also hope that you find these tips useful while caring for a cancer patient or interacting with them.

In the next chapter, I also suggest a few tips for cancer patients to make life easier for themselves and their families.

More about Cancer:

Breast cancer survival statistics[47]:

- It is good news that more people survive breast cancer today than 40 years ago.
- In the 1970s, just over half of women with breast cancer survived the disease beyond 5 years. Now it's more than 8 out of 10.
- Almost 8 out of 10 women survive breast cancer for at least 10 years.
- Almost 2 out of 3 women diagnosed with breast cancer now survive their disease beyond 20 years.

---

[47] Cancer Research UK. "Breast cancer Key Stats." Last modified November 2014. http://www.cancerresearchuk.org/cancer-info/cancerstats/keyfacts/breast-cancer. Last accessed December 05, 2014.

How can a cancer patient help their family?

The chapter above was dedicated to how others could help a cancer patient. However, there is also something that the cancer patients can do to help their families. A cancer patient needs to understand that caring for someone with cancer, or just knowing that a loved one has been given the cancer diagnosis, can be terribly stressful.

So, what can you do to help out your friends and family? I'd like to share some ideas with you.

Stop feeling guilty: Feeling guilty would just make the situation worse for everyone. As I said earlier: don't be guilty about the cancer diagnosis, or about being an encumbrance to your loved ones.

Put yourself first: You may have been culturally programmed to put others before yourself, but in times of critical need like a cancer diagnosis, it is OK if you put yourself first. If you put yourself first, you are more likely to do what is required for you to recuperate. That will be the biggest gift to your loved ones.

Be self-reliant, as much as possible: Every illness is different, and I appreciate that people can be so ill that they need serious help with everything. But if you are able to do it, this will be very helpful to take complete ownership of your treatment. This is linked to the point above – you place your recovery as the topmost priority. In my case, I took complete responsibility for my treatment. I literally spent hundreds of hours in the hospital, over innumerable visits, but Abhi has so far been in the hospital with me only on nineteen occasions (right through the diagnosis, chemotherapy, Herceptin, surgery, an emergency hospitalisation, and follow-ups).

Imagine the kind of stress Abhi would have undergone if he had had to coordinate my surgery and hospital appointments, and subsequently accompany me there. It would have been impossible for him to keep up with a high-level job, because of his frequent unavailability. That would have impacted his career. With me ill and at home not working, that would have put such a humongous pressure on us financially. In our case, I had decided that I would let him concentrate on his work, and I would concentrate on my recovery. Putting my health first was the best thing I could do to help myself and him.

Manage the transition well: My experience says that the transition period, between your old life and the new life that you move into post-cancer, is the most intimidating and unsettling period, after the diagnosis. Just like any situation involving change, the uncertainty of a new life heralds fear. But we must step right into the transition, in order to get better. This is how the situation may look:

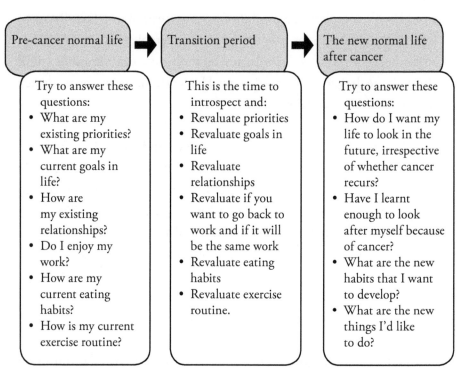

The transition from the life before cancer to the life after cancer

Source: We discussed this transition model in the 'Living well, moving on' course at The Haven. It was conducted by Eve Warren, a life coach who worked at The Haven. Thank you, Eve.

The transition period is the most intimidating time, because it is during this time that a cancer patient has to let go of the old, and make changes for a new life. As people come to terms with the new 'them', some questions that they need to answer are:

- Have I been kicked enough in the guts by cancer to motivate me to take ownership of my life? (I am not suggesting that you didn't take ownership for it before; you just need to do more of it now!)
- If so, what are my new priorities in life?

- Am I happy to continue investing in relationships like I did before? Which ones? Do I need to value certain relationships over others? Should I take charge and step out of relationships that have no real meaning?
- What can I do to proactively recover from the side effects of the treatment? Should I explore things like acupuncture, homeopathy, massage, and counselling? Maybe meeting other people who have been through similar experiences will bring me solace?
- When am I ready to go back to work? Will it be the same work as before, or will it be something different, that I always wanted to do but never actually did?
- Should I volunteer with an organisation of my choice?
- What are the lifestyle choices I will make with respect to physical and emotional health?
- How am I feeling? Am I feeling low or hurt due to the recent pain, or have I started healing?
- Am I ready to let go of the pain, learn from the journey, and move on in my life?
- Despite the trauma caused, what am I grateful for?
- Am I evolving spiritually as a human being?

Answering these questions requires a lot of work. There are no right or wrong answers, but the questions definitely need some serious introspection. This stage can be like when a child is learning to walk. While there is a need to start walking, there is also the fear of letting go and standing on your own. You need to remember not to rush, and learn to walk again with baby steps – one small step at a time.

Visit a cancer support centre: The UK has several cancer support centres, and they do fantastic work in supporting patients and their families. You can avail of their support mainly in two ways:

a. **Take various therapies:** The centres provide a variety of therapies and you can choose what suits your requirements. Acupuncture, different types of massage, aromatherapy, hypnotherapy, yoga, nutrition advice, mind-body therapy, and counselling are just a few options to choose from. The centres provide most of the therapies at minimal or no cost.

b. **Meet other cancer patients:** It is unbelievable how soothing it is to meet other cancer patients. No matter how much support you have from family and friends, spending time with people who have been through similar experiences is unparalleled. They understand your situation like you want them to. They don't judge you, nor do they patronise you. They understand when you feel depressed. They don't pressurise you to feel better or to move on with your life. When you speak to a fellow cancer patient, you know that you are being listened to and understood, which is simply priceless.

Stay away from negativity: During the course of the treatment, some people tried to offload their negativity on me. They were scared of cancer (which I appreciate) but consistently told me that things would get rough for me. For example: If I was at work, instead of appreciating that I was trying to manage work along with the treatment, they would paint vivid images of how being at work could make me severely ill. If I went out for a walk, which I was strongly advised to do, they would tell me not to, as I could collapse from fatigue. After a while, their overt concern started bothering me. I decided to stay away from such people. I did not want to bear the brunt of their negative thoughts. I told Abhi that I planned to minimise contact with them and he fully agreed. It helped enormously. Stay away from negative people, and do not let them hold you hostage to their negativity.

If you get stuck with someone who continues to say demotivating or negative things, remember that you don't have to listen to them. Staying away from such people will be helpful; otherwise they can easily sap your energy, and as a cancer patient, I am sure that you have none to spare.

With the help of these tips and complementary therapies, my recovery gradually picked up. I spent August struggling emotionally, but my psychological healing commenced in September. As time passed, the healing happened at a holistic level – not just physically but also emotionally and psychologically. You will be able to find the details of how this healing happened in the next chapter.

Amongst all the complementary therapeutic remedies, the most effective was Abhi's love.

Self-awareness or my spiritual quest

Cancer causes stress in ways that we cannot even imagine (all right, maybe I can imagine a few ways now). Even if a cancer patient is well supported by family and friends, is financially stable, and has a fabulous healthcare team looking after them, they often feel stressed. Stress manifests in different ways for different people: it could impact sleep, or lead to anxiety, or make people depressed, or have them worrying about a recurrence of cancer, or it could be a mix of all these things.

Whatever the impact of stress, the first step is to recognise that you are stressed. When you recognise this, you are more likely to do something about it. In my case, when depression hit me, I recognised it, because being depressed was just not me. I am not someone who wails about situations often, or feels low about them all the time. I would rather do something about them. I did berate myself for feeling this, in the beginning, as I wanted to stay happy. But when I was told at The Haven that it was OK to be sad and that it was a normal response to what I had been through, I got in touch with my real feelings. I took some time to make peace with the fact that it was OK to feel low. This didn't go with my self-image, and my need to be strong all the time. But how liberating it was to not put up a brave face! I explained to Abhi what I was going through emotionally, and he seemed to understand. I must say that I did not share this with anyone else, except a little with Sachin, because I was not sure if they would understand. Maybe others could have understood, but I was not comfortable sharing my emotions. Being depressed for several months at a stretch was a new experience. It also meant that I was not in denial or shock over my life-threatening illness and the perils it posed to my well-being. I went through what I could call the grieving stage, and when I felt ready, I looked for help in the form of complementary therapies and courses that would help me heal psychologically.

At Paul's Cancer Support Centre, I went through a course called 'Coping with Cancer Stress', wherein several self-help tools to manage the stress caused by cancer were discussed. The 'Coping with Cancer Stress' course is an adapted version of the Healing Journey Programme, created by Professor Alastair Cunningham, and researched and run for over 30 years at the Princess Margaret Hospital in Toronto. For the original Canadian course, you can visit: www.healingjourney.ca. I am extremely grateful to Alastair Cunningham and Paul's Cancer Support Centre for granting me permission to present this work in my book. Thank you, Alastair and Paul's.

While this course was spread out over almost nine months, I want to collate all the learning from the course in one place, so that it is easy to assimilate. So, here we go:

Being an active participant in our own recovery was one of the initial ideas that we discussed. We were invited to evaluate the options of playing a rather dormant role and letting others look after us, or playing an active role in our recovery in addition to the help that we had from others. The self-help idea resonated with me. I wanted to do something, to help myself come out of the miserable situation I was in. I had gone through all the complementary therapies with the sole intention of expediting the recovery process. As discussed in the course, many of the complementary therapies do not have a plethora of evidence to support them, although case studies abound. Therefore, it was important to find the therapy or the complementary solution that chimed well with my needs. The 'Coping with Cancer Stress' course helped me to explore these options.

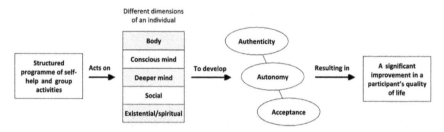

Process diagram from 'Coping with Cancer Stress' course

Source: The 'Coping with Cancer Stress' course: http://www. paulscancersupportcentre.org.uk/

As the diagram above illustrates, 'Coping with Cancer Stress' is a structured course with several tools which act on all the five dimensions of an individual. The aim of the course is to develop the three A's – Authenticity (what feels true to us), Autonomy (standing up for what feels true to us) and Acceptance (the ability to accept things that cannot be changed). There were several concepts that were gradually introduced. I am sharing the ones that helped me to enhance my self-awareness and to cope with the stress cancer brings.

Concept one: The first concept that I found really interesting in the course was the Stress Pathway. I have picked up the diagram from the course material for your reference below:

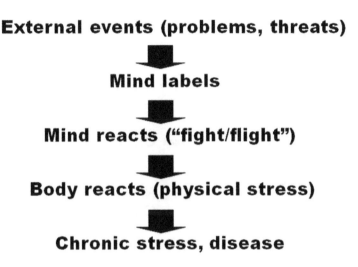

Stress Pathway

Source: The 'Coping with Cancer Stress' course: http://www.paulscancersupportcentre.org.uk/

What this concept says is that, if there is a crisis (be it any small problem or a big one like cancer), our mind labels it as good or bad, desirable or undesirable. This labelling, in turn, serves as the stimulus for our Autonomic Nervous System[48] to get into a fight-or-flight response. The reaction of the mind causes our body to react, which typically happens in the form of stress, which in turn leads to ailments. There is increasing

---

[48] Autonomic Nervous System (ANS): It is the part of our nervous system that regulates the functioning of our internal organs. It also controls some muscles within the body. The most commonly known function of the ANS is the fight-or-flight response.

scientific evidence that when we are under stress, the immune system of the body gets impaired.

So, is there anything we can do to prevent this from happening? Fortunately, there is, and the concept is explained through the diagram below:

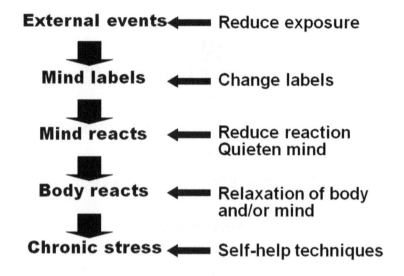

External events ⬅ **Reduce exposure**

⬇

Mind labels ⬅ **Change labels**

⬇

Mind reacts ⬅ **Reduce reaction Quieten mind**

⬇

Body reacts ⬅ **Relaxation of body and/or mind**

⬇

Chronic stress ⬅ **Self-help techniques**

What can we do to manage stress?

Source: The 'Coping with Cancer Stress' course: http://www.paulscancersupportcentre.org.uk/

We can reduce our exposure to situations and people that we find stressful. Maybe you are getting stressed with not having the energy to work for a couple of hours at a stretch. Breaking work into smaller tasks to spread out exertion could be a solution to this situation. If there is a person who is hurting you with insensitive remarks, maybe staying away from them will be helpful as a short-term solution. However, as a long-term solution, you will need to do deeper work with yourself.

If a stressful event takes place, we need to change the labels that we assign to it. So instead of reacting with something like, 'Goodness, this is the end of the world,' maybe we could say, 'This is difficult, but I have been through cancer and survived, and I can handle this.'

This is to be followed by deliberately quietening and relaxing the mind. I learnt that learning to relax deliberately is the basic requirement to set healing in motion. It is important because it gets our mind and body into a state conducive to healing. This is where relaxation and visualisation are of help. Our body does not differentiate between the real and the imaginary. Therefore, if we imagine that we are relaxed, our body believes it. This brings mind and body into an equilibrium, which subsequently reduces stress and illness. There are several techniques that I used for relaxation and reducing stress:

a. I found hypnotherapy very useful to get into state of deep relaxation.

b. Meditation helped to quieten my mind. It gave me peace.

c. Mental imagery, which I explored through visualisation, gave me results that were simply mind-boggling. I have discussed these experiences later in the chapter.

At times, you may feel that your life is very busy, especially after cancer, and that accommodating these self-help tools will be cumbersome. But the fact is that once you figure out which tools are beneficial for you, they will improve your quality of life so much that the investment will be more than worthwhile.

Concept two: The second concept I discovered in the course was 'Connectedness', which is represented in the diagram below:

The Connectedness model

Source: The 'Coping with Cancer Stress' course: http://www. paulscancersupportcentre.org.uk/

The 'Connectedness' model shows that our physical self is just one aspect of us. In order to be healthy and to heal, we must look at all the dimensions of ourselves. What conventional medicine cures is primarily 'A' – the body. We need to nourish our mind, too – the conscious as well as the deeper or subconscious mind. The next is our social interactions, or relationships. This is followed by our spiritual self. While healing, if we nurture one dimension while leaving out the others, it will not be a holistic change.

While we can start working on all the dimensions at any time in our life, a lot of times we don't do so, because we are too busy doing regular things – pursuing education, hobbies, work. An event like cancer makes us stop, forces us to take time off, think, feel, introspect, and so it serves as a great opportunity to make some changes. I am writing about how to nourish the four levels, except the body, below.

1. **The conscious mind:** Mind-watching and journaling were introduced as tools to look after our conscious mind. Let's look at them one by one.

   Mind-watching: I found mind-watching or thought-watching a very powerful concept. It enables us to look after our conscious mind. This concept propounds that our thoughts are *an* option to us, instead of being *the only* option we have.

   During the course, the facilitator compared our minds with water. At times, this water flows torrentially, while at other times it is stagnant. The water can be clear, or it can carry mud or other kinds of debris. Usually, we tend to think that we have no choice whether this water is torrential or stagnant, or whether it is clear or muddy. But thankfully, this is not true.

   To explain – There is always some chatter that goes in our heads. Let us call this mind-chatter (this is the mud, or debris). Unfortunately, some of our really difficult and negative thoughts tend to become repetitive, thereby leading to 'stuck thoughts'. A stuck thought is a negative thought stuck in a loop that does not find an exit from our minds. Such a perpetual negative thought pattern may cause anxiety or depression. We go through the same thing, again and again (in our mind), and get stressed or angry. The good news is that we can train ourselves to become aware of what is going on in our heads.

   When we think that something is terrible, it distresses us. Similarly, if we think that something is great, we feel happy about it. When we have an awareness of our thoughts, we have better control over our emotions, because it is our thoughts that cause emotions. Therefore, it is important to watch what we think, so that we can deal with our emotions and, in turn, manage stress. We know that there is a link between how we deal with stress, and the illnesses we get. If we can manage our thoughts, it may contribute to keeping illness at bay.

When I watched my thoughts closely, I realised that I had a negative thought stuck in my mind. As I became more aware of what I had been thinking, whenever this thought cropped up in my mind, I consciously changed it. Soon, I managed to come out of the stuck thought pattern, as I could clearly see how counter-productive it was.

The deliberate changing of thoughts should not be confused with their denial. While managing my thoughts, I stay aware of what I am thinking. When I realise that it is unproductive or negative things that I have been thinking, I make a conscious decision to let go of those thoughts. But it is extremely important to be aware of both 'good' as well as 'bad' thoughts.

So, the mantra is to:

Acknowledge our thoughts and feelings → express them → substitute unpleasant thoughts and feelings with the pleasant ones, because we have a choice!

Therefore, we must remember that:

a. We have a *choice* in what we think – Watching our thoughts makes us aware of what we think, thereby giving us a choice of what to retain and what to let go.
b. Our thoughts precede our emotions.

It was my father who brought to my attention that I was constantly clinging to my phone, and that I had a huge need to answer every message or email immediately. Later, when I learnt to watch my thoughts, I realised that I was doing so mainly because I would get distracted by the tiniest external stimulus. Whether it was a beep signalling a new text message or an email received, or whether it was the post that the postman put through the door, I had an inner urge to rush and respond. Most of the time, a slightly delayed response would have done no harm. So, if travel made me feel sick, and if this motion sickness was worsened by reading, I could just wait for the travel to finish and respond to the email when I got home. Earlier, this was a difficult thing to do. Now, I have come out of the need to respond or act immediately. The external stimuli do not distract me as much as they did before.

Journaling: Journaling was introduced to us during the course as a tool to explore our thoughts and feelings. It involves not just writing down things that happen, but more importantly, how you feel about them. I really benefit from journaling, because I struggle with sharing my feelings with others. When I felt isolated during the cancer treatment, journaling helped enormously.

Journaling also complements mind-watching very well. We often do not know that we are carrying certain thoughts or mind labels. But when we pour down our thoughts onto paper, we have an opportunity to explore what is really going on in our minds. It is all about self-discovery, which can be used later to take the required action. In fact, journaling not only helped me to understand my feelings, but it also worked as a catharsis for me. I began to pour out my thoughts and repressed feelings and the process finally shaped this book.

We also need to accept that our thoughts may be destructive, and at times they may not necessarily be true. We get so accustomed to our thought patterns that often we are not even conscious of what occupies our minds all the time.

231

Often we get so used to being stressed that we don't notice how it is affecting our health and mental peace. Tools like journaling and thought-watching can help us achieve this self-awareness.

Hmmmm – so, what are you thinking now?

2. **The deeper mind:** The deeper mind, in the connectedness model, is our subconscious mind that holds a great deal of content, of which we are not aware. In psychologies such as Psychosynthesis[49] and other transpersonal psychologies[50] that have developed out of the work of Carl Jung, the deeper mind

---

[49] Psychosynethesis: The Psychosynthesis approach affirms the reality of spiritual experience as an integral part of human experience. Psychosynthesis acknowledges our individual uniqueness and our connection to the whole. Where suffering can be caused by a loss of contact with who we really are, the psychosynthesis approach seeks to restore and renew this contact. The first step in psychosynthesis is the acquisition of self-knowledge and the ability to move within our inner world with ease and confidence. For this to happen, we must first enter into relationship with those feelings, thoughts and memories that society tends to alienate us from. We can then contact aspects of ourselves we've repressed because we found them too painful to experience, or because they conflict with the conscious image we have of ourselves, or with the dominant cultural norms. Instead of being consistent and unchanging, in this work we find ourselves to be a mix of contrasting, changing elements, which in psychosynthesis are termed subpersonalities.
The Psychosynthesis & Education Trust. "What is Psychosynthesis." http:// www.psychosynthesistrust.org.uk/about-psychosynthesis-and-education-trust/ what-is-psychosynthesis. Last accessed December 06, 2014.

[50] Transpersonal Psychology addresses the spiritual nature of humankind. Unlike religion and theology, its interest centres on the mind and behaviour; hence it is a branch of Psychology. All the major spiritual and mystical traditions of the world incorporate teachings about the nature of mind and promote behavioural practices intended - amongst other goals - to bring about psychological transformations. Transpersonal psychology addresses these teachings and practices, researching their value and evaluating their relationships to ideas promulgated in Psychology. In essence Transpersonal Psychology seeks to integrate non-scientific spiritual insights with observations and models associated with the rigorous methodological approach of psychological science.
The British Psychological Society. "Transpersonal Psychology Section." http:// www.bps.org.uk/networks-and-communities/member-networks/transpersonal-psychology-section. Last accessed December 06, 2014.

is understood to contain not only aspects of ourselves that we consider negative, but also a great deal of creative potential and many latent positive qualities.

The developmental work that we undertook in the 'Coping with Cancer Stress' course included making conscious many of the aspects of ourselves that had been in the shadow.

We explored the deeper mind, and the potential it contains, through visualisation and free drawing in a group setting. Thoughts affect the body through emotions (as discussed in the section on the conscious mind), as well as through mental images. Imagery is the mental representation of our experiences.

I always thought I was one of those people who were not creative enough to paint images in their minds. But in the course, our facilitators mentioned that if we knew how to worry, then we knew how to build images. How true! If you are like me, you must be guilty of creating worrisome images of things that do not exist, or imagining things to be worse than they really are – like imagining demons in your bedroom after watching a horror movie. Now the choice is whether to continue building unproductive images, or consciously work on images that are capable of healing. Healing means moving towards a greater sense of balance and wholeness, a holistic wellness which goes beyond the physical. The course provided us with several audio tapes of guided imagery, which I used to relax deeply and expedite my healing.

Goal-setting: Most of us are familiar with setting goals in the corporate work environment. Some of us set goals when a new year begins. But here, goal-setting is about exploring what we want to achieve in life, rather than gaining specific things like a job or a pair of boots or a car (of course, it is perfectly all right to set your eyes on that special lingerie or bungalow or anything else that catches your fancy). Having gone through cancer, the reality of finite time had been driven home to me. And because time is finite, I knew I ought to figure out what I really wanted to spend my time on. But in order to understand what I wanted to do, I first needed to look at what I was already doing. I made a list comprising: (a) Activities that I had done over the last week; and (b) Activities that I would have liked to do, but hadn't done.

The million dollar questions that I asked myself were: Where do I have a choice, and how much choice do I have? If I have a choice, do I exercise it? Do I try to exercise control on things that I can't change? I needed to know what I could influence, and act accordingly.

Then I divided the list that I had prepared into three categories – had to, ought to, and wanted to:

- Did I do them because I had to?
- Did I do them because I thought I should? Who decides what I should do – family, friends, cultural norms, society, or the conditioning that happened when I was a little child?
- Did I do them because I wanted to do them? When I do these things, is there a flutter or a happy song in my heart, or is it more akin to a frustrated bawling?

Having understood the motivation behind my activities, the key for me was to figure out how to increase the things that I wanted to do, over the things that I had to do or should do. This could be achieved by adding more activities in the 'want to' category, and taking as many items as possible off the 'have to' or 'ought to' list. Or, this change could also be achieved by doing the same things differently. For instance, I might have eaten broccoli because I thought I should eat it; but if I considered the benefits it gave me, it could fall into the 'I want to do it' category. The motivation behind doing what I had done would be greater in the latter case.

3. **The social level:** It is important to invest your time and effort in meaningful relationships. After cancer, I decided that I would spend more time and invest greater effort in connecting with people who mattered to me. I didn't want geographical distances to be a good enough reason to dictate how my relationships should be. I saw how important it was to support my loved ones, and also to draw the support I needed from them.

Forgiveness: The concept of forgiveness was introduced when we were about one-third of the way through the course. This was something that I had been really keen to work on for a long time. When the topic was introduced, I was delighted, as I saw this as an opportunity to fix a few things that were damaged or broken within me. The lesson on forgiveness was so powerful that I would like to reproduce it here in its entirety for your benefit. My course facilitator, Ella, was fabulous in explaining the concept. I want to share with you the key ideas that I learnt from Ella here:

> *When you hold resentment toward another, you are*
> *bound to that person or condition by an emotional*
> *link that is stronger than steel. Forgiveness is the*
> *only way to dissolve that link and get free.*
>
> - Catherine Ponder

The second quote was equally powerful and it captured exactly why I wanted to work on forgiveness:

> *When a deep injury is done us, we never recover until we forgive.*
>
> - Alan Paton

Remember the work that I had done with Gosia on letting go? That was just the beginning of the most difficult but precious part of the cancer journey.

We discussed how blame, resentment, anger, and the absence of trust cause stress at all the five levels of the connectedness model, as follows:

- Body – They induce stress responses, which manifest as ill health.
- Mind – They lead to a whirling mind, which affects concentration.
- Deeper mind – They produce lots of unproductive emotions, such as anger, shame, guilt, frustration and bitterness.
- Social – They adversely impact our relationships, not only with others, but also with ourselves; our hearts and souls get fragmented.
- Spirituality – They rob us of peace, shut us down, and make life joyless.

What a massive price we pay because of the negative emotions of anger and blame! There is scientific evidence that when people let go of angst and forgive, it reduces the various ill effects mentioned above. Consequently, their health and overall quality of life improves. Below are the most crucial, beautiful things I learnt about forgiveness. It:

- Is a choice we make.
- Is a mode of release.
- Is moving on.
- Is appreciating the larger picture.
- Is healing.
- Is setting healthy boundaries with others.
- Can be directed at others as well as ourselves.

(And this is where it gets interesting.) Also, it is:

Not about changing the other person: Forgiving someone does not mean that we are trying to change them.

Not about condoning hurtful behaviour: In the early stages of my learning about forgiveness, I confused it with granting tacit approval to undesirable behaviour. However, when I learnt that they were two separate things, I felt better. This is also beautifully linked to the 3 A model. Here's an example to better understand this:

I had never been able to figure out how people can forgive others for the hurtful things they say or do, like emotional and sexual abuse, female foeticide, murder or rape. In order to understand the process of forgiveness, I decided to work with something that was important to me. This thing was important because someone had said terrible things to me and I had been very hurt. My hurt had festered over years. All this while, I had been aware that it was all talk, and that it had not affected any real life event (for instance, imagine someone talked about killing someone precious to me, but no one was really killed). I had been angry with the person who did this, because I did not approve of what was said to me. It felt grossly unjust. At the same time, I was angry with myself because I had not stood up to them for what was hurting me, and had let them say the same thing to me time and again – all in the name of social relationships.

Ella suggested that accepting and acknowledging what had happened was the beginning of the forgiveness process. She said that accepting that I had been hurt was important. I also should be true to myself (authentic) and recognise that I had no control over how others behaved or what they said. Therefore, acceptance of the situation and the person's attitude came into play here. Acceptance does not mean that I approve of their behaviour. It simply means that I accept the things that I can't change. It was time to accept that I could not be the control freak that Gosia had suggested I was. Maybe I could choose to be authentic, and share with people the impact of what they said to me.

After accepting the situation and being authentic in my response to it, I was now exercising autonomy, and choosing to move on from the hurt these events had caused. I learnt that it is feasible to forgive and let go at the same time. I don't want to be bound to the past or these people forever because of my anger. Harbouring anger towards them will do no good, and will not change the situation either.

Not about allowing hurtful behaviour to continue: In reference, again, to the above example, I decided that if something like this happened again, I would make sure that I told these people respectfully how such talks hurt me (being authentic to myself). I would hope that they would process this information, and act on it. But I would not try to control what they thought or how they acted. And I wouldn't let anyone exploit me because I was willing to accept or forgive.

Not about taking responsibility for others' actions: No, forgiving does not mean that I become a party to others' actions. Nor does it mean that I am reconciling with them. It just means that I am choosing to move on.

Not easy: I so wish that it was otherwise – it is so easy to hurt and get hurt, but so difficult to forgive and move on!

With the help of what I learnt from this course, I have begun to view relationships in a different light. Earlier, if someone said something unpleasant to me, I would be hurt and hold on to that hurt for a long time. Now, with help from self-care tools, I am able to view the same difficult relationship differently. Now, I evaluate if holding on to hurt is what I need. The answer invariably is no, and it helps me to move on from what others have just said to me. Self-help tools have also enabled me to become calmer, and so I react less to the situations that served as stimulants or irritants to me before.

4. **The spiritual mind:** Here, spiritual is not synonymous with being religious; although being religious can be a subset of being spiritual. We may be Christian or Hindu or Buddhist or agnostic or atheist, but being spiritual refers to something more than what we can see, feel and rationalise. It may be God for some, while it may be Nature for another; it may be some unknown higher power for still others, or it could be the interconnectedness of life. Spirituality is different things to different people. By spending time with myself and connecting with my inner self, I began to explore what spirituality meant to me.

This course was very special to me, as it served as the vessel for my spiritual quest.

Through Dinesh, Abhi and I also became better acquainted with the power of praying. Abhi and I had always been spiritual, but I had found contentment merely by placing my faith in God and not necessarily by praying. 'Why do we need to pray when the Lord knows that we trust Him?' was my usual predicament as well as rationale. But as I went through the cancer experience, my attitude towards praying changed, without my even knowing it. As my faith deepened, I developed an inclination towards praying, even if there was no tangible reason or outcome in sight. Before cancer, I always needed to know why effort should be invested in a particular prayer or ritual. (Hinduism is a religion that has many rituals.) Now, I am happy to trust and let the Almighty sort things out for me. I think this change occurred because during this journey, I learnt to trust others, including God, more than I had ever done before. With every passing day as I learn from cancer, my gratitude towards God for looking after me and for giving me the opportunity to be alive increases.

I am sure that I must have been impatient with Dinesh innumerable times. But he put up with me every single time, taking my impatience in his stride – and I am and I can be very, very impatient (yes, despite all the introspection and self-improvement after cancer). *I, surely, am a pampered sister. Thank you, brothers!*

I had heard from others that events like cancer stimulate people to look for meaning in life. I had heard from so many people that cancer is a journey, where the higher objective is to evolve, and this evolution means different things to different people. It could mean getting in touch with your inner self, or endeavouring to understand what really matters in this world, or developing a strong religious inclination; or it could be your perfect opportunity to change into a better person. Having gone through cancer and survived, I agree that it surely is a journey. It is a journey where the travel matters as much as the destination, where the experience is painful but the learning priceless. There is struggle every single day and night, but there is also the exhilaration that comes with every little victory. How many times do we appreciate a good night's sleep? Isn't it something that we have become accustomed to doing and getting every night? But after cancer, a good night's sleep is one of the most precious things for us. At home, Abhi and I look forward to my sleeping well every night, and whether I have been able to sleep or not is quite a discussion; and the cancer diagnosis seems to have happened so long ago! The day I am able to go for a run is so very special for me; because until a few months ago, the breast that had gone under the knife hurt badly at the slightest movement in my body. It is not that I have resolved all the knots in my soul, but the spiritual journey that commenced with cancer is definitely a promising beginning.

Concept three: The 'Finding Meaning' pathway was introduced early on in the course, although we explored it in greater detail when we discussed spirituality. I loved how Ella explained this pathway:

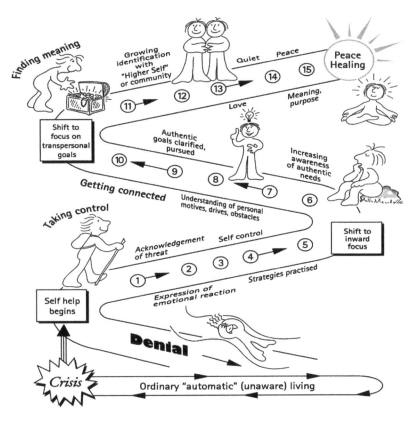

The 'Finding Meaning' Pathway

Source: The 'Coping with Cancer Stress' course: http://www. paulscancersupportcentre.org.uk/

We continue living 'automatically' and rather ordinarily, while life gradually unfolds. We are less aware of the choices we make. A crisis situation (cancer in this case) acts as a wake-up call. We could be in denial in the beginning, but gradually come to terms with what is happening. Once acceptance comes into the picture, we may choose to take the path of self-help. What happens when we start this process of self-healing via self-education is that we start to *unravel* this loop of thinking in our minds; we start to notice what we do; we notice our thoughts, and the habits that keep us anchored in the loop. While the journey here is depicted in a progressive way, in real life we tend to go back and forth, as we become aware, explore, assimilate and further move on. This process enables us to learn about ourselves, and the journey continues as we find deeper meaning in our being.

In my spiritual quest, there was both the flavour of 'finding greater meaning in life' as well as the religious aspect.

We explored several other concepts with the aim of increasing self-awareness so that we could understand our authentic needs and goals. I have discussed the key concepts below:

Judgement: Our judgement about others, as well as ourselves, is something that we discussed at length. We agreed that:

- Judgement is not discrimination.
- Judgement is not discernment.
- Judgement is not useful.

We explored our judgemental streaks with the following exercise:

- Question: What situations or people lead you to judge yourself or others?

  o It was interesting to note that judgement was primarily born in my head due to expectations – the expectations that I had of myself, or those that others had of me. Most of these ideas had been planted while I was growing up.

- Question: What judgements have you experienced from others, regarding your cancer experience?

  o I was thankful that I didn't have to face much judgement of this sort. I was also unsure whether what I thought of as judgements were reflections of my thoughts or those of others.

- Question: What judgements have you made or are you making of yourself?

  o The inner critic is the part of me that is always ready to make judgements, and it treated me more severely than it treated others. The inner critic, like guilt, can be a useful means of bringing in discipline (making healthy choices, getting rid of procrastination). The trick would be to remain aware of what it said, and make it work for me and not against me. The realisation that my inner critic was judgemental and hard on me was useful, as I decided to be easy on myself. There was enough to deal with throughout cancer, without beating myself up.

Guilt: We explored guilt, and whether it could be a useful thing for us. In the group, we agreed that when used cautiously, guilt can help us in many ways, some of which are depicted in the picture below:

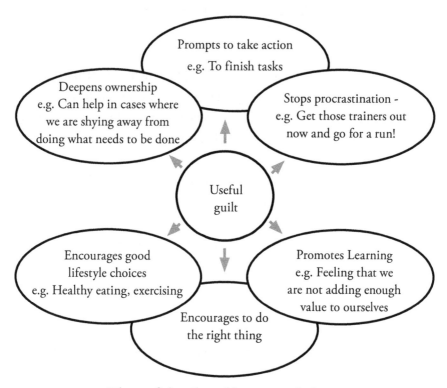

The useful guilt and how it can help us

The concept of good and bad is typically imposed on us by other people, who have had authority in our lives. It was worthwhile to delve deep inside myself, and examine the guilt that I was harbouring inside me. As my self-awareness rose, the definition of good and bad and what I felt guilty about changed. I must aim to have more useful guilt, while minimising the harmful guilt.

The inner child: Out of the various exercises that I tried while recovering from cancer, probably the most powerful was working with my inner child. When I began the exercises to heal my inner child, I had no idea how deep-reaching the results would be. I also had the opportunity to touch upon the inner child in the 'Coping with Cancer Stress' course. But it was during my relaxation and visualisation sessions that I did much deeper work. Healing the inner child is an important concept in the world of psychology, and there is a lot of literature available on the subject. What I did with my therapist, Catherine, was this:

- Based on my needs, we decided the issue or situation that was bothering me. For example: one of the situations that I chose was my lack of confidence in getting through a particular type of assessment during the recruitment process.
- The process began as she induced my body and mind to enter a state of deep relaxation.
- After I went into a state of deep relaxation, she asked me to bring my attention to the problem that we had chosen.
- She asked me to travel back in time, and reach the age when I experienced that emotion as a child. Fear in specific situations was the key problem that I was trying to deal with; Catherine asked me to feel this fear as a little child.
  After a while, she encouraged me to face my fear – visualise it as a person or a shape, to look at it, to speak to it when I was ready. The objective was to face my deep-set fears in a managed way, and to console that little child who was scared back then. Through this exercise, I was revisiting my childhood to make those things right that weren't perfect then, and which had left some kind of undesirable impact on me.
- At the same time, she encouraged me to speak to my younger self, and assure her that I (the present me) was there for her and would always be there for her. I held my little self in my arms, and comforted her. I told her that it was OK to be scared. I told her that it was OK to feel what she felt then, but that she did not have to be scared anymore. I told her that now I had the means and the strength and the wisdom to confront that fear; I was not so vulnerable now. I assured her that I would always continue to protect her.
- After this interaction with the fear and my little self, we completed the exercise, and Catherine guided me back into complete awareness.

- I completed this visualisation exercise for several issues that I had long carried as baggage (knowingly or unknowingly) from my childhood. What was interesting was that while it seemed to have little correlation to the real world, something deep within me had begun to change. I realised that my fear of assessment tests didn't debilitate me as much as it had before. After working on some relationship issues through visualisation, the hurt in my relationships felt less intense. The anger reduced, and so did the other negative emotions. I was amazed to realise that this work also had an impact on other aspects of my life that had seemed unrelated to it. For example: I had been working on some anger issues for some time, and had made little progress. It was the healing produced by the inner child work that really gave me results. Unlike before, the anger reduced for good, and stopped coming back with the same frequency and intensity. The situations that had triggered anger before did so less frequently now. The rendezvous with my little self had lit up my path to moving forward.

The orchestra with a personality: We discussed that our personality consists of several sub-personalities. Some of these smaller but important dimensions of our personality are:

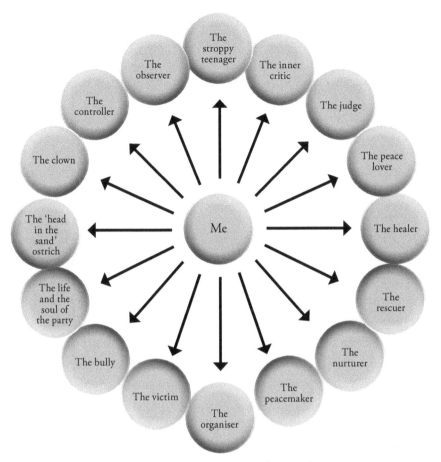

Is the 'orchestra in your personality' in harmony?

While all these sub-personalities are critical to our whole being, the inner critic and the victim stand out for me. The inner critic is the chattering voice that goes in our heads all or most of the time, and it does a fabulous job of reprimanding us. The inner critic gets muscle from the voice of others as well as our own thoughts. Being in a victim's shoes must also be familiar territory for most of us. I think almost everyone has derived solace in being a victim at least once in their lifetime. Many times, being a victim also absolves us of the responsibility for taking action, as the onus to make things right lies on the other person.

Each of these sub-personalities, I realised, was an important component of my personality. If I could make them work together as an orchestra, I would be in greater harmony. Over the course of the 'Coping with Cancer Stress' course, I gave more space to the observer in me, so that it made me aware of what was really going on inside me.

Fear: We had all spent the last one or two years of our lives amidst fear and uncertainty. A cancer diagnosis is synonymous with both of these feelings. Therefore, a discussion about fear seemed necessary and inevitable.

We discussed what we were afraid of, and the entry that topped the list was the fear that cancer may come back. The fear of recurrence is very real for anyone who has had cancer and there is no way to run away from it. Whenever a scan is organised for us (and there are plenty), it gets anywhere from stressful to scary. I remember that I was almost overtaken by a crippling fear during the two weeks' wait that led to the scan. We were trying to establish the reason behind the swelling in my arm. I was diagnosed with a very mild case of lymphoedema, and rest of the scan was clear. Thank Goodness! I had been going bonkers about the lymphoedema diagnosis, as one of the factors that cause lymphoedema is metastatic cancer. It turned out that I had been reading too much into this scan and its potential outcomes. As I said, the fear of a recurrence of cancer is very real, and we need to learn to manage it. Here is an exercise that we did to explore our fears, in safe environment:

- Relax, let go, and get fully grounded by placing your feet firmly on the ground.
- In your mind's eye, go down to the beautiful garden which is your safe place. A safe place is a nourishing place that you can visualise, a place where you feel good. The concept is to get used to the idea that within you, you have great resources that you can call upon, to feel energised and reassured. You can evoke

these resources in the form of the image of a safe and nourishing place, which you can then draw upon.

- With all your senses, really appreciate bring there – See the beauty of the place, smell the fragrance of the flowers, touch the morning dew, hear the chirping of the birds, and the rustle of the wind.
- When you are ready, bring your fear symbol into the garden. The fear symbol is a matter of visualising whatever comes to mind that you are frightened of – whether this is a person or a situation. It could have a distinct shape, face or size, or it could be something absolutely abstract.
- Talk to it and listen to what it says.
- If you find the fear overpowering, remember that it is a visualisation, and that you are safe.
- In your mind's eye, see if you can also bring in your internal loving friend to support you. The internal loving friend is the figure you evoke which symbolises your inner wisdom and unconditional love. It is a way of concretising the qualities of love and wisdom which we all have latent in our psyches, but often don't realise. This friend could be a part of you, or a friend, or a wise person – anyone from whom you would like to derive support.
- After the conversation, allow the fear to fade away.
- Come back from your safe garden, and feel your feet on the ground.

This exercise enabled us to face our darkest fears, gradually, and in a safe environment. While doing this exercise was when this beautiful thought occurred to me for the first time:

Being in a fearful situation is a circumstance; being stuck in it is a choice!

Grounding: We did two interesting exercises to explore grounding. The first one was: 'I am a tree.' It went like this:

- Imagine yourself to be a tree.
- See it grounded; imagine your arms as the branches.
- Imagine that this tree is experiencing different seasons – visualise the lushness and the hope of the spring, the blossoming of the summer, the shedding of leaves in the autumn, and the bare and the cold tree in the winter. After the cold and the barren tree, visualise yourself again experiencing the spring.
- Think which season your tree is in at the moment.
- Draw your visualisation on a sheet of paper.

The exercise was intriguing. I was able to visualise myself as a tree and see the changing seasons. However, when I tried to feel how deep my roots ran into the soil, I kept on getting the feeling that my roots were thin. My roots almost felt like the feeble and the slender creeper that entwines itself on a tree, instead of the thick roots of a banyan tree that become undistinguishable from the trunk as the time passes.

In the second exercise, we imagined ourselves to be a mountain, and viewed the world from the peak (Gosh! I can't help recollect the movie title *The hills have eyes!*). In this exercise too, I was able to imagine myself as a tall mountain and look at the world from my peak. However, when it came to feeling how grounded I felt as a mountain, I was not too sure. Clearly, there was something funny about my 'grounding'; at least I had a funny feeling that there was something funny about it.

I further explored 'grounding' in one-to-one coaching sessions, and became aware that there were aspects of my roots that I was uncomfortable with. For various reasons, I had rejected parts of the culture that I came from. At times, I thought that I did not agree with the traditional norms, while at other times I thought that I was building walls to protect myself. Was this the reason that I felt my roots were frail and thin? Well, I don't know. There may be a correlation between the two, or they may be completely unrelated. But it was nice to be reminded of my perspective on the outer world and my place therein.

As Oscar Wilde said, 'The final mystery is oneself.' I was gradually unravelling the mystery called me.

Karma, destiny's doing or the randomness of life: The discussion about *Karma* was intense, interesting and invigorating. I recollect that during the discussion, a friend who subscribes to the Eastern philosophy was thinking aloud about her *Karma*. What had she done to deserve cancer, which had robbed her of a year of life and caused so much pain and loss? It was a poignant moment for all of us in the room – for those who felt let down by their bodies because cancer had happened despite making healthy lifestyle choices, for those who subscribed to the philosophy of *Karma*, and also for those who assigned no particular reason to the events of life. The last category of people were surprised at how strongly we judge ourselves when we correlate each event that happens in our lives with our actions. When we say that every event is predestined and that our deeds or *Karma* define what happens to us, there is an awful lot of judgement to which we subject ourselves. This is when our friend, Liz, asked us to consider the idea that there could be randomness in life. Having contemplated *Karma* for a long time, I did think that I had done nothing to sow the seeds of cancer in my life. And so, when the possibility of randomness was put before me, I found it absolutely liberating. I toyed with the idea that we don't have to judge ourselves all the time, and assign a reason to everything that happens. If there were no randomness, nothing bad would ever happen to good people. So maybe some things happen in life randomly. Maybe it is not our right to understand every single thing that happens.

While I was contemplating my *Karma*, and how it could have contributed to cancer, Liz suggested that *this* (read: going through cancer) was probably my *Karma*. What if I was meant to do something bigger related to cancer, like helping out others? There is no telling if having to go through cancer is a punishment for bad *Karma*, or if my cancer experience (through this story) is meant to give hope to others during their difficult times. And if my cancer diagnosis was not a random but a meticulously planned event, maybe the impetus was not chastisement but instead the opportunity to make a positive difference.

The randomness of life was and remains a new idea to me, and I need lots of time to think it through, but this is definitely an intriguing start. I guess that my journey into the unknown will continue for a long time. But thank you, Liz, for initiating the idea.

I do think that the whole concept of *Karma* is misconstrued at a social level, and also contributes to the stigma against conditions like cancer. Some people tend to think that what we get in our lives is dependent solely on our past *Karma*. At a social level, this judgment prevents people from talking about cancer in the open...because if you have got cancer, you must have brought it upon themselves with your bad actions or *Karma*! This is the awful judgement that Liz was referring to. This, in turn, impacts cancer awareness, as people do not come out into the open about their cancer experiences.

Through this book, I want to do my bit to change that situation. I want to come out into the open about my diagnosis and treatment. I want to share with people that cancer is a medical condition and not a taboo. I want to affirm that cancer happens when cells go crazy and multiply more than they should, and not when our *Karma* punishes us for not being good. I want to bring that change into society – because it is required, and because I want to do something about it! Maybe people who think that cancer is a punishment for their bad *Karma* can ponder over this discussion.

And finally... The three A's, revisited and re-assimilated:

Authenticity: Authenticity is being in touch with your real self, finding out who you really are. It is about living the life you choose to live, and not the one prescribed by others.

Autonomy: Autonomy is acting from your own wishes when you can. Life is not about constantly putting other people first or doing what others think is right. At the same time, it is not about being self-centred. It is about striking a balance where we are thoughtful of others and also true to ourselves, without putting on a facade.

Acceptance: In an exercise, we explored the things that we have to accept and also the things that we struggle to accept.

When I looked at the first question, I thought about how I had to accept ill health, despite having made mostly good lifestyle choices. The same thing applied to my work situation. I loved working, I was good at what I did, but I had to let go of it when the illness struck. There was nothing I could do about it.

When I introspected about the things I struggled to accept, I discovered some key things. I found out that 'unfairness' is one of the things that I struggle to accept the most. So, it was not the comment that 'I invited cancer upon myself' that hurt me, as much as the discomfort that it was not fair to cast such blame on anyone. Similarly, it was not just about what was actually said to me when my cancer diagnosis brought home the reality of mortality, and forced people to face their own fears; instead, it was about the fact that I considered it unfair that people should project their own fears onto others.

I also thought of the vulnerability that a cancer diagnosis brings with itself, which is very hard to accept. Remember how after cancer had struck, for several months, I was angry that there were some loved ones who bailed out of my life at a bad time? The anger reduced slightly when, instead of worrying about these people, I decided to pay attention to those who stayed with me. But the anger actually went away when, as per the 'Authentic' in the 3 A's model, I decided to be authentic to myself and confront one of these people. I shared with her how hurt I had been over the last twenty months. She told me that she had found it difficult to talk about cancer, and had no idea what to say to me or how. Because she could not figure this out, she decided to stay away from me completely. Hmm – while I agreed that the decision to completely stop talking to someone with cancer is not the best course of action, knowing that I had been in her thoughts was enough for me. This simple ten-minute discussion was proof of how being authentic to ourselves can resolve issues and enhance the quality of our lives.

We also did an exercise wherein we acknowledged the pain, struggles, and grief of ourselves, one person whom we loved, and one person with whom we had a difficult relationship. We brought the person into our thoughts and acknowledged that they had faced challenges, they had been through pain, and they had been afraid. With loving kindness, the aim was to develop compassion for all. It was a powerful exercise, as it enabled us to empathise even with those who had troubled relationships with us. It was all about increasing our acceptance.

I felt privileged to attend this course with Caroline Clark, Christopher Salter, Jenny Dennehy, Liz Aram, Roya Aram, Sarah Thompson, and Sonia Markham. When I embarked on this course, little did I know that soon I would have each of these persons as my dear friends. As members of the same group at Paul's Cancer Support Centre, we developed a strong bond. Our differences in cultures, nationalities and age seemed completely irrelevant. We had seen each other at some of our most vulnerable and weakest moments. We had stood for each other in solidarity, and we continue to support each other in difficult times – such as, 'Goodness! Has it come back?' When someone stands with you in your times of struggle, it is very likely that they will stand with you in good times. This precious faith and bonding is not something that money can buy, nor can any MasterCard in the world! Thank you, friends, for sharing your lives with me and letting me share some of mine with you. You have helped me learn; you have helped me grow and you have helped me heal.

I would also like to thank my course facilitators, Ella Titman, Petra Griffiths and Pauline Withers-Born for their patience and empathy, for their love and kindness and for their commitment to pull us out of our misery. Thank you for guiding me on my spiritual quest.

Obviously, a cancer diagnosis is not a pre-requisite to set out on a journey of self-discovery or spiritual quest. However, all my life before cancer, I had been too busy gathering educational qualifications, striving for high performance ratings and promotions at work, learning to improve my public speaking skills, cooking, and doing activities I don't even seem to remember. And so, earlier, I'd never had much time or inclination left to think about the spiritual aspect of life. So, thank you, cancer! Thank you for facilitating this rendezvous between me and me.

He who knows others is wise. He who knows himself is enlightened.

- Lao Tzu

Love helps to cure cancer

I have heard that a new parent is intuitively conditioned to wake up whenever their baby needs them. If the baby stirs in the middle of the night, needs a feed or a change of nappies, the parent's instinct gets to know even when they are in deep sleep. I have seen it happen with one of my friends. She is such an amazing mum that no matter how many times her baby needs her, she is there. No matter how many times he stirs, she comforts him in the night. How beautiful it is, the feeling of protection and comfort that a parent gives to their child!

During cancer treatment, there were several nights when I couldn't sleep. There were many others when I was in pain, and there were innumerable times when I could sleep very little and with much difficulty. I would toss and turn in bed for hours, trying to get into a comfortable position which would bring sleep; or I would toss and turn because of too much pain. With each of these turns, Abhi would stir too. Somehow, right from the day when we had the first heart scare in the middle of the night, Abhi got programmed to wake up with my every movement and ask me if I was OK. Because of all the drugs that were running in my blood, I felt horribly dehydrated. The fact that my treatment was happening during the severe winter seemed to make little difference to this dehydration. I drank water and then I drank some more. On most of these sleepless nights, I would consume several glasses of water. This also meant that I would need to use the loo multiple times. Each time I stepped out of bed, Abhi would get up and check on me. I felt bad that his sleep was getting disturbed, and offered to sleep in another room; but he would never let me do that. He knew it better than anyone else that I needed him. He also wanted to make sure that he was available right when I needed him.

There were days when he was putting in 14-15 hours at work to meet project deadlines, but that weariness did not interfere with his attentiveness in his sleep. During many of these nights, when I was sleepless, he would hold me and put me off to sleep like a baby. I cuddled up against him and that *always* calmed me. I have never been able to understand the reason; but it worked. On more difficult nights, he held me close and gave me Reiki, which he had learnt several years ago. A cuddle from Abhi and Reiki was the sure-shot nemesis of insomnia. I tried to use it only when nothing else worked, because I didn't want to be super-selfish and put an additional encumbrance on him. At times I shudder to think, 'What if I was alone while going through cancer? Would I have been able to cope with it all by myself?' Maybe; but even if I could, it would definitely have been far tougher than it was.

Love may not cure cancer, but it definitely helps to cure it!

When I look back at my cancer journey, I realise that I handled it confidently. I had my fair share of uncertainties and not feeling great, but most of the time, I did well. I believe that Abhi's support was a major contributor to my confidence.

Abhi and I know someone whose spouse is unwell. Each time we spoke to this person, they would complain about how embarrassed they were of their spouse, because of their unkempt looks. No matter whether I spoke to them after two days or after a month, they would inevitably mention the shame they felt because of their spouse.

I have already shared with you that cancer messed up my looks completely. I think that I looked worse when I was losing hair than after I had lost all of it. At this stage, I was reminded of the common acquaintance that I referred to above. I asked Abhi if he would feel ashamed if I stepped out of the house with no hair and with my head uncovered. He said he would not be bothered by my hairless look at all. I told him there would be things that would be out of my control: things such as the weight gain due to steroids, or the deteriorating skin; but I could cover my head if he wanted me to. He asked me if I would be comfortable stepping out without hair. I said, 'Yes.' I saw cancer as an illness that could happen to anyone. Hair loss was a part of the treatment. I know that I was not thrilled about losing hair, but it did not bog me down. Abhi said that he would be OK, if I was OK with it. And so, during the entire period when I had no hair (which lasted for more than seven months), I went out and socialized without feeling the need to cover my head. I went to work and moved around just like rest of the people – with my head held high. My chemotherapy had started in September and it went on until January, during the most severe winter months in the UK. The only reason why I covered my head was because I felt cold due to the enormous heat loss through the scalp.

I think I could be my confident self when I looked my worst because I have a husband whose love for me is greater than an admiration of how I look. His desire to support me went far beyond his concern for the weight I put on, or my awful-looking nails, or my hairless head, or a face without eyebrows and eyelashes.

I know that not everyone is fortunate to have this kind of love – love that stays strong when several other people walk out. Those of us who are this lucky must hold on to it, no matter what it takes, because love is what matters, when everything else, including life, is at stake. I am not sure why I had to go through cancer, but I am thankful that I had the love of a few people to help me walk through it. Their love gave me the power to face the most dreadful moments when my fear was at its peak. It helped me get back on my feet when my fighting spirit was wounded. There were times when I wanted to give up because of too much pain, but I clung to the unconditional love I received from some people, and carried on. At times I held onto this love for a week at a stretch, at times for a day, at times for an hour, at times for a minute, and at times moment by moment.

I am immensely thankful to cancer, because it enabled me to rediscover how powerful love is. While some relationships went out of the window, several others were strengthened. It definitely reminded Abhi and me how precious we were to each other. It prevented us from going back to being individuals instead of remaining a couple, something that often happens in marriages over a period of years. It was also a testimony to 'To have and to hold, from this day forward, for better, for worse, for richer, for poorer, in sickness or in health, to love and to cherish, 'till death do us part', something that we had solemnly vowed before the Almighty nine years ago.

Thank you again, cancer! (However, even though I am thankful to you, please can you stay away from us and not touch our lives again?)

The cancer scare

It was a regular Friday evening in September. Abhi and I were watching a movie at home. While engrossed in the movie, I happened to place my hand on my right thigh, and was startled to find a lump-like swelling about two inches above the knee. Goodness! I almost froze. Abhi felt it as well, and suggested that I report it first thing on Monday morning to the breast care nurse. The forbidden word hung in the air between us – recurrence? I was scared. With a deep breath I said, 'Oh God, let this not be cancer.' Abhi comforted me, and said that we must keep a close watch on the lump or swelling and get it investigated; but I could clearly see that he was shaken too. The fear in our eyes, hearts and minds had nowhere to hide in our little apartment or our turbulent lives.

Later at night, I found myself lying in bed worried about the recurrence. Exactly one year ago, Abhi and I didn't personally know anyone who had cancer, and therefore, we didn't really know what we were up against; but this time we did. Now we know how intense cancer and its treatment are. The faintest possibility of having to go through the same experience again intimidated me. Throughout the weekend, my hand would reach the swollen area inadvertently and I would check if the swelling had reduced. By Sunday evening, it actually did, and I heaved a sigh of relief.

I did report this swelling to my breast care nurse first thing on Monday morning. She listened intently and suggested that I see my GP. She said that having a cancerous lump just above the knee is highly unlikely. It was so comforting to be reassured. Cancer was scarier to me now that it had been a year ago.

My acupuncturist, Chris, helped to sort out the swelling. What would I have done without his expertise to manage the side effects of this treatment!

After a few days, a new anniversary would get added to my personal list of important dates. It would soon be time for my first cancer anniversary.

Special dates

It was the 10th of September – one full year since I had received the heads-up for cancer. I would be celebrating my 35th birthday in five days. Abhi and I had, together, battled a difficult illness and had emerged stronger and wiser from the experience; at least that is what I'd like to believe.

It had been eight months since I finished chemotherapy, and four months since I finished radiation therapy. I still had several side effects from the treatment: insomnia, fatigue, poor stamina, sensitive skin, a sensitive scalp (due to the regrowth of hair), severe pain close to the site of the operation, and low moods, were a few amongst a long list. Despite so many side effects, my oncologist was happy with my recovery, and she thought that I was doing pretty well considering that I had been through the mill. I had not resumed work yet, I was just concentrating on recuperating at home. I intended to regain my stamina before getting back to work.

My 'chemo hair' looked like salt and pepper; it was rough but precious. The texture of the hair looked uneven, and some of it was growing curly. One day I picked up a ruler and asked Abhi to measure how long my hair had grown. '1 to 1.5 inches,' he measured. Great! I had been restless to go for a haircut for almost a month now. We would see for how long I could resist the temptation.

It was the 12th of September, and my eagerness had taken over. 'I must get it done today,' I decided. Waiting any longer for the haircut felt torturous. And so, I picked up the phone and booked an appointment with a hair dresser in the vicinity of my home. When I reached the salon, I was greeted by two very experienced hair dressers. I had shared with them over the phone that this would be my first hair cut after chemo. They certainly understood that my little hair was precious to me. With a lot of love, the lady trimmed my hair. There was another client at the salon who was getting her hair styled. When the hair dresser finished with her, she looked at her hair and screamed, 'Gorgeous, gorgeous, gorgeous!' She was delighted with the results. The rest of us in the salon turned to look at her, and joined her in appreciating her new hairstyle. After about a minute or so, the lady who was working on me said, 'Just give it another year, and you will be able to have your hair styled as gorgeously as her.' Her colleague (the one responsible for creating the gorgeous haircut) agreed with her. Although at that particular instant I was focused on appreciating the other lady, and not really feeling bad about my frizzy short hair, I was won over by their empathy and kindness. I walked out of the salon with trimmed hair and a happy heart. I didn't remember the last time I had felt so happy after spending money on a haircut. This was my little gift (in addition to lots of shopping) to myself for my birthday.

Cancer had been a turning point in life; I would take time to get back to what is called 'normal', whatever that means. After being on this rollercoaster ride for twelve months, I knew that the definition of normal had changed for me. With the learning from cancer, life was gradually coming back to (the new) normal that I had defined for myself. As my lovely friend, Liz Aram, said in a session we were attending together, 'How do you achieve a good balance between celebrating every day in the knowledge of death; but also begin to return to a "normal" life?'

Now, in September, the time I spent at the GP's surgery or the hospital was much less than before. In May or June, I visited my GP's surgery often and I made an abnormally high number of trips to the hospital. The number of times I topped up my oyster card for trips to the hospital had now reduced. The size of the needles had reduced, and so had the number of pricks. Now I didn't need to go for blood tests often, nor did I have to run to the hospital for different types of scans. It had been a few months since my last heart scan. There had not been any emergency rush to the GP for some time, nor had there been any panic calls to the oncology unit. The frequency of phone calls to my breast care nurse had reduced significantly. Unlike before, if there was a phone call made to the GP or the breast care nurse, they asked me to wait and watch, and I was not asked to leave everything and rush to the hospital.

By the way, this did not mean that the insomnia or the severe pain in the operated area or migraines or the weakness or the poor stamina were resolved. It just meant that the ill effects of the treatment were decreasing, and my health was better than what it had been six months ago. The definition of what is OK or acceptable is different for someone who has had an encounter with cancer or has looked after someone with cancer.

And so, my life was more in balance, and this was how I intended to keep it. In my day, I would make time for a short meditation, cook and eat healthy food (mostly), go for a walk, read, rest, watch TV, minimise negative emotions, and invest time in relationships. I was still unemployed, but I didn't *feel* so bad about it, because work was not as big a factor of self-esteem for me as it had been a year ago. I was not losing focus in life; I was just taking time out to appreciate other things that life had to offer. I wanted to build a reservoir of memories from all aspects of life, and not just work.

I intended to return to work when I felt better – maybe next year. After cancer, I did wonder if returning to work would be difficult. Would I get the right type of work, which would give me the salary and the challenge that I wanted? Would prospective employers be worried about my health condition, and shy away from selecting me, even when I was the best fit for the job role? Would they worry if I would be psychologically traumatised after cancer, or be able to cope with the challenges that the workplace brings? Whether they singled me out or not, I definitely felt cowed down each time a job application did not get converted into a job offer. But this was not something I could change; I must remember the 'acceptance' that I had learnt in the 'Coping with Cancer Stress' course.

After cancer, I don't know exactly how and why, but I went through a phase when I became a shopaholic. I had never been much of a shopper. In the past, all my shopping trips had been need-based. I knew what I wanted to buy, and would get to it straight away in the store. I almost never walked around in the market or the stores, just checking out stuff. I always liked to buy good quality stuff, but never bought too many things at one go. But earlier that year, during the summer, I seemed to have spent more on my wardrobe that I had spent over the last three years (and I didn't feel guilty about it). I did go out and buy that handbag from Radley that I had been appreciating in the John Lewis store for more than a year. I went out and bought new shoes, several tops, jeans, sleepwear and a jacket. This was over and above the large number of books that I purchased from Amazon. I got to the point when Abhi noticed that I was shopping yet again. Clearly, I was behaving like a shopaholic. I had to hold myself back from supporting the economy by pushing more money into the retail market – I think supporting home finances was a cleverer thing to do! Thankfully, the shopping spree stopped soon, but it was an interesting change. It seemed to be motivated by the thought that I must enjoy what I wanted now, rather than later. It was a reflection of savouring the present instead of saving for the future.

My self-doubts were gradually decreasing as I picked myself up after cancer, and I was putting together a new life. The new me allows more time for my brain and body to relax. Unlike before, at times I just sit, do nothing, and enjoy nothingness. There is more me-time, and I know that I must put my own needs first, rather than let others always come before me. I am moving on to explore new interests in life.

We celebrated Diwali on the 3rd of November, and it felt like a very special day. I was so happy about Diwali, and prepared for it so enthusiastically. I think that I had never been in such high festive spirits. I shopped for the traditional earthen lamps and the sweets, and dressed up for the celebration. I offered the prayers and I was joyful like never before.

I did briefly think about the previous year, and what I had been going through and how I had looked. In that year's pictures clicked on Diwali, there is not even a single hair on my head. Now, my head was adorned with thick black hair. I was thankful that things had changed for the better over the past year. Two days later, I shuddered, as the memory of the oesophagitis experience and how I had struggled to keep any food down crossed my mind. Somehow the painful memories made me appreciate my blessings and the delicious food that I was eating even more. While I celebrated Diwali, I hoped that there would be many more such celebrations for me. I hoped that I would be around for not just ten but several more years.

November was an extremely special month. On the 22nd of November, I had the last dose of Zoladex and Herceptin. Everything seemed to go wrong that day, but I was not bothered; I was too busy revelling in the fact that it was the last dose. I first went to the GP's surgery, for the Zoladex injection. The nurse who usually did it for me had left the surgery, and the other one said that she could not do it. She went looking for a doctor who could give me the Zoladex injection. The doctor arrived in a while, and we did the injection. With all this, I got delayed for my Herceptin appointment. When I eventually got there, there seemed to be a long wait. I might have been restless with all the waiting on some other day, but not today. I had booked a reflexology session for 11 am at the hospital, and I went for it. After a relaxing reflexology session, I got hooked to the machine for Herceptin for the last time. I happily ate the sandwich and the yoghurt provided in the chemo day unit, and even enjoyed the food. I remember that I clicked my picture on the phone and sent it to my family; the title being 'The last Herceptin'. Oh! We had so much fun on chat while the Herceptin snaked through my veins. Dinesh, Sachin, Abhi and I were exuberant about the last intravenous dose of the cancer treatment. By the time the Herceptin finished, it was 2:45 pm. I had carried a box of chocolates for the nurses in the day unit, just as a little thank you for looking after me. The nurse unhooked me from the machine and said, 'It was great to look after you, but please don't come back here. I mean it in a nice way.' I smiled, and said *Amen.*

I gathered my belongings and walked out of the hospital. How carefree I felt as I walked down the three flights of stairs that took me away from the Oncology unit! I decided to treat myself, and went to an Indian restaurant near the hospital. I ate happily and leisurely. After that I picked up a few things from the market and boarded the bus to get home. It was 5:30 pm when I reached home. I was exhausted but felt on top of the world.

Four days later, on the 26th of November, I went through a small operation to remove the port that had been part of me for exactly fourteen months (26 September 2012 to 26 November 2013). After the operation, the white dressing under the right shoulder felt pretty. Although my arm took more than three weeks to heal from the surgery, I did not resent the pain and the discomfort. Wasn't it nice to be able to turn onto my right side without feeling an obstruction just under the collar bone? When the incision healed, it was nice to be able to turn onto my side without disturbing my sleep. I had so been looking forward to this!

Two days later, on the 28th of November, Abhi and I were at the hospital for a meeting with the oncologist. It was a special day, as I was officially signed off the cancer treatment. I was given something called 'Open Access' to the oncology unit, under which I could call my breast care nurse directly if I developed some worrisome symptoms. This would eliminate the need to go to the GP. The final discussion with a member of the oncology team was not really a happy discussion, I must say. For several side effects, I was told that I would probably have to live with them, as conventional medicine could not do anything about them. 'Seriously?' I asked. 'Yes,' was the reply. For the sensitive hair follicles, they reckoned that the chemotherapy drugs had probably damaged the hair follicles that were causing all the pain. 'But they cause a migraine every day, which is severely debilitating,' I moaned. 'Isn't there anything that you could do to resolve the situation?' Apparently there wasn't. I was devastated. I had been suffering from terrible migraines for the last six months, and the thought that I may have to live with them for the rest of my life was unnerving. We talked so much about the existing after effects of the treatment, as well as what to do in case of a recurrence, that I got depressed. We discussed a few more things and then Abhi and I took leave from the oncologist.

I was sulking as we left the hospital. But after thirty minutes or so, I realised that sulking was not the best thing to do. It made no sense to be sad, now that I had been signed off the cancer treatment. Who could say for sure whether the hair follicles would continue hurting or not? Who could say for sure whether I would have migraines every single day for the rest of my life? When there were no certainties about anything, how could there be certainty about my suffering in the future? It was all speculation. If it was nothing but speculation, why not rejoice in the bliss of today? And all said and done, my doctor was sharing information about the worst, to make me aware of what could happen. She was doing it so that I could be safe in the future. This thought process helped me to recover from the upset caused by the meeting, and I was able to savour the joy of officially being signed off the cancer treatment.

The 4th of December was very special as I had an opportunity, through Paul's Cancer Support Centre, to speak at the House of Lords. The objective of the event was to tell the sponsors, patrons, and trustees of the Centre about the fabulous work the Centre had been doing, with the hope that they would continue supporting the Centre. The event started with allowing time for the guests to get to know each other. After some food and drinks, there was a welcome talk by the main patron of the Centre. It was followed by a presentation on the treatment of cancer in the UK by a senior surgeon from the NHS. After this talk, the Director of Paul's Cancer Support Centre delivered a presentation on the work that the Centre had been doing. Then came my turn; my talk was like 'the voice of the customer'. It was after two years and two months that I was back on the podium. Apart from the long time that had passed since I had faced an audience to speak in public, my difficult personal situation had not done me any good. I had prepared well for the talk and I spoke sincerely. I shared with the audience a little information about my cancer journey, and then talked about how Paul's had helped me. I specifically talked about the benefit that I had derived from biodynamic massage, counselling, hypnotherapy, and the 'Coping with Cancer Stress' course. I spoke for a little over eleven minutes. During the entire time, I could see that the people were riveted to every single word that I said. The response was fabulous. After the speech, Abhi - who was there to support me like he always is – and I spent the following seventy minutes gathering compliments from the audience. It felt great to return to the podium, with a talk that was simply loved by people in the audience. It was also a special evening for me, as it helped me to regain some confidence after the cancer experience. Apart from being appreciated for the content and the delivery of the speech, I was also appreciated for the fact that I had managed to pick myself up in just fourteen months after the diagnosis, and had delivered an impactful speech. It was a great evening!

Over the next month, it became easier to sleep on the side of the operation site. I had been suffering from shooting pains like electric shocks, in and around the operated area, for eight months, when homeopathy came to my rescue. Homeopathy first helped me to get rid of the shooting pains, and subsequently alleviated the pain in and around the area of surgery. The nails on my fingers and toes recovered from the discolouration, but for the ridges and brittleness. They kept on breaking with the lightest pressure, but how wonderful it was to see normal looking nails!

Some days later, it was New Year's Eve, and I was at home. I had been actively participating in various discussions in the Macmillan's online community. There was a particular post that reflected how someone going through chemotherapy felt so low on hope and so unwell. There was nothing Happy about the imminent New Year, for her. This person seemed to have hit her lowest point. I felt a little sad when I read the post. I could empathise with her and recalled that one year ago I had been exactly where she was now. Life had seemed so difficult and every single day was full of pain. One year later, I was all excited about the beginning of the New Year. Like other festivals and important days, this day felt very special too. My family and I had worked hard to ensure that I got better. I guess this happy feeling was well-earned!

I was gradually healing, and I seemed to be approaching a kind of closure with cancer.

C=Cancer, C=Cure, C=Choice and C=Courage!

After going through cancer, I knew that I must do whatever I had always wanted to do, sooner rather than later. I appreciated that time may not be as unlimited as people, in general, take it to be. If time could not be taken for granted, I had better get started now. This included improving my health, becoming a successful trainer, spending more time with Abhi, lots of travelling, spending time with my family, and eating a variety of good food. All these things felt important, and I had assigned no particular order to them except one, which was at the top of the list: spending quality time with Abhi.

In December 2013, Abhi had attended a funeral, and had seen the grief of the bereaved family, especially of the spouse. Witnessing the pain of that woman brought back so many memories for us. Abhi was shaken when he got home. He found it difficult to go off to sleep in the night. We were both reminded of how scared we had been when I was diagnosed with cancer. It is true that my prognosis had always seemed positive, and we had never even discussed death with my doctors; but we were constantly aware of how things could go wrong in cancer. How scared Abhi and I had been that we might end up losing each other. We always noticed when the doctors said that they would try to cure me and that my chances of survival were 80%. We were never in denial that the remaining 20% could also happen. It was the unsaid truth at our home. It was the fear that we lived in, until I was declared free of cancer after the surgery. I can't even imagine what people go through when a poor prognosis stares them in the face, or when they lose their loved ones to cancer. While the fear of recurrence continues to reside in our hearts and home, we try to look at every day as another day, and make the best of what we have got.

I was meeting up with some friends for the New Year (2014) celebrations when I shared with them that I was writing a book on my cancer experience. As we talked about my writing project, they expressed a desire to listen to some excerpts from my book. 'Sure thing,' I said. I decided to read out the gratitude poem, and the other composition, 'The Mighty Cancer', to them. This was the first time I was discussing my book in detail with anyone other than those people who had been closely involved with me in the cancer experience. I realised that while I was reading, I felt a lump in my throat. I felt as if I was back at Addenbrooke's Hospital, scared and alone, when I was given the heads-up for cancer. I felt my eyes grow moist – it was like reliving the experience, albeit at a much smaller level. It definitely hurt! While I do intend to continue talking about my cancer experience, in order to build awareness about cancer, at times the memories hurt me. Hopefully, time will prove itself to be a great healer, and I will talk about my cancer experience without pain in the future.

In 2014, Abhi and I began thinking that maybe it was time we got ready to become parents. But while I pondered over parenting, I did ask myself – was there a chance that I might pass the 'Let's go bonkers and multiply like hell' gene to my baby? *Sigh!* If yes, would I be able to cope with my guilt? *Another sigh!* But then I thought, *We'll cross that bridge when we come to it.*

Life is a beautiful journey, and there is no sense in skipping such an important aspect of it. Life is too precious for that. Ask any person who has had a brush with the Big C, and they will be able to corroborate this statement. This may be the 'I told you so' moment for dozens of people who have always predicted that Abhi and I will at some point in our lives want to be parents. You see, now that the cancer was gone, it was time for me to look beyond the illness and celebrate life. Cancer had brought with it immeasurable pain, but I also got in touch with my inner courage, to bear that pain. Cancer broke off some relationships, but it also blessed me with the ones that would stay. Cancer severely hurt me emotionally, but it taught me that I could make a choice no matter what the situation: the choice to place hope over despair, the choice to opt for information over ignorance, the choice to value life over death, the choice to treasure love over betrayal, and the choice to look beyond the hurt and have the empathy and willingness to act differently. I am glad that I have been able to learn from the cancer journey, as Dr Charles suggested: 'Let it be an experience that changes things for the better for you.' Getting through the treatment was not the end of that journey.

I was aware that I had several scars from cancer, and they weren't pretty. The crown that adorned my head was now short and curly (in place of longer straight hair; I prefer straight hair over curly hair), I had thinned eyebrows, acne on my face due to the hormonal treatment, persistent dark bags under my eyes due to fatigue, surgical incisions on my breast and under the collar bone, extra flab on the abdomen due to steroids, the nightmare of a breast cancer survivor – unequal sized breasts, and perpetually un-moisturised looking hands and feet. Of all the after effects of the treatment, what bothered me the most was the painful hair follicles that were growing back at a funny angle and causing migraines every other day. Maybe it sounds funny that when I touched my hair, it hurt. Yes, I know that hair is dead keratin, but mine hurt really badly. But each of these scars reminded me that I was stronger than my adversary: The Big C. Each of these scars reminded me that they were the reason why I was still here, and I was immensely grateful for that. My scars were my life-affirming tattoos! Yes, I may never have managed sitting on the giant wheel at the local fun fair, but I had beaten cancer!

Since October 2013, I had been asked a few times if I had not lost my hair in chemotherapy. Ah! What an amazing question. Remember how happy the other girl had been when I had asked her this question? People frequently mistook my short chemo hair for my regular (smart) hair. I thought that short hair looked fabulous on me. While my hair grew back, I was taking this as an opportunity to experiment with short hairstyles. I was *not* marked with cancer anymore.

I also trained for the 'MoonWalk[51] at London' half marathon, scheduled for May 2014. It was on the night of my ninth wedding anniversary, and participating in the marathon to raise money for breast cancer was a fulfilling way to celebrate the special day. In my pre-cancer era, my highest laurel in running had been being able to run for fifty metres (all huffing and puffing) to catch the bus. After boarding the bus, all I could manage was to collapse into the chair. Now things were different – I had trained for the MoonWalk by going for a run every alternate day. Eventually, I managed three kilometres of running at a stretch. While I found it challenging to go for a run regularly, due to migraines and poor stamina, I did not let these hurdles stop me. As I write this, I am fully aware that the MoonWalk is about power walking and not running. But let me confess: often power-walkers in the park walked faster than when I was running or jogging! Therefore, I was confident that I would fit in the criterion for power-walking during the MoonWalk.

So on one of these training days, I was going out for a run and wanted to wear a hat (because it was freaking cold in January). While searching for a hat in my cupboard, I came across the pretty (cancer) hat with a peak, that I had been unable to wear during the treatment. I stared at it for a minute, and wondered if wearing it could signify a bad omen.

---

[51] Walk the Walk – Uniting against breast cancer. "the Moonwalk london." http://www.walkthewalk.org/Challenges/TheMoonWalkLondon. Last accessed December 06, 2014.

Then I almost giggled at my weird thought, and wore the hat. While I was using the hat without any predicament, it definitely served as a reminder of cancer.

The MoonWalk on the 10th of May 2014 was fabulous, and what a night it was! The gusts blew at more than 30 kmph, it was wet, and the temperature was 5°C. Amongst 15,000 participants, we walked through the night in the freezing cold and painted the city pink. When we approached the finish line at Clapham Common, several people applauded us. It was such a proud moment for me – it was the first major event that I had participated in after cancer, and I had managed to complete the walk. The aching legs and the torn tendon muscle were so worth it, to receive that applause. Abhi and I also raised funds for the event, which would be passed on to various beneficiaries of WalktheWalk.

I have decided that this is how I will make my little contribution to help people going through cancer, as they helped me during my cancer experience. I will raise funds for organisations associated with cancer every year, by participating in walks and runs. It will be a win-win situation – I will improve my fitness, and raise funds at the same time. In addition to raising funds for cancer charities, I will also volunteer my time to help people who have been diagnosed with cancer.

Homeopathy and all the spiritual work have been such a life-saver. As I write this in May 2014, the pain in my hair follicles is almost gone. My leg is still messed up, but so what... sooner or later, I will get there! There is a streak of progress, and so I must 'Keep Calm and Carry On'. What has also helped is that while I may have lost bits and pieces of me, one thing that I didn't lose during cancer was my sense of humour.

I am aware (all the time) that I am so lucky to have won this battle. I feel gratitude towards the Almighty, and towards everyone who prayed for me or undertook the journey with me. I feel grateful when I look at the beautiful sunshine, the rain, or the magical snowfall. I feel thankful when someone says a kind word to me, or looks after me, or pampers me. I feel hurt when someone shows apathy or is rude to me, but I promise myself that I will not repeat that hurtful behaviour in similar situations, and I feel gratitude for this attitude. I rejoice when I say that I *had* cancer and I am cured now. I am immensely thankful that I don't want to forget any part of this experience, because I believe that it has humbled and grounded me. Abhi and I are now eagerly waiting for the next cancer milestone: the remission!

I want to continue being the new me – except, of course, without the cancer-ings: poisoning (chemo) causing nausea and vomiting, slicing and scarring (surgery), tanning (radiation), limping (leg pain), hurting (all over – physical, emotional, psychological), fearing (synonymous with a cancer diagnosis) and last but not the least, dying (The Ultimate event and the Truth).

Big C: While I hope that you never come back and that I stay out of your clutches, thank you for making me, in your own way, a better person. Thank you for reminding me that no matter what happens, life is beautiful and worth fighting for. Thank you for reassuring me that love is what matters the most, something worth living for and to be grateful for.

I may have fallen, bled and groaned,
I may have coughed a lot of blood
I may have lost patience time and again,
And every moment may have been full of pain.

I know I have reason to be scared
That cancer may come back and get me
I know that there are enough scars
That cancer has given me.

But what really matters
Is that I am here today,
I choose to be stronger and wiser
And live fully every single remaining day!

- A breast cancer survivor
(member of cancer incidence statistics in the year 2012,
and member of cancer survival statistics in the year 2013)